# THE
# CAPE
# OF
# STORMS

# THE
# CAPE
# OF
# STORMS

A Personal History of
the Crisis in South Africa

## ANTHONY HAZLITT HEARD

Foreword by Archbishop Desmond M. Tutu

THE UNIVERSITY OF ARKANSAS PRESS
FAYETTEVILLE    1990    LONDON

Typeface:  New Baskerville

The paper used in this publication meets the minimum requirements of the
American National Standard for Permanence of Paper for Printed Library
Materials Z39.48-1984.  ∞

*Library of Congress Cataloging-in-Publication Data*

Heard, Anthony Hazlitt, 1937–
    The Cape of Storms: a personal history of the crisis in South Africa/ by
    Anthony Hazlitt Heard.
        p.    cm.
    Includes bibliographical references and index.
    ISBN 1-55728-167-X (alk. paper). — ISBN 1-55728-168-8 (pbk.: alk.
    paper)
    1. South Africa–History–20th century.   2. Apartheid–South Africa.
    I. Title.
    DT1945.H43   1990
    968.06–dc20                                                    90-11022
                                                                        CIP

*To a free South Africa*

*"People crushed by law have no hope but from power. If laws are their enemies, they will be enemies to laws. . . ."*
*Edmund Burke, letter to the Hon. C. J. Fox, October 8, 1877*

*"In South Africa, just living is a political statement. . . ."*
*Leslee Durr, Stellenbosch University white student activist, explaining her stand in* Los Angeles Times *interview, December 31, 1989.*

*"Ag, man. I just want to sell tickets."*
*Bus conductor on Brighton Estate, Cape Town, route, having to decide who was white and who "non-white."*

*"With a wild rattle and clatter, and an inhuman abandonment of consideration not easy to be understood in these days, the carriage dashed through streets and swept round corners, with women scream-ing before it, and men clutching each other and clutching children out of its way."*
A Tale of Two Cities *by Charles Dickens, Penguin Classics Series (1985), 140. (All future references to* A Tale of Two Cities *will be to this edition.)*

*I do not know where I've been*
*But, brother, I know I am coming.*
*I do not know where I have been*
*But, brother, I come like a storm over the veld.*
*Wally Serote (1971)*

# ACKNOWLEDGMENTS

Warm thanks are extended to those who, in various ways, helped to make this chronicle possible. They include the editor of the *Cape Times,* Koos Viviers, ex-colleagues at the paper Roger Williams, Lynne Clement, Peter Ibbotson, and John Scott; University of Cape Town political scientist David Welsh; the anonymous Cape Town advocate (barrister) who gave me *pro amico* advice; Cape Town attorney Richard Rosenthal; Bill and Merlee Harrison, of Fayetteville, Arkansas, U.S.; institutions at the University of Arkansas, Fayetteville, that sustained me while preparing and writing—the Fulbright Institute, the Walter J. Lemke Journalism School and the University Press; and particularly individuals associated with these institutions, Hoyt Purvis, Miller Williams, David Sanders, Ellen Beeler, Brenda Zodrow, and Scot Danforth; the late Howard Simons and the Nieman Foundation at Harvard University; the Mullins Library at the University of Arkansas, Fayetteville, the Metropolitan Toronto Reference Library, and the Centre for African Studies at the University of Cape Town—and, not least, three people in particular: Oliver Tambo who gave me an illegal interview in London in 1985; Gerald Shaw who provided critical loyalty and sound advice all my professional life; and my wife, Mary Ann Barker, who shared dismissal from my job and preparation of this book with me.

# CONTENTS

# PREFACE

The 1980s saw one form of tyranny crumble in Eastern Europe and another due to crumble in South Africa. This is a personal view of that country's turbulent times written by a journalist and editor who was there.

Generally, the style and spelling used are South African English. Where deemed appropriate, local terms are explained or translated.

South Africa's history of discrimination makes it unavoidable to identify people frequently on the basis of colour. South African law has for years distinguished between African, coloured, Indian, and white persons and these terms are used when referring to those groups separately. The term black is generally used when referring to the first three groups collectively, but sometimes is used for African.

The use of these terms does not imply acceptance of the statutory divisions of the South African population—divisions which have largely caused the crisis in the country.

At the time of going to press, the most recent reliable estimate of the size and composition of the total South African population was

|  | Numbers | Percent |
|---|---|---|
| African | 29,000,000 | 75.9 |
| White | 5,000,000 | 13.1 |
| Coloured | 3,200,000 | 8.4 |
| Indian | 990,000 | 2.6 |
| TOTAL | 38,190,000 | |

In May 1990 a South African rand equalled 38 U.S. cents. Its value had fallen sharply against the dollar, having stood at $1.30 in January 1980.

# FOREWORD

In May 1986 I had the honour of addressing the International Press Institute at its annual conference in Vienna. I gave my address on the South African press titled "The Esau Principle". Esau in the Bible is the older twin brother of Jacob. He sacrificed his birthright of primogeniture and exchanged it for a mess of potage. He abandoned a rich future benefit not easily encashable for a short term immediate advantage easily attainable without much effort. My basic thesis was that the South African press, controlled exclusively by powerful white bosses, had by and large been pandering to white interests at a time when they should have been opening the eyes of the white public to the dangers to which our country was exposed by the iniquitous system of apartheid and its draconian state of emergency measures. They were lulling whites into a false security, usually telling them those things which they wanted to hear. The South African press was on the whole at that time giving the impression that our country was passing through a time of calm and stability when in fact it was facing traumatic times.

We had appeared to have learned nothing from the Rhodesian experience when the white community had been kept singularly uninformed of what was taking place in their country so that most white people genuinely believed that Bishop Muzorewa enjoyed massive support among the African populace and that Robert Mugabe was really a blood thirsty terrorist no better than the devil incarnate. Those poor whites were shocked out of their skins when Robert Mugabe won a landslide victory at the first free elections and were even more flabbergasted when on the night of his election victory Mugabe appeared on television. He was no firebrand demagogue, but a well-spoken, articulate and urbane man who, far from spitting the brimstone and hell fire of revenge and hatred, unbelievably spoke of reconciliation, rehabilitation and reconstruction in their common motherland.

Much of the South African press have appeared to have the three monkeys for their emblem, hear no evil, see no evil, speak no evil. They were far more concerned that their balance sheets should reflect large profits and they dared not upset their apple cart by annoying the white public by telling it the often unpalatable truth of the injustices of apartheid, of the reasonableness of black aspirations and demands and the moderation of the black liberation movements. It was better to keep on the right side of the government and the public by giving one sided and slanted accounts of all these matters. Very few white newspapers, and I mean English newspapers, told the world Robert Mugabe was not anti-white or anti-South African but was anti-apartheid and injustice and oppression. These same papers were quick to relate the alleged reverses of the government and those they identified as anti-South African. They did so with ill concealed glee. They are still up to their old tricks even in 1990 as evidenced by how they have enjoyed describing the so called rebuff Nelson Mandela received in Miami in a United States tour that has been an unprecedented triumph for him. Or note their gloating in describing the actions of six or so Jewish demonstrators on an occasion when over 4000 people gave the Archbishop of Cape Town a rousing welcome in Pasadena.

Those are the characteristics that I referred to in my address in Vienna.

On that occasion I also mentioned the wonderful exceptions. Newspapers like the then defunct *Rand Daily Mail, Sunday Express,* as well as the *Cape Times.* And I mentioned warmly Raymond Louw [Editor of the *Rand Daily Mail*], and Tony Heard then Editor of the *Cape Times.*

Tony Heard has had journalist ink as it were coursing through his veins living up to the high standards of a newspaperman father who had in the 1940's, exposed the pro-Nazi sentiments of many leading lights in the Nationalist Party during Word War II.

During his editorship of the *Cape Times* Tony tried to tell it as it is. And had a few brushes with the law. His greatest moment was when he published a full page interview that he had had with Oliver Tambo, the President of the then banned ANC. It was a serous contravention of the security and the emergency laws. He had acted on the hallowed journalistic principle that his readers had to hear both sides of the story and then be free to make their own judgement about which side to support. In doing this highly laudable thing, he was taking on not just the government but fairly those powerful moguls who control the press and who were so concerned about profits and the reaction of the white public (not caring two brass farthings about that large and ultimately more powerful, in all kinds of ways, black public).

It was not the government which got him, indeed the government ended up throwing in the towel against him for it withdrew charges preferred against him for publishing the Tambo interview. It was the white business interest which controlled the press which had it in for him. He was really sacked for daring to want to tell the truth. It was a sad day for the Cape Times and for the white press in South Africa.

When the true history of South Africa is written, Tony Heard will be depicted rightly as a leading light for liberation, truth and justice. No wonder he has been awarded the Golden Pen for courageous journalism. It is a richly deserved recognition of a South African newspaperman and I am proud to have him as a friend telling the story of how the government can try to intimidate, cajole and control because their policies are fundamentally evil and can only be defended in the end by equally evil and indefensible methods.

The Most Reverend Desmond M. Tutu
July 3, 1990

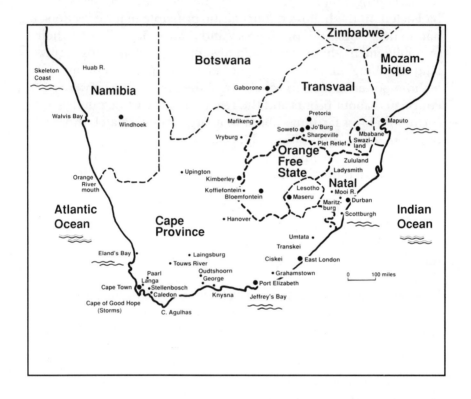

# CHAPTER ONE

# PRELUDE
# MIDNIGHT, MARCH 21, 1960

Lombard lay dead in the unmade gutter of a township street amid the beautiful surrounds of the Cape Peninsula.

Francis Drake called this place "a most stately thing and the fairest cape in all the circumference of the earth." It is one of the world's floral kingdoms. Far above the city towers a massive mountain, springing more than three thousand feet out of the chill, often wild, Atlantic Ocean. Vertical stretches of bare rock rise up the mountainside, clasping the flat summit against the sky. The wind drapes a white cloud over it, the "table cloth." The foothills are decked with varieties of protea flowers, heaths, daisies, and occasional soft-leafed silvertrees. The flora forms a gentle, hip-high covering called "fynbos" (fine bush). Occasional blood-red disa flowers dance in the spray from streams that glitter on the slope. Deer, imported mountain goats called "thars," scurrying rock rabbit-like "dassies," lizards, Cape cobra, and baboon take their chances on the heights.

The animals would warm themselves in the direct African sun. They would retreat to remote places when man, fire, or weather threatened. They would eye the city and listen to its noise . . . their kinds more endangered than the troubled people below.

The mountain and sea could suddenly lose placidness and kill. A wisp of cloud on the horizon and a breath of wind could presage violent weather. Mountain climbers, surfers, and mariners showed healthy respect for the signs. Each year the weather wrought human tragedy on the mountain and in the water below.

There was tragedy of a different kind in the townships that lay on the far-flung Cape Flats where only the longest shadows of the mountain reached.

William Hazlitt wrote that man is the only animal who laughs and weeps because man is the only animal that is struck with the difference between what things are, and what they ought to be.[1] Cape Town had done much weeping. Political unrest stalked these gaunt and neglected areas, which were in many cases treeless, pavementless, windswept, powerless; the roads were rough, the homes were boxes, and electricity was nonexistent. Wood fires in winter would cast a polluting cloud over the city.

The Cape Flats were where the "blacks" lived—Africans and so-called "coloured" people—regimented into their own "group areas." On still nights, the faint sounds of police gunshots, the whining of armoured vehicles, and victims' screams —the shock-waves of apartheid—could be picked up by whites living close by. Some showed concern; they turned to protest, activism, emigration, or lapsed into amnesia. Others remained at all times unconcerned in their racially cosseted world. They enjoyed one of the most affluent lifestyles in the world and, of course, the protection of the South African police.

This Peninsula had many names. It was known as the Cape of Good Hope in colonial and pre-colonial days. But it had also been called the Cape of Storms by those passing in tall ships to and from the east; indeed, Portuguese visitors referred to it as *Cabo Tormentoso.*

## CAPE TIMES DRIVER IS KILLED

A Cape Times driver, Mr. Richard Lombard, of Winchester Road, Walmer Estate, was killed in the Langa riot last night.

He had driven a Cape Times reporter and photographer into the location just before the clash occurred.

The reporter and photographer left him with the car and climbed on the roof of a building some distance from the car.

**Car on fire**

No one saw what happened to Mr. Lombard, but the reporter and photographer were rescued by the police.

A car was seen on fire but it was not known whether the driver had escaped or not.

Four hours later, when Mr. Lombard failed to report to the Langa police station, his badly-mutilated body was found beside the car. [2]

The report appeared on page one. It was written in shock and sadness at midnight, on deadline, in a busy newspaper office eight miles from Langa, the township closest to Cape Town.

In a crude gutter all that had been left of a gentle, humble man was a log-like object lying next to a burnt-out Chevrolet. The gasoline dousing and burning by the crowd had shrunken him to an unrecognizable lump. A limb lay severed from the rest.

The squad of white policemen who had escorted us to the scene kicked their heels impatiently as we set about trying to identify our colleague, Richard Lombard, who had for years been an editorial driver at the *Cape Times.* The police stood with their short-barreled sten-guns at the ready and kept their armoured vehicles idling. Thousands of eyes peered from black faces around us. The faces, causing dancing shadows in rooms back-lit by candles, were pressed to countless windows. Makeshift drapes were pulled back just enough for the township people to see the last rites of a terrible night.

The backdrop to the scene was the immovable black shape

of Table Mountain. The night sky was still . . . township fires flickered against it.

For the police, too, it had been a busy night. They were tense and exhausted. Rioting could flare again any moment. We had driven deep into the township in a convoy through burning streets and debris to discover our own *Cape Times* tragedy.

Langa had passed its most turbulent night. But this was mild compared with what had happened elsewhere.

In parts of the country countless thousands of South African blacks had turned up at police stations to say no to apartheid with the only thing they had: their bare hands. Their challenging, Ghandi-like protest had been organized by the newly formed Pan-Africanist Congress (PAC), a militant offshoot from the main vehicle of black nationalism, the African National Congress (ANC).

The PAC campaign was directed against the "pass laws." These hated rules required Africans in designated white areas to carry documents authorizing them to be there on pain of summary arrest and jail.

Thousands of Africans heeded the call and presented themselves at police stations after leaving their passes at home. They offered themselves for arrest. The police and prisons could not cope. Crowds gathered. There was shooting. At least two blacks died in Langa after six thousand protesters were given a three-minute police warning to disperse from an "illegal meeting."

There was no such warning at Sharpeville near Vanderbijlpark in the Transvaal, a thousand miles to the north, where blacks gathered peacefully, as a leader said, "To talk, not to fight." The police arrested him, panicked, and opened fire. There was a massive death toll of sixty-nine. A doctor found that 70 percent of those examined were shot in the back. Tumbling sten-gun bullets caused gaping wounds.

Sharpeville and Langa shocked the world. The Eisenhower government in the United States issued the strongest rebuke South Africa had received from that quarter. The South Africans retorted that the U.S. should first have acquainted itself with the

4

"facts" about this alleged "attack by many thousands of Bantu on a small police force." Many people were shocked by the remark in Parliament by a government member who, before the full extent of the shooting was apparent, betrayed some surprise that—at that stage—only one black was reported dead. Dr. Carel de Wet went on to become a cabinet minister and ambassador to London. De Wet said, "Just a final word before I sit down. Serious riots have taken place at Vanderbijlpark. My information is that one Black man has been shot dead. They have marched on the police station and the White people in the town are very alarmed and I want to make an appeal to the Government to-day. The one thing that I am concerned about is that when there are riots whether on the part of Whites or on the part of Blacks, if it is necessary to shoot, only one person is shot dead. [Time limit.]"[3]

The Sharpeville and Langa incidents brought journalists to South Africa in large numbers. Parliament changed overnight. New accents were heard in the green-carpeted lobbies where ministerial private secretaries scurried around and stern faces of former Speakers gazed from oils on the walls. There was an invasion of drain-pipe trousers and slicked-back hairstyles then fashionable in Britain as Fleet Street journalists came to listen to debates and interview the grim, biblical men of apartheid. Ironically some of those journalists had just left South Africa, having covered a historic visit the month before by British leader Harold Macmillan. (Little did they know that another big story, a prime ministerial assassination attempt, lay around the corner.)

Overnight, Sharpeville and Langa became synonymous with black opposition and state violence in South Africa . . . bloodstained milestones in the struggle between white overlord and black subject . . . part of the long march against apartheid.

As 1960 unfolded amid growing racial unrest, visiting British Premier Macmillan had pinched a phrase from a predecessor, Stanley Baldwin, and warned South Africa of a "wind of change" blowing through Africa. As Macmillan spoke in the dining room of Parliament in February, people of colour who walked the streets almost within earshot had no meaningful political rights. Africans were not welcome in the cities except to work for whites.

5

They were strictly controlled—and not even allowed to buy liquor. Apartheid repression was reaching its height and black defiance simmering.

On January 24, 1960, nine policemen had been killed while raiding illegal liquor stills in the Cato Manor African ghetto in Durban. There had been recent black unrest in Paarl, near Cape Town, and in Windhoek, capital of South West Africa (Namibia), and elsewhere. Many innocents were yet to die.

As we peered at the remains of Lombard, smoke and flames from fires caused by arsonists still rose above the township buildings. The Southern Cross, the mariners' pinpointer for north in that hemisphere, rode aloof in the sky.

Police in Langa township had opened fire on blacks attending a meeting at 6 P.M. that day. Some blacks claimed later that they had gathered to receive the authorities' response to their earlier demands. Elliot Magwentshu, an official of the Pan-Africanist Congress (PAC), later told a judge investigating the events that when the police arrived he had rushed up to a Saracen. His story:

"I said in English to the man who was holding a megaphone on top of the Saracen: 'Please, if you must tell us to disperse, do not give us only three minutes. Give us longer.' He said: 'Voertsek!'"[4] ("Voertsek" is a much-resented term meaning scram!, and worse. It is generally directed at dogs—or at blacks by racist whites. Some young black nationalists would, in days to come, chant in Angola training camps or Soweto streets: "Botha . . . voertsek!")

Magwentshu testified further: "The next thing, I got a blow on the shoulder with a stick from an African policeman. Others joined him and chased me away."[5] As so often happens in South Africa, it was a person of his own colour—paid and protected by a white government—who hit Magwentshu. That was to be the reality for years—with black police and civic puppets of government paying dearly in vengeance killings.

After the breaking up of the meeting and the police shoot-

6

ings, there was terrible violence in Langa. Mob anger spilled all over the township. Cars and buses were overturned and fire engines stoned. Several buildings, including two schools, were burned and destroyed. Makeshift roadblocks were put up in the townships to hinder the police. The Langa police station was besieged for more than two hours until troops and police reinforcements arrived. Four white women were injured as cars were stoned on nearby highways (pro-government newspapers published horror pictures of bleeding faces). The white community of Cape Town, including the all-white Parliament which was in session in the city, was awash with rumour and fear.

A mile or two away lay the middle-class, whites-only suburban town of Pinelands. A prominent Cape Town family had taken the lead in establishing "Garden Cities" like this one. They were leafy, largely English-speaking havens with an abundant supply of churches, schools, shopping centres, and black labourers. Thatched roofs could be spotted among the high Norfolk pines. Lawns were manicured and well watered. Special "service roads" kept the fast-moving traffic separate from houses and children for safety. On Sundays, hearty Wesleyan hymns mingled with high church chants as whites offered respect to the Almighty. Any blacks were in Pinelands to work, to deliver goods, to tend gardens, children, and homes—not under any circumstances to live. Pinelands, on low ground, was regarded as "a bit damp," but otherwise "ideal." If you could forget about Langa across the way, it was English village life at its best.

That frightful night of March 21, 1960, Pinelands did not forget. Residents, including friends of mine, heard the shots and fretted. Some living closest to Langa considered moving temporarily to relatives' or friends' homes in other parts of Cape Town. The rhythm of white privileged life was disturbed.

Indeed, Langa was much too close to Pinelands for white comfort on nights like that. When visiting friends in Pinelands, we were always acutely aware of Langa, that densely populated black township. A faintly revolting smell from the Athlone sewerage works nearby could hang in the air, like an omen. The summer

7

southeast wind blew it onto white Pinelands—the winter north-wester sent it over "coloured" areas, like Athlone. Sometimes streams of Africans would take shortcuts to their work through Pinelands, a physical reminder of a vast unresolved presence so close. Some whites resented such passage and complained.

As blacks flocked to Cape Town over the years, they were as a matter of policy settled farther and farther from white areas. Townships and roads were planned with strategic intent, providing for quick access and containment by security forces in case of black unrest. Places like Langa, awkwardly close to white settlement, had been a warning to South Africa's rulers. (Alexandra Township, cheek by jowl with Johannesburg's affluent northern suburbs, was another. Whites driving home or relaxing over drinks after work in spacious surroundings might just get a whiff of tear gas or hear shots—evidence of "unrest" so close in a world apart.) Prime ministers were known to take special helicopter trips to decide where to build more townships as the unstoppable black tide swept the cities. New urban settlement—routine in other lands—was security business in South Africa.

"Ja, that's Lompie," said John Peter Florus, the colleague who had driven with me to the spot. The words remained with me all my life.

With news and pictures of the rioting in South Africa cascading into the newspaper office, the editor of the *Cape Times,* Victor Norton, terse as usual and puffing the pipe that was his trademark, had sent us off to burning Langa.

"Get hold of the top cop. find out what's happened to Lombard. Get the death toll clarified," he had said.

Eight miles from the office, we had found him. Florus uttered three words. Matter-of-factly, hiding his shock and grief at seeing the remains of his murdered friend, Florus thus provided the information we had sought.

How Florus recognized Lombard from that shrunken mass I could never fathom. But they were close friends—both had worked as drivers at the *Cape Times* for many years in a small team. Something had made him sure.

Lombard's death was, for me, a harbinger of coming conflict and destruction in South Africa. It spoke with grim eloquence and tragic irony. It showed how indiscriminate the violence could become.

Lombard was olive-skinned. He was a so-called "coloured" person, and thus shared many injustices with black Africans. It was this fellow-oppressed, of all people, who was caught in the midst of this black fury after the shootings. He had driven a *Cape Times* editorial team to the meeting at the township which erupted in rioting. It was prudent practice at the newspaper to leave the firm's car some distance from potential trouble. Lombard had parked the Chevrolet near the single men's hostels, large barracks-like flats, on a road near Vanguard Drive that would give the team quick escape out of the township if necessary.

The reporter, Terry McComb Herbst, and the photographer, Cloete Breytenbach, had been caught up in the riot. They had found themselves in danger. They were rescued by police who had baton-charged the crowd to reach them. The police then hurriedly put them in a van and drove them away—leaving Lombard sitting peacefully around the corner in the car, waiting for them. Herbst had taken a direct hit on the head when a protester threw a cold-drink bottle from an upper floor. Fortunately for him, the force was broken as he was jumping down from a low roof. Lombard was less lucky.

As the police sped away with the newspapermen, the two tried desperately to get them to turn back to ensure Lombard's safety. But in the clamour and confusion their entreaties were ignored. The loyal driver was left to his own devices.

Richard Lombard was in all likelihood taken by surprise. The crowd came running from the broken-up meeting, threading their angry way among the hostel buildings. He may have been alerted to trouble by gunshots and clamour minutes before he died. His last moments have never been described. Almost certainly, he felt his duty was to his newspaper team in spite of the obvious danger hurtling toward him. He probably faced death torn between a sense of duty and terror. His fate was reminiscent of those hanged in fury on lampposts in the San Antoine district of Paris in the French Revolution.

"The swinging sentinel was posted and the sea rushed on."
*A Tale of Two Cities,* 294

The fact that Lombard wore a peaked chauffeur-type cap could have led the crowd to believe he was a policeman. The police wore such caps. Moreover, he was light-skinned enough to look white, particularly as night approached. Perhaps the rushing and angered sea was beyond discriminating after the police shooting. (Years later, in another upheaval in the Transvaal, a white woman futilely screamed: "I'm English!" as if her non-Afrikaans descent would curb the crowd bent on stoning her car. She lived to tell the story on South African television, to the unconcealed jeers of the ruling white Nationalist Afrikaners. They had always held that when blacks rose against whites there would be no discriminating. That was the dynamic behind the call to all whites to join the Nationalist *laager* (defensive ring of ox-carts). A prominent Nationalist academic's wife, responding to some strong remarks I had made about black grievances at a dinner in Washington, D.C., in the 1980s when we were in a visiting party, rasped in my ear in Afrikaans: *"Hulle sal jou ophang, net soos die res van ons!"* "They'll hang you, just like the rest of us." Maybe. Maybe not, I thought. Maybe we'd all be okay.)

Lombard was taken out of the car. He was shot. He was doused with gasoline and burned. A limb was severed.

The blaze was out and the place quiet when we arrived to identify him.

All the time those eyes watched from the windows. . . .

Lombard died where apartheid was felt most keenly by blacks: outside those single hostels, the several-storey high buildings standing in this blacks-only township. (Other races required

10

written permission to enter African townships.) The hostels were drab monuments to apartheid. Housing single migrant workers who were not allowed to bring their wives or children with them from the far-off Transkei or Ciskei "homelands," most of the accommodations were ceilingless, doorless, tiny, and depressing. They were a collection of cubicles. These zones were well-known breeding grounds for prostitution and vice—and for political education fuelled by alienation, bitterness, despair.

Our job done, we turned from the scene, distressed and weary, and picked our way by car through the still-burning township under police escort. The Saracen armoured vehicles took the lead as the small convoy headed toward the police station, and the relief of the township exit.

Except for the roadblocks and fires, there were few signs of the rioting. (A police colonel told me in great confidence outside a neighbouring township, Nyanga, a few nights later: "These native chappies don't riot after dark." But that did not deter my companion reporter that night, a devout man touting a big revolver. He sat with it cocked at the car window as we drove past the Nyanga Township houses in the dark. We had not ventured in, except briefly and dangerously earlier that day, after which editor Norton had banned staff from entering the townships till things quietened down.)

At the Langa police station at midnight on March 21 we found young white constables, some in their teens, rushing around with rifles and sten-guns. The siege of the station was over, but they were on edge. Some had shot and killed or wounded people that night. The busy foot soldiers of apartheid were dressed in their neat khaki uniforms, peaked caps, and "sam browns." Those were the days before the setting up of a special riot—or "reaction"—squad in the police, which, in camouflage dress, would swoop down on unrest. The police vehicles (aptly dubbed "nylons" by township-dwellers) had wire mesh at windows to protect against the "African bomb," stoning. These vans were, with the whining, trundling Saracens, the mainstay of anti-riot activity in 1960—and they were everywhere in Langa that night. (Later the police and army developed all sorts of heavily armed

11

vehicles. It was a serious business, this, keeping ahead in the technology of repression. There were Casspirs, army Buffels, and Ratels—and in the 1980s the unveiling of a mean-looking vehicle called *Nongqai*, roughly translated as "peace-keeper.")

Numbed by the night's events, Florus and I faced our most difficult task. We had to break the news to Lombard's wife. We drove to Walmer Estate, an old residential area on the side of Devil's Peak. The Lombards lived there in a modest house on Winchester Road. Mrs. Rhoda Lombard knew instinctively. Her middle-aged and punctual husband was supposed to be home much earlier and had not telephoned to say he would be late. She and the rest of Cape Town knew there had been rioting. We had just started to tell her the news when she drowned our words in a long wail. We offered the company's mumbled condolences and returned to the office.

Sitting next to Terry Herbst, who was picking shattered cold-drink glass from his bloodied head as he wrote, I typed the six-paragraph report about Lombard. It took a single-column place beneath the banner-headline news and historic pictures of Sharpeville and Langa on the front page.

I was exhausted and returned to my Rosebank home to bed at 3 A.M., creeping in under the mosquito net and groaning the news to Val, my bride of three months.

Aged twenty-three, I felt wretched about that whole night—and about my country.

Three memories would remain indelibly with me: the body, Mrs. Lombard's cry, and those faces at the windows. They were accompaniments to a tragedy unfolding in a beautiful land.

> ". . . it was the season of Light, it was the season of Darkness."
> *A Tale of Two Cities,* 35

CHAPTER TWO

# GEORGE ARTHUR HEARD

The course that brought me to Cape Town and the events of 1960 in its townships covered all of South Africa's four provinces. Birth in 1937 in the keen "highveld" air of the Transvaal in Johannesburg. Schooling in the warm, conservative, sugar-rich province of Natal. University and work in journalism in the Cape where cold Atlantic and tepid Indian oceans meet. But my roots were in the other province, the Orange Free State—landlocked in the centre of South Africa and bounded by the Cape, the Transvaal, Natal, and Lesotho (formerly the British protectorate of Basutoland).

It was in the capital of the Free State, Bloemfontein, where my father, George Arthur Heard, was born of British immigrant parents on October 28, 1906. His father, Arthur Henry Heard, was from Hastings in England. Together with thousands of young Britons when Empire offered duty or adventure, Arthur had come to South Africa to fight in the Anglo-Boer War at the end of the nineteenth century. Like many other British "tommies," he settled for the African sun and was to become inspector of works in Bloemfontein. George's mother, Millicent Agnes Elliott, came from Folkestone, England.

George grew up in the atmosphere of a Free State English-speaking community till recently at war with the Boers, but working hard at peace. He went to Bloemfontein's St. Andrews High School and did his B.A. in politics and economics at the embryonic University of the Free State, then called Grey University College. He was totally at home speaking English and Afrikaans, which was to serve him well in later life as a journalist. It was natural for whites to speak both languages in that province because relations between the two white language groups were particularly good in the Free State (compared with the more divisive experiences of the Transvaal). This was in spite of the war's having drawn much English and Boer blood from 1899 to 1902. George just missed a Rhodes Scholarship to Oxford and went into journalism on the *Farmer's Weekly* and the *Friend* daily in Bloemfontein. (The *Friend* was in its day regarded, not all that over-frivolously, as the *Manchester Guardian* of South Africa. Its public service ended when it was closed in the 1980s by its owners because of declining fortunes in a province where Afrikaans had become dominant among whites.)

George married a girl from London who was descended on her mother's side from English essayist William Hazlitt. She was Vida Stodden, whose whole family had packed up in England after the first World War and gone to South Africa because her brother, Roy, had tuberculosis and needed the sun. They got sun in South Africa. They got a lifetime of it. In the mid-twenties, Vida began a fifty-year tryst with this harsh and beautiful land. One of her first "South African experiences" was when she was asked, when going to the butcher in Bloemfontein, to buy "boys'"—or servants' meat—for black domestic workers. Her adventures included editing publications, writing books, rearing two sons, and marriage to a journalist who left her a lifelong conundrum.

George became one of South Africa's best-known journalists. In the mid-thirties the family moved from Bloemfontein to the hub of South Africa, Johannesburg, where George joined the

*Rand Daily Mail.* (It was in future years to become a prescient liberal voice and a thorn in the side of white conservatives who were delighted when the paper was closed in 1985. The shabby deed was done, not by the government, but by the *Mail's* wealthy mine-industry owners, for "financial" reasons—just when the *Mail's* voice was most needed in the black townships and white suburbs of South Africa. The government applauded.)

On the *Mail,* and later writing a special weekly column for its Sunday stablemate, the *Sunday Times,* George's pen became a force in the land in the late thirties and early forties.

My earliest recollections are of moving from north to south and back again by train. George was parliamentary correspondent of the *Rand Daily Mail.* This occupation involved working for six months a year in Cape Town, the legislative capital of South Africa (Pretoria being the administrative capital and Bloemfontein the judicial capital). Each January we would come south from the Transvaal in what was called the "zoo train"—a horde of parliamentarians, officials, and journalists taking a two-day ride across the hot Karoo to the "mother city" for the session of Parliament. Our family life was alternately spent in a large Parktown house in Johannesburg and for the next six months amid mountains and mist, hard against the sea in Cape Town. There we would stay at a rambling two-storey Victorian house, Craigmillar, owned by Vida's mother, Margaret Jane Stodden.

George covered Parliament for the *Mail,* and early in 1937 he managed to scoop everyone, including Minister of finance N. C. Havenga, by publishing a remarkably accurate account of the national budget two days before it was delivered to Parliament. The *Volksblad* of Bloemfontein said that it "coincided in almost every detail with the minister's announcements." I have never been able to find out from whom George got the information, although I have suspicions. Vida was always Delphic when asked, and she put it down to intelligent guesswork based on research and a bit of official help. The forecast was too accurate to have been totally unassisted. I think he was given some figures by an official and did the rest himself. He kept the secret.

The *Mail* story created a *cause célèbre*. It followed on the heels of a sensational budget leak in Britain in 1936 leading to the resignation of a colonial secretary, J. H. Thomas. In George's case a magistrate was appointed under the Criminal Procedure Act to hold a special inquiry in Cape Town to force George to reveal his source. He refused even to take his place in the witness box, maintaining that he was not going to disclose anything. So the magistrate sentenced him to eight days in prison for contempt of court. (Journalists in South Africa have no legal right to refuse to name sources, and the prison term for refusing has since George's case been increased considerably. Absolute confidentiality is reserved only for lawyers in their dealings with clients.)

George would pace the floor at night, under pressure to give in. But he refused, with his journalist wife supporting him. Facing jail, he lodged an appeal and this was heard in the Cape Supreme Court in April 1937. Important issues were at stake. The case raised the question of whether journalists had the right to be silent. It also touched on the constitutional issue of whether British statutes covering such matters as official secrets were applicable in South Africa—a country which had become a full-fledged dominion while still technically under the British crown.

The appeal was lost in the Cape court. The Appellate Division in Bloemfontein was now the only avenue available to George. But before the case could go to Bloemfontein, the government discharged the committal order. In other words, George was let off and he never went to jail. People flocked to him with confidential information, knowing he could be trusted.

It was George Heard's public commitment to the Allied cause against Hitler which secured him a national reputation. In September 1939 South Africa entered the war on the Allied side by a thirteen-vote majority in Parliament. It was touch and go, and George was one of those who worked, wrote, and lobbied day and night to secure the pro-war vote.

The prime minister at the outbreak of war, General J. B. M.

Hertzog, wanted neutrality with Hitler, but his deputy, General J. C. Smuts, won the day in Parliament and became the country's wartime leader. J. G. N. Strauss, a member of the Smuts cabinet and in later years a leader of the opposition, provided Vida with a testimonial which said of George Heard: "In those crucial days in September 1939 when the South African Parliament had to decide whether to remain neutral or to side with the United Kingdom and its Allies, he was wholly committed, not only professionally as a member of the *Rand Daily Mail,* but also personally, to leave no stone unturned to swing the vote in favour of participation on the Allied side and to keep the sea route around the Cape open. Much is owed to George Heard for his untiring and valiant efforts."[6]

Then, in the words of Joel Mervis, a distinguished newspaper contemporary, George went on to become the key figure in a "massive, prolonged campaign" by the *Sunday Times* against the different groups of subversives in South Africa.[7]

Much of George's weekly column in the *Sunday Times* was devoted to ferreting out those who were working for a Nazi win. And there were many Afrikaner Nationalists—some of whom might have played with George among the prickly-pear bushes and *koppies* (hillocks) on the Free State veld as boys—who were praying for a Hitler victory. That would give them their goal: a "Christian National" Afrikaner republic freed from British influence. Some were fanatically pro-Nazi. Others were simply anti-British, seeing a Nazi win as a tactical means to an Afrikaner end. In the desperate days of world war, the difference between "pro-Nazi" and "anti-British" was vanishingly small.

Mervis writes of Heard's articles: "This spectacular campaign, carried out in the darkest months of the war, shows the extent to which the *Sunday Times* felt obliged to intervene directly in the war effort and to alert people to the grave dangers on their doorstep."[8] Mervis said George's exposure of the fifth column in South Africa, his analysis and his warnings, constituted a "journalistic highlight in the long history of the *Sunday Times.*"[9]

In late 1939 George exposed what he claimed were security lapses and Hitlerite sympathies in the South African Broadcasting

Corporation. After an inquiry, some staff were dismissed and even interned for the duration of the war.[10] George and his colleagues coined emotive wartime words like "Malanazi"—a play on the name of the leader of the opposition, Dr. D. F. Malan—to describe such sympathizers. (In postwar South Africa, Malan became prime minister in 1948.)

Explaining to *Sunday Times* readers what was going on, George wrote:

> Throughout the country today, aspiring politicians and "culture" leaders are gathering around them the nucleus of a "fighting" commando, pledged to defend the interests of Afrikanerdom and to confound its enemies. . . . South Africa's 'private armies' are not banned: their pamphlets and 'prophecies' and threatening letters circulate without let or hindrance. Members of the defence force, the public service and the police are free to join up with them, and there is probably no town in South Africa today where officials of these departments are not actively associated with one or other of the unofficial "commandos" operating in their districts.[11]

These writings were not calculated to endear him to those opposing the war. There were threats to his life. Mervis said that "Heard fought with the heart of a lion and the courage of a soldier. Anonymous threats did not deter him."[12]

A *Sunday Times* headline read: **MEN OF FIFTH COLUMN IN SOUTH AFRICA: QUISLINGS WANT NAZIS TO WIN THE WAR.** Beneath it, seven months after South Africa had declared war on Germany, George wrote: "The time has come for South Africa to start war against Germany. For more than seven months Hitler's fifth column has been operating almost unhindered in every part of the Union. Already it has gained great strategic objectives. It now threatens to accomplish in South Africa what its counterparts have already accomplished in Austria, Czechoslovakia, Poland and Norway."[13]

He criticized the Smuts government for its policy of early release of internees: "Men who have been interned on the most devastating police evidence (and who would have faced a firing squad in Germany) are being released because they 'look nice,' because they promise to be good, or because some of their friends and social acquaintances are satisfied that they are 'decent fellows.' No doubt many of them are decent fellows. According to some writers, Hitler himself is quite a 'decent fellow.' It does not occur to the benevolent folk who labour unceasingly for the release of internees that these self-same internees are mainly concerned in wrecking South Africa from within."[14]

All this made him a marked man. Leaders of the anti-war Ossewa-brandwag (O.B.) organization peppered their speeches and writings with attacks on him and on the editor of the *Sunday Times,* J. Langley Levy. Dr. Hans van Rensburg, the O.B. leader and commandant-general, speaking at the town of Parys on January 16, 1941, described one attack as the "foulest" to date, and Van Rensburg betrayed hardly veiled anti-Semitism: "It was in a Sunday newspaper edited by a 100% English Afrikaner descended from the tribe of Levy [*sic*]."[15]

The Ossewa-brandwag—literally, "ox-wagon sentinels," i.e., those who guard the interests of the Afrikaner nation—was a militant mass movement of Afrikaner nationalists working actively for a German win. Its violent, extreme wing was called the *Stormjaers* ("storm troops"). Their philosophy was anti-democratic, anti-Parliamentary, and fascist. Their methods and objectives included secret oaths, killing informers, sabotage, and political assassination. This treachery on the home front was carried out while South African forces fought a desperate war against fascism. They included many Afrikaners—and also seventy-five thousand African, coloured, and Asian troops.*

There is much irony in the fact that in 1942 at roughly the same time O.B. operatives were blowing up installations and endangering lives inside South Africa, a black South African

*Whom the Smuts government crassly refused to arm—thus illustrating its conservatism. Blacks could drive vehicles, fix machinery, and be of general help—but not shoot. A disillusioned coloured man who had been driven by this racism to join the wartime British army, where such discrimination did not exist, later settled in San Diego, U.S. He told me in 1990: "The reason for not arming blacks was simple. Smuts did not want blacks to kill white Germans." That's how some coloured people saw it.

taken prisoner by the Germans in North Africa was busy blowing up a German steamer in Tobruk harbour, using a jam tin and some cordite he had found. The man, Job Masego, died in obscurity in 1952—voteless like all other blacks.[16]

During the war, the O.B. grew so powerful and violent that it fell out with its political soul-brother, the National Party, which was the official opposition in Parliament. There was intense animosity—and violence—between them. The O.B. faded after the N.P. won the general election in 1948, and many O.B. figures gained government jobs. O.B. "General" Balthazar John Vorster went on to become prime minister of South Africa, and Hans van Rensburg was given a top job on the Group Areas Board, the body which segregated living areas.

Vida and George, while at a wartime dance in Johannesburg in 1942, were warned by the commissioner of the South African police that George was number four on the death list of the O.B.[17] "I hope you have a gun," said the commissioner. Vida does not recall George's ever carrying one. (Years later in Cape Town, in the early 1970s, the managing director of the *Cape Times,* Guy Cronwright, burst into the editor's office, at the height of some right-wing threats against the newspaper and myself, and blurted: "Do you want a revolver? We have a couple of old ones in the safe upstairs, from the war years." Mainly because they would endanger my untrained self more than the right wing, I said no thanks—probably echoing George's reasons thirty years before.)

George became highly controversial on other counts. He had discovered that he was a gifted public speaker. He began addressing rallies in favour of the war effort. These included calls for the Allies to take pressure off the Russians by opening a second front against Hitler. He also strongly supported the international campaign for food and aid parcels for the West's beleagured ally, Russia. He was vice-president of Medical Aid for Russia. He was no Communist—although official reports I saw later were to suggest that he had "leftist sympathies." Judging from his speeches and writings, and the personal assessment of his wife Vida, he was a left-leaning social democrat and a liberal. His strong feelings against racism and injustices like low black wages would have put him at odds with the capitalist forces bent on exploiting black labour while bolstering white privilege. Particularly controversial was his open support of militant servicemen's causes like the Springbok Legion, which in its early stages had pillars of the establishment on its ruling bodies. Among other things, the legion was working for a more just South Africa—not just for whites but for all its people—when the war finally ended. Later, after George had joined up in the navy, the legion did become Communist-inclined—and Vida resigned on behalf of both of them. George's support for that organization, even before it was openly far-left, was no doubt viewed with hostility by his employers. It came to breaking point. In 1942 the *Mail*'s board of directors issued this ultimatum to him: Stop your public speaking or leave.

George chose to resign. The news got around quickly. South Africa's best-known journalist was out. Vida recalls newspaper posters on Johannesburg streets saying **GEORGE HEARD SACKED.** When he and Vida got into a taxi to go to their Parktown home, the driver recognized George and immediately turned his meter off as a gesture of support.

Ignoring offers of a naval commission from friends in government, George joined up as an ordinary able-bodied seaman. After basic training, he served in coastal minesweepers. He felt that, of the war service options, at sea he would be least likely to have to kill his fellow man. He benefited physically from the active naval life and never looked fitter. He earned twenty-five pounds sterling a month and sent twenty to his family. Overnight, from being well-off, with a large house in Parktown, the Heards got used to a more frugal life in the modest suburb of Kensington. George went off to fight Hitler, but without his pen.

Things had become so dangerous for him at the *Mail* and *Sunday Times*, in view of the murderous activities of the O.B., that friends heaved a sigh of relief when George submerged himself among enlisted men—ironically finding safety in war service.

He was away from home for much of the period from 1942 to 1945. He would visit his family at our small house in

Kensington, Johannesburg, or in Cape Town if we were staying there with Vida's mother, Jenny Stodden. George went to Scotland in 1944 on secondment to the Royal Navy with a party of South African naval men to take delivery of three Loch-class frigates presented to South Africa by Britain as the war drew to a close. His ship was called the *Good Hope.* It was the most modern type of escort vessel.

Victory-in-Europe Day (May 7, 1945) found him on leave bicycling around the domain of the Earl of Antrim at Glenarm, Northern Ireland, and writing warmly to his family. He and a fellow officer had crossed from Scotland on the ferry to Larne. He stayed at an inn nearby called the Arms of Glenarm.

In mid-1945 the *Good Hope* picked up some former prisoners-of-war from England and sailed for South Africa, putting in at various West African ports including Walvis Bay in South West Africa (now Namibia). The ship arrived in Cape Town on July 2, and a big reception was held in the city hall for the returning men. George's name was mentioned in the press as one of those who had returned. People would have noticed he had come back to South Africa. His comments on the embryonic South African Navy were widely published and broadcast.

Having been promoted to a full lieutenant with two "rings," he was the signals officer and captain's secretary on board the *Good Hope.* George, from all accounts, got on well with his fellow officers. In Scotland he had shared a cabin with Alan Elgar, who later became the British consul-general in Cape Town. Elgar told me of a quiet, thoughtful man—in his late thirties, somewhat older than many of his colleagues—who did not "live it up," but who used to go down to London a lot. It is likely that, as a confidant of cabinet ministers in South Africa and a well-known figure in the propaganda war against Germany, George would have kept contact in London with South African and British political sources. Whether his involvement went beyond that is a matter of conjecture. He was offered a job in London, apparently to act as naval liaison between the South African and Royal navies, as the war in Europe ended. He turned this down because he wanted to return to his family in South Africa and resume his journalistic career. In letters home, he noted that he was *persona non grata* with the major newspaper groups and that he was nearing forty and anxious to get back to civilian life. He declined to volunteer to go to the Far Eastern Theatre against Japan, and began negotiations with his friend John Cope, editor of the *Forum* weekly in Johannesburg. The plan was that George would edit a new magazine in the *Forum* stable called *Photonews*—with backing from the prominent liberal, Cabinet Minister Jan Hofmeyr.

On arrival in Cape Town, George immediately took a train north to visit his family in Johannesburg. He went to Pretoria where he was offered a public relations post in the government agriculture department, which would have been employment, but would have bored him to tears. He signed a contract with Cope to edit *Photonews*. After finishing his leave, he returned to his ship early in August. He sent Vida three guineas, earned from a radio interview, to mark her birthday which was on Sunday, August 5. He went with his mother-in-law to a cinema in Cape Town on the night of Saturday, August 4. He was very anxious to avoid going east with the *Good Hope*, but he was having trouble getting demobilized from the navy. On the telephone he expressed dissatisfaction to Vida about this. He needn't have worried.

The atom bomb was dropped on Hiroshima on Monday, August 6, and news of the bombing was all over Cape Town. George animatedly and at length discussed the bomb's implications with John Cope, who was in Johannesburg, by phone. (Cope confirmed this to me in London years later.)

George would know this meant the end of the war . . . that he would not have to go east . . . that he would soon be demobilized . . . that he could get back to work with his friend John Cope.

At the time, the *Good Hope* was in Table Bay docks in Cape Town being fitted with ack-ack guns to deal with Japan's kamikaze planes when it went east. Its sister frigates were already on the way there. George had permission from his captain to sleep ashore at the home of Jenny Stodden because of the refitting and general disruption on the ship. Her modest house was then at number 31, Blackheath Road, Green Point, in a terraced row of cottages on the slopes of Signal Hill a few miles from where the *Good Hope* was docked. It was a five-minute bus ride and a short walk up a fairly steep Rhine Road to get there.

Vida's letter thanking George for the birthday telegram never reached him.

It waited on the *Good Hope,* to which he never returned.

> The court is therefore left with this: that at some time on the afternoon of August 8, 1945 (or thereafter) Lieutenant Heard disappeared and that no trace of him has since been found; that no reason of any kind for a voluntary disappearance has been shown, but, on the contrary, evidence exists which makes such conduct on his part most improbable. There is however no direct evidence to show either that Lieutenant Heard is dead or the manner in which he did meet, or might have met, his death.—Acting Justice Herbstein, refusing leave to presume death, in the matter: ex parte Heard, Cape Provincial Division of the Supreme Court, February 28, 1947.

There was some confusion about dates; but the last day on which he was seen was either August 8 or August 7. As indicated above, the Supreme Court worked on August 8 as the date of disappearance. He did not keep a dinner date with Jenny Stodden: she had specially prepared steak-and-kidney pie and waited for him in vain. He had ridden in a bus from the docks with a fellow officer, turned down an offer to have a drink, and begun walking up Rhine Road . . . not to arrive at the Blackheath Road address.

Earlier, George had turned up late to a lunch date with a journalist colleague working for the *Cape Argus.* They had sat chatting in the newspaperman's office because George did not feel like eating. George gave the clear impression that he was not cheerful.

George was seen that evening under the clock at Cape Town railway station—the most popular meeting spot in the city—by three able-bodied seamen. He was also seen walking in the Main Road, Sea Point, not far from where his mother-in-law lived but away from the direction of her house and his ship. He seems to have been under some sort of pressure. He had had demobiliza-

24

tion problems; but, after the widely publicized bomb, he would have known the war was about to end and that he would not have to go east. He may have sensed he was being followed. If so, why did he not tell someone he trusted? He had many friends in Cape Town. If he was seen, as some claimed, near the docks the day after missing dinner and planning to sleep at his mother-in-law's, the question is: where was he—without his shaving kit, etc.—that missing night?

In the excited atmosphere of the aftermath of the dropping of the atomic bomb, and also because he was staying ashore overnights, there was a delay of several days before he was posted missing. There was a confident belief that he would "turn up" after a few days. By that time any trails were no longer fresh . . . and memories were fading. This delay led to much confusion as to dates and details. There was also confusion between the navy and the police as to whose responsibility it was to investigate the disappearance.

The police criminal investigation department officer who handled the case, George Cloete Visser, assured me in Johannesburg many years later, not long before his death, that the police did their best. Interestingly, in that year of 1945 it was Visser who was appointed by the Smuts government to travel to Germany to take statements and seek documents concerning the activities of South African anti-war activists during the 1939–45 conflict.

George was known to have very little money on him. His naval kit was accounted for on his ship, down to his last vest. His shaving set lay untouched in Blackheath Road, ready for use. He had his greatcoat on; he would have needed it, for it was winter and chilly. It would have been dark by about 5:45 P.M. in August in Cape Town.

Vida flew to Cape Town as soon as she got the belated news. That was about August 14. In flight the passengers received news of the end of the Second World War. The world's troubles were lessened. Hers were beginning. She walked the streets of Cape Town and personally questioned scores of people. As the police and the naval authorities tried to find him, newspaper stories were written, and Vida offered a reward.

She later swore that while staying in the room where George slept at Blackheath Road she heard his voice in the middle of one night, saying: "It's no use." She was so convinced it was his voice that she woke her mother and told her. Vida knew that she, herself, would say: "It's no good." George would say "use."

Mediums, cranks, and sundry experts offered advice. Con men did so for profit. Almost everyone in Cape Town seemed to have seen George on his last day, but no one could prove it. Friends of George's scoured the city and dug the beaches. John Cope told me years later how he had dug with his bare hands in the sand at Llandudno, a rocky beach just along the coast from Sea Point. The navy sent out special parties to search and drag the seashore. Divers went down beside the *Good Hope* in case George had fallen overboard. Years later I went with a friend, on a hunch, to an old mine on Signal Hill above Green Point. We carried spades. We dug into the collapsed, dusty shaft. . . .

Nothing.

On August 8, 1945, George Heard just vanished.

It was South Africa's most famous and baffling missing-person mystery.

I discovered years later that a known O.B. assassin was in Cape Town at the time. There is evidence that he discussed the Heard case with a naval acquaintance later traced to Rhodesia (Zimbabwe). That discussion was a short time after the disappearance in 1945. The suspect was not around when I chanced upon the link. He had been hanged in Pretoria Central Prison in the early fifties for a murder committed in the eastern Cape. The bid to get to the bottom of the George Heard story continues. . . .

# CHAPTER THREE

# QUEST

George Heard disappeared when I was seven and my brother Raymond nine. I recall my father only in faded snapshots: fashioning a wire golf club; resting after falling down a hold on his minesweeper *Immortelle*; trying to coax a Rhodesian domestic worker into ironing his naval trousers in the "seven seas" style, flap-over-flap to fit into a kitbag; taking the phone from me as I informed him importantly, "It's Hoffie on the line" (his liberal friend Jan Hofmeyr, number two in the government); explaining to his sons how submarine-detection equipment called Asdic worked (with its "ping" noise). I recall crowding round the radio to hear South African naval men in Britain broadcasting Christmas messages home, and George said nothing memorable—only: "The beer's lousy."

Vida never received a war widow's pension, in spite of the presumption of death—turned down in 1947 but granted in 1952—and the fact that George was in full uniform when posted missing.

The men who hated George, the Afrikaner Nationalists whom he had attacked so severely in the war years, had their day. They came to power in 1948. It became obvious that there was no way that Vida would receive a pension from that government. She was told as much by people high up in the party. She petitioned Parliament on several occasions for a pension—even trying again in later years when war tensions and memories had mellowed. She was always turned down. So she kept writing and editing for a living.

In her old age, living in Cornwall, Vida was thrilled to chance upon recognition of George's war record, of all places, in Plymouth, England. There was his name inscribed on the naval war memorial on the seafront promontory, Plymouth Hoe. George's name was in the section for naval personnel who had no known graves, hewn in rock.

Whatever the South African Nationalist government might think of him, George's name was captured there forever.

The family never gave up. We pored over documents, talked to countless people in different parts of the world, checked court records and newspaper files. We went through the story with Vida a hundred times. And a hundred times we would think the matter solved.

The search went on all over South Africa—involving talking to journalists, members of Parliament, retired naval officers, his friends, even enemies. If *anyone* knew what had happened to him, they should. During a private discussion in the 1960s, I bluntly raised the matter with the former O.B. general and wartime internee, John Vorster. He was minister of justice, before becoming premier. He answered without hesitation.

"All I know about your father is that he scooped Klasie Havenga's budget," Vorster said—referring to the budget story in 1937. Vorster was either a bigger liar than I thought or instinctively telling the truth. To me, he did not seem to be hiding anything. When I was a young Parliamentary reporter I had had private discussions with M.P.s about my father, and some of those in the opposition were adamant that George had been "rubbed out" by the O.B. One M.P. had a story to rival the "bluebeard" murders.

As I sat in the lobby with hair on end, eyes wide, he pointed a finger to a certain extreme Afrikaner Nationalist walking around and claimed that he knew only too well what had happened to George Heard—and to others who had died in a string of political murders dating back through the turbulent war years to pre-war days of political intrigue in the (white) mineworkers' union.

Nothing conclusive was revealed . . . except for the powerful suspicion about the hanged O.B. man. It was strange that, all those years, no one gave anything away when inebriated or emboldened by time. It seemed pretty obvious that if, in fact, George was killed by the O.B. it was a private grudge—paid off in some dark alley, with the body disposed of and knowledge of the event limited. There were enough anti-war elements, including ex-internees emerging from camps, who had cause for a grudge.


There was compensation for the frustrations of the search.

I made the acquaintance of my own father. I learned much about his pen and his public speaking, his courage and his commitment to free expression and his rejection of totalitarianism and regimentation. And, indeed, I learned about his optimism for the triumph of liberalism; what he once was to describe as "a new outlook . . . that is foreign to the fear-conditioned politics in our country."

His egalitarianism in matters of race came through strongly. He posed this question to a Springbok Legion meeting: What value would there be in wartime victory if whites came back to well-paid jobs while blacks earned the same pittance on the gold mines?* He believed in a South Africa for all South Africans—an ambitious notion in the days when "South Africans" were seen as axiomatically white, and "the natives" as "the problem." It took time for whites to realize who the problem was.

*These pittances, over the long period from 1911 to 1969, remained static at a low level in real terms, and it was only after 1970 when this scandalous situation was addressed by the mining houses under pressure of black organized labour and other factors—see *Uprooting Poverty: the South African Challenge*, by Francis Wilson and Mamphela Ramphele, published by David Philip in 1989, 194.

George Heard's views, which I came across in yellowed speeches and clippings kept together by rusty pins, and gleaned from people who knew him, were an inspiration. He was a man before his time.

CHAPTER FOUR

# MOOI RIVER

My brother Raymond and I had most of our school years in
the province of Natal. Primary school years were spent in the hilly
midlands at Mooi (meaning "pretty") River. High school years
were spent in the sweltering port of Durban, which was our home.

When George disappeared Vida took the family to Durban
and secured a job on the local morning newspaper, the *Natal
Mercury*. She was editor of the women's pages, which had been
suspended during the war.

Vida trained five socialites in journalism and did the rounds
in a part of the country much devoted to horse racing, polo, pink
gins, and white superiority. Durban, she says, was "convoylessing"
after the eventful war years when hundreds of Allied ships had
called and were entertained by Durbanites. The Durban social
whirl culminated each year with the country's premier horse race,
the July handicap—when the women would vie with one another
in fashion, watched by binoculars-clutching, well-groomed,
frequently empty-headed men. The privileged whites were

waited on hand and foot by sweating Zulus and Indian waiters.

Though July was mid-winter, it was usually pleasantly warm in subtropical Durban. So dates of business and professional conferences were carefully manipulated to coincide with the "July" or the other big race, the Gold Cup. These events attracted the top dogs of the South African white establishment, such as Rand mining moguls who would bet more on a horse than they would pay a gold miner in a month for working in intolerable conditions two miles underground. They would mingle with the handsome and sunburnt sugar-cane barons of the Natal coast and the racehorse owners of the province's lush midlands.

Elsewhere at the races, in segregated public places, would be the hoi polloi having *their* fling.

In the July season Durban attracted hordes of ordinary white families taking advantage of the holiday warmth. They stayed in good but cheap, whites-only beachfront hotels. They would come from Johannesburg, Pretoria, Bloemfontein, and country towns and farms. The main tourist dangers were sunburn, stings from jellyfish or the Portuguese man-of-war (or "bluebottle," with trailing tails), drowning, and sharks. The last-mentioned offered tourists a fair choice of terror—Tiger, Ragged Tooth, Zambesi, and Great White, and others. These swift-moving monsters we called "johnnies," with due respect.

Criminal elements would descend on Durban in the July season like flying ants after rain.

This was Durban, our "holiday home" from where we went off to boarding school, Treverton, a hundred miles inland at Mooi River.

Treverton life was invigorating. Winter was cold; for Mooi River, unlike Durban, was several thousand feet high. In winter the domestic water pipes had to be swathed in burlap or they could burst in sub-zero temperatures. A thick evening fog rivalling San Francisco's would roll in at certain times of the year, and we would sit on the scrub-grassed hillside waiting for its dank grip. The Drakensburg peaks, visible on a horizon near Basutoland, would be capped in snow, sending icy winds toward

Treverton. Lightning could maim or kill locals, particularly as they walked over the highly conductive ironstone rocks.

We went through standard boarding-school experience—fear of a legendary axe murderer roaming the hills; catching the debilitating bilharzia disease from taking dips in the stagnant pools of the Mooi (the cause: a micro-parasite that burrows through the skin and makes for the bladder); misery at being separated from family; running away (one lad was delivered by train in Durban in a milk-can); playing rough veld games like "bok-bok" involving back-cracking leaps on other boys in line against a wall; falls from horses, trees, trains, you name it; embryonic sex education peeping at the elocution teacher and science master necking outside our dormitory; and lashes of "cuts" from Headmaster Peter Binns with his feared malacca cane.

It was an exclusively white life. Only whites were enrolled at the school, and that was seen as perfectly natural and routine. (Parents wanting a racially mixed education for their children had few options. In time the well-off came to transport them across international frontiers to non-racial schools like Waterford in Swaziland. During the 1980s the pattern gradually changed, and private schools in South Africa—but still not government schools—increasingly admitted all races.)

Our school life in the 1940s went on as if blacks did not exist. They were, in fact, remarkably versatile. They were everywhere and nowhere at the same time. Living evidence of the power of bilocation. They were the familiar dark shapes who waited on us, worked in the kitchen, cleaned the grounds, shuffled through the cold nights emptying bucket toilets.

The sound of a spade or a pick was a surefire sign of an African at work, shovelling something for whites. There was a rumour in school that African workers licked the stamps that were placed on the loaves of bread at the bakery down the road. This did not please us one bit—as if white spittle would have been any different.

Blacks were not really recognized as people, certainly not in the way that *we* were people. They were servants. They were part of the necessary furniture of life. There were two worlds—and no meeting-points between them, except as master and servant. That was how it had been. That was how it was. That was how, we thought, it would remain.

The Zulu workers had their own "khaya" (or place) way beyond the rugby field, on the far side of some high gum trees. There they ate their own "putu" (corn meal) between thumb and fingertips, drank their "maas" (sour milk), brushed their shiny teeth with charcoal from open fires. They did their living there.

Near the "khaya," obscured among the rocks and heath on a "koppie," were several British war graves, marking where "tommies" had fallen in warfare against the Boers. These bore faint testimony to the giant and distant conflicts in the nineteenth century. Nearby to the north lay Ladysmith, Colenso, and Estcourt, where fierce battles had been fought half a century before between Boer and Briton. There had been white-black conflict too. Not many miles away was Weenen, where the Zulus had slaughtered Boers in whole families, and Blood River, where the Boers had had their revenge, formally asking God's help in advance. They wiped out three thousand Zulus for the loss of none of their own, which can perhaps be noted as somewhat over-enthusiastic divine intervention. (The Boers thanked God profusely every year, till further notice, by making December 16 a public holiday to commemorate the event.) There were places like Isandhlwana, where Zulus overran the British; and Rorke's Drift where the British held out against the Zulu flood and won several Victoria Crosses; and Ulundi where the British Empire crushed Zulu power in 1879. The prince imperial of France, Napoleon Eugene Louis Jean Joseph, had been ambushed and killed by Zulus on June 1, 1879, while on a mounted "recce" with British soldiers, causing tension between the thrones of Britain and France. The hills were drenched in treachery and blood.

Those hills of central and northern Natal hoarsely screamed out history at us, pointing to old conflict that would echo in the present and the future. There was enough evidence there to sharpen our interest in race relations and the central dilemma of how South Africans could live together in one land. But the impressions made on us were small and indistinct, as I recall. It is all a matter of conditioning.

We used to clamber "out of bounds" over the barbed-wire fence at the top end of the school grounds, pick our way to the koppies, and gaze at the graves.

The little mounds covered the bones of those who had (like my grandfather) come to Africa for Empire. They were sad little graves, forgotten in the hills of Natal and cut off from English home.

In 1947 the British Royal Family detoured to that area while on a state visit to South Africa, and they visited the historic Boer War battlefields of Colenso and Spionkop not many miles from Treverton. I was among the Treverton boys, clutching Union Jacks, who waved to them as they passed through Estcourt in the governor-general's shiny white train.

At Treverton we learned some Zulu, which I found useful in later life—in the Xhosa-speaking Cape where there is the same language root, Nguni. It struck me powerfully later that I had learned to express my needs in Zulu—"mena funa isinkwa" (I want bread), for instance—but not, with the same facility, to offer anything to others. Take, not give. This was how it was. Blacks were there to provide for needs.

Reminders of racial history abounded. Not too far from our school, in the province's capital city of Pietermaritzburg, a young barrister had been thrown off a train in 1893, his luggage turfed out after him. His name was Mahatma Gandhi. And, as he wryly noted, he had possessed a first-class ticket.[18]

It was always good to get away from Treverton to escape to the relative comfort of home in Durban. The first thing we would do was guzzle the local municipal water. It was tastier than Mooi River's rain water, caught in tin tanks, heavily treated with chemicals, and served in shiny tin buckets. That was our immediate luxury of home. But the real value was living in a liberal, tolerant atmosphere at home—despite the countervailing influences of school and society, which were powerful.

35

Yet it was overwhelmingly a cosseted life in a sea of black shapes. We were never told to be unkind to or distrustful of blacks. It was just how one grew up at school—or, at least, some schools. People of colour were "different." Their world lapped over into ours, but only at the convenient level of manual labour. Yet they were the majority in the land . . . a growing presence, an awakening giant, if anyone cared to notice.

I remember, many years later, arriving at a luxurious home in Durban with an acquaintance. Without betraying any sensitivity, he said stereophonically to our host, for everyone to hear, "Feed my coon!" The "coon" was his car driver. This disposed of, we whites went in to an exquisite dinner. The remark showed some brusque concern for the driver's stomach, granted; but his dignity needed feeding too. This everyday incident reflected a knee-jerk cast of mind widely in evidence in Natal, the "English" province. Natal whites can be every bit as racist as the most conservative Afrikaners, as anyone who went to school there can confirm.

The beginning of wisdom in South Africa is to appreciate that the politically dominant Afrikaners undeservedly took the blame for almost everything that happened under apartheid. Because of their bluntness and forthrightness, they certainly asked for it; but they didn't deserve all the blame. They played the leading role in formalizing and enforcing apartheid, particularly after the National Party came to power in 1948. But the process of segregation was aided and abetted by English-speakers.* This was particularly so in reactionary places like Natal, where segregation was applied with indecent haste and enthusiasm by local authorities. The irony was that Natal, at the same time, produced major contradictions—liberal voices like Alan Paton who wrote the classic indictment of apartheid, *Cry, the Beloved Country*,

*For a discussion of the gold-mining moguls' role in buttressing repressive measures such as pass laws and single-sex migratory labour in South African history, see Wilson and Ramphele, *Uprooting Poverty: the South African Challenge*, 197.

his fellow-liberal Peter Brown, and many others. This, also, was the province of ex-chief Albert Luthuli, the Nobel prize–winning leader of the ANC.

The spoils of apartheid were not confined to the Afrikaners. Far from it. Despite being well looked after by the National Party government, they always lagged financially behind their English-speaking compatriots. The Afrikaners were, indeed, at the political coal face—the public sector. They were the bureaucrats of apartheid. They did the dirty work and got the flack.

The joint beneficiaries of white privilege, comfortably at one remove, were the urbane commercial and professional classes who were English-speaking (a population group that numbered about 40 percent of the whites). They were the "uninvolved minority" who spoke in liberal-sounding clichés but, in many cases, expected blacks to use the "back door." After dining well on tripe or roast beef in their gentlemen's clubs, they would bank apartheid's dividends. There were exceptions, marvellous ones . . . and changed times brought better attitudes. But the generalization holds.


## FIRST BLOOD: JANUARY 1949

My introduction to racial violence was in Durban—in fact, it was the first major riot to face the new government elected in 1948.

The long summer school holidays were ending, and we were preparing to return to Treverton in Mooi River. It was the steamiest time of the year. That was the moment, the night of January 13, 1949, when the Zulus rose against the Indians. The people of Shaka, known as the "Black Napoleon" in the nineteenth century in Natal history, clashed with the descendants of the so-called "coolies" imported from India to work the Natal sugar-cane fields.

The Indians were no match. By 1949, the Zulus of Natal numbered several millions; the Indians were a community of about three hundred thousand. The Indians' commercial success

37

was a cause of friction—it generated envy and resentment from other races.

Although the causes of the riots, and the events themselves, were shrouded in controversy and confusion, it seems that a minor, spontaneous incident—a young Zulu boy being maltreated by an Indian—led to the carnage.

In the two days of rioting Indians fled before Zulu impis (armies), whites were terrified, and police were heavily extended. The Zulus were disciplined and harsh. They brandished their traditional "knobkieries" (a stick with a knob at the end), knives, and sugar-cane machetes or "cane knives."

The death toll will probably never be determined. A commission of inquiry put it at fifty Indians and eight-seven Africans, which would be on the conservative side. A thousand or more people—including a small number of whites—were injured. The commission spoke of the Indians having been "slaughtered like sheep." The government complained about the newspaper coverage, particularly foreign reporting. The *New York Sun* conveyed something of the atmosphere in a dispatch quoted in Parliament: "Residential areas were put to the torch by Natives shouting battle cries."[19]

At home and abroad, political lectures were delivered to the new South African government about the causes of the riots—lectures which it resented. General Smuts, who had become leader of the opposition after losing the 1948 election, described the incidents as the first fruits of the government's policy of racial repression.[20] Smuts said, among other things: "What happened in Durban is a sign. We are now taking away small rights which have been enjoyed for generations by the non-European population."[21]

Black nationalist groups showing a sense of responsibility urged rioters to be calm and not to play into the hands of political quarters that wanted to foster racial hatred at the expense of the African cause.

The staff correspondent of the *New York Times*, G. H. Archambault, was critical of the fact that little had been done about black housing. "They squat and build shanties," wrote Archambault, a remark that could be made with the same justice a generation later. He also observed: "British South Africans still retain the 'outpost of empire' attitude and Afrikaners the patriarchal attitude toward the non-Europeans."[22]

The Durban racial explosion brushed right past me.

I was at Vida's apartment on the eighth floor of Chelsea Court on the Victoria Embankment, also called the Esplanade.

That apartment looked out over the Durban Bay. In the distance stood the green-clad Bluff, a large promontory which created a natural harbour. A whaling factory operated on the Bluff at a point marked by blubber, blood, and ravenous sharks. "Moaning Minnie," a dredger given this name by local insomniacs, clanked day and night clearing the bay. On the Esplanade lay the Durban Yacht Club, frequented by the smart-casual white yachting set amid the high masts. In the shallows of the bay shimmering above the sand banks were schools of mullet. Halfway across the bay was Salisbury Island, to us a place of exciting mangrove swamps, mamba snakes, and egrets' eggs, where the British and South Africans had secretly built a major naval base during the war. The Esplanade was dotted with high palms and clustered rockeries. A statue of Dick King, who had undertaken a six-hundred-mile ride from Durban to Grahamstown in 1842 to bring reinforcements to the British garrison under Boer pressure, showed him wearily astride his equally exhausted horse. The scene was palm-fringed tranquility.

Until January 13, 1949.

My teenage recollection of the incident was fleeting but powerfully permanent.

A terrified Indian youth ran down the esplanade, vaulted a wall, darted down the railway track. Thirty or forty Zulus pursued him wielding cane knives and knobkieries. From behind the window on the eighth floor of Chelsea Court, no noise could be heard. Just this crowd chasing a man, like predators in a wild leap after an antelope.

That was all. A lone man's terror. A boy aged twelve, nose pressed to windowpane, transfixed. . . .

39

I realized, with a chill, what was happening. The man was being chased *because he was an Indian and for no other reason.*

Pursuers and pursued disappeared along the railway track in a blur, in the direction of the customs house.

# CHAPTER FIVE

# DURBAN HIGH

Durban High School presided in red brick on a hill called the Berea overlooking the city of Durban. It had produced everyone who mattered, we thought . . . indeed, one memorable year, half a South African Springbok cricket team. Then there was a former Speaker of the house of assembly who became governor-general of South Africa, Dr. E. G. Jansen (not much mentioned because he was a Nationalist); poet Roy Campbell who achieved international fame; British playwright Noel Langley; Bill Payne, a massive war veteran who rather light-heartedly taught us Latin and religion and ran the fifty-five-mile Comrades' Marathon between Durban and Maritzburg in rugby boots, stopping for steak-and-eggs halfway; and master bomber Capt. Edwin Swales, awarded a posthumous Victoria Cross in the Second World War for air bravery over Pforzheim, Germany, in the dying days of the war in Europe.

There was a mixed assortment, including beach boys, marijuana-smokers, kleptomaniacs, even a hypnotist. One "old boy" became a travelogue producer in Canada. Another died in the South African Air Force defending white South Africa. Another died after being injured on the rugby field before our horrified eyes in a game against prestigious Anglican private school Michaelhouse. Yet another, Robert Brandon Kirby, became a satirist who would quote on the stage the very expressions banned by the puritanical South African censors.

Another, a prefect of our "house" at school, shot and killed himself when his girlfriend ended the relationship on the phone. Another's mother was charged with keeping a brothel.

We were given a solid, bland English grammar school–type education. Natal was the only United Party opposition stronghold after the National Party came to power in 1948. Since education was a matter reserved for the provinces by the Act of Union in 1910, Natal was able, at least for some time, to go its own "English" way even when the Afrikaner Nationalists came to power. In some measure it could thus resist introduction of the concept of "Christian National Education" forced on white schools by Nationalists. (C.N.E. was aimed, *inter alia*, at turning out good, God-fearing citizens for apartheid.)

Academic standards at Durban High were adequate to good. We learned lots of Latin and lots of history and never to split infinitives. We knew all about ablative absolutes and Caesar's campaigns. There were lots of experiments with Bunsen burners and test-tubes.

The school had borrowed some British traditions, notably caning by "masters" and prefects and callous initiation rites. Also, the system of enslavement of younger boys. The prefects arbitrarily allocated themselves several junior helpers or slaves (called "poops") who fetched and carried everything—even washing rugby kits and warming toilet seats for them in winter. Life was Spartan for newcomers.

The Berea where Durban High was situated was a well-heeled suburb with high mango and avocado trees and the sound of "hadedas" and Indian mynah birds in the sky. "Intensely red outbursts of poinsettia," noted by Mark Twain on a visit back in 1897, were still much in evidence on the Berea.[23] It was marginally cooler than the humid city bowl below. We lived a privileged life. We were waited on by Zulus dressed in faintly ridiculous "house-boy" garb—aprons and long shorts not quite covering the "house-maid's knee" caused by a lifetime on all fours cleaning floors. It gave them the appearance of eunuchs.

In Durban, a big city with growing squatter areas like Cato Manor, the shadowy black presences were more in evidence than at rural Mooi River. We got to know more blacks by name, but still on a master-servant basis. Like Frans.

The kitchen staff were masterful at carrying plates in and out of the dining room. They would load up in the kitchen and walk gingerly in with a teetering array of plates. These were perched on hands, arms, sometimes almost up to shoulders. Frans, I think, held the school record at about twenty plates.

On one occasion, Frans (no one seemed to know his sur-name) emerged with a load of chocolate blancmange, something we abhorred and had secretly conspired to boycott. Frans was turned down by everyone he tried to entice to take a plate. His face sweating profusely, he exclaimed "aikona!" (more or less "shucks!") and gave the click of irritation delivered so expertly from the side of the mouth—and which means more than mere "tsk! tsk!" He staggered back to the kitchen, the burden telling on his aging frame. The boarding-school masters, who sat at a high table and said grace in incomprehensible Latin, had a simple remedy.

No sweets courses were served for weeks, which was a relief to kitchen staff. This was the masters' stiff-upper-lip approach to rebellion.

Discovery that bilharzia had accompanied some of us to Durban from Mooi River was excellent news. It provided the excuse on three days each week to secure an *exeat* ("let him go out" in Latin) to have injections at Addington Hospital. This was just across the road from South Beach. After having the serum mainlined into the forearm, one could "hit out" with other surfers and "catch slides" (waves). Only a punctured arm cramped one's style.

43

Beach life was beguiling and remote from the realities of South Africa which, by the 1950s, were starting to press in. (The National Party had come to power in 1948, and, living in the opposition "English" stronghold of Natal, we were aware of this "bad news." The riots of 1949 had confirmed big trouble ahead.) The sun would roast people on the beach a golden brown. Sensitive skins would turn pink, causing pain and requiring soothing calamine lotion. The beach sand could be so hot that it was necessary to throw a towel down ahead, like playing hop-scotch, to dull the heat for each step taken. The surfers, particularly the members of our South Beach Surf Board Club, the first such club in South Africa, were reputed to be the "Greek gods" of the beach. They got the waves and the "allies," girls. They would ride twelve-foot long Hawaiian plywood boards, or use canvas-covered paddle-skis. Those were the days before the short, light boards—with easier portability and manoeuvrability which popularized surfing worldwide. The old dreadnought-like craft we used—called "guns"—were far more difficult to steer and control. Surfers would take off on "slides," with no skeg or keel to hold them in the wave, and they would have to dip hands or feet in the water for direction finding. To cut across a wave was the ultimate experience, called "broadsiding." Even a short distance side-slipping away over the face would almost match the euphoria of being "locked in the tube" which came in later years. With no "dog-leashes" to tie around our ankles, loss of the board in a "wipe out" would mean a long swim in, while the board scythed dangerously toward swimmers, rocks, or beach.

Surfers sported gashes, broken ribs, even cracked skulls—testimony to the dangers of the sport. These were marks of honour, as in tribal fighting or Germanic fencing. A friend of ours, a pupil at rival Glenwood High School, was taken by a shark off Addington Hospital in the early 1950s. He yelled a warning to friends and disappeared in a swirl of blood while body-surfing.

Other surfers had shark bites and close shaves, including one whose surf-ski's bow was bitten off. Later, when shark nets were laid off the beaches, the danger receded.

Life was full of tales of slides, broadsides, johnnies, jellies, and blues. And "allies." The girls were essential surf equipment, camp-followers of the beach. Some would surf solo, or "two-up" with a boyfriend; others would ooh and aah from the beach.

Beach life was almost non-dimensional. There was little to discuss apart from beach and girls. There was no women's lib, no gay rights, no pollution, no AIDS, no hard drugs, no politics, no blacks except labourers. Just slides and allies. Those were the days of London jive, Ike, bobby-soxers, and Brylcreem. We hadn't heard of Joe McCarthy, and Korea meant Chesterfield cigarettes and chewing gum—because that's what U.S. sailors en route there gave us.

In those days there was no pill, no loop. Pregnancies happened and were invariably unwanted. Abortion was back street. "Dagga" or marijuana (but nothing stronger) was used by some beach boys, with the choicest variety brought in from the Transkei to the south. Liquor was freely available and consumed—and cheap at sevenpence a tot for cane spirits at the railway bar; sometimes with a bar brawl thrown in.

The lifesavers worked hard; but, like fashion models, their career days were numbered. In their thirties they could become too old to perform rescues in the taxing surf. The constant exposure to the sun could addle the brain, and the years on the beach would take their toll. Some would filter off into other jobs, such as bowling-green attendant or toilet attendant, barman, surfboard-maker, or looking after boats in the kiddies' paddling pond. A few did well in life, including some who were brilliant at school and university, and, after stints as lifesavers, took up promising careers. One became an Oxord blue and a barrister; another became a prominent butcher in Cape Town.

There was a dark side to beach life. One of the "boys" was jailed for three years for rape. Another was charged with having sex with an underage girl (under sixteen)—a warning to others which went unheeded. Another got into a scuffle with a millionaire at a party; a "contract" was put out on him, but he was lucky because the person "contracted" turned out to be a beach boy. One resourceful printer, among the best surfers on the beach, was jailed in the United States and South Africa for scattering counterfeit U.S. dollar bills around Disneyland, California. Another beach boy was jailed in London for faking an attack on a rich widow for insurance purposes.

There were frequent fights with visiting toughs from Johannesburg, and a reported fracas with Indian youths in the sleazy Point Road area—the only serious "racial" incident I recall. Life took its toll.

The main horizon in life was surfing. The only other places we wanted to visit were the Channel Islands, north Cornwall, the U.S. West Coast, Australia, and Hawaii—all rich in surf spots. We knew all about renowned places such as the Pipeline, Waimea Bay, Sunset, and the Wedge. There were regular "surfaris" to the South African equivalents—Scottburgh, Jeffreys Bay, Victoria Bay, and Cape St. Francis on the warm East Coast, and Eland's Bay on the icy West.

Vida wondered whether our desire to spend our lives as professional lifesavers required some mature and detached consideration. In time, so did we. Raymond and I both entered journalism, in Bloemfontein and Cape Town respectively. He left South Africa after Sharpeville and Langa and made a successful communications career in North America.

Matters racial were simple to understand. "Non-whites" were banned from the main beaches in Durban, except to work for whites. Indian waiters in high-necked white tunics padded on the hot sand offering refreshments. Zulus did heavier work, carrying loads of umbrellas and deck chairs and preparing them for sunbathers. Apart from the massed armies of black labour in evidence, whites had the beach and the surf to themselves.

As beach boys, I recall no open hostility toward blacks. We were simply unconcerned about them and their problems. Africans had their "own" swimming places somewhere up the remote coast, and in any event we knew *they* were not keen on swimming. We knew that there were excellent Indian surfers who caught slides on "their" beach, also up the coast. But they all

46

had their recreation place "somewhere else"; that was how it was.

It was years before I caught my first wave with a black South African—a "coloured" surfer on a shimmering stretch near Muizenberg, Cape Town, at a spot called the cemetery. The same north-wester blew in our faces; the same crumbling, gentle False Bay breaker took us to the shore. A refreshing "first" for me.


The Africans we would encounter in Durban were mainly local workmen; or occasional up-country blacks dodging the law at a white beach to scoop a bottleful of sea-water for medicinal purposes back home; or "ricksha boys," powerful men with feather head-dresses and bead anklets who pulled tourists around in festive carts—and would die young because of the physical exertion; or gas station attendants who would open pink palms (as at communion) seeking their "tip" after filling up. "Thank-you baas," they would say coaxingly.

We got friendly, to a degree, with Indian lads who worked with us on the "Surf-o-Plane" (surf cushions) business on South Beach. We white youngsters went into the water to fetch the "planes" when the hirers' time was up. The Indians, not allowed by law to swim at a white beach, earned their pay stacking the rubber cushions.

They did not bother to bring the costumes they knew would never get wet.

Our beach income was made on the "Surf-o-Plane" job and in two other ways.

We would look for "tom" (money), lost by tourists and thrown up by the high tide. We would grab it when it rolled down the steep sand inclines as the waves receded. The cry, "The tom is rolling," would bring us running to find it.

And, more dangerously, we would lay shark bait on our surfboards for anglers who could not cast out that far. With shark attacks common in those pre-nets days, laying bait concentrated the mind wonderfully.

Durban High School, rooted in discipline, was keen on cadets for its pupils. Cadets mustered each Monday on the blaz-

47

ingly hot school grounds in smart khaki uniforms, shiny buttons, belts, and unloaded rifles. The surfers and "beach boys" were widely regarded as undisciplinable slouches. They were confined to a remote corner of the parade ground where they could cause minimal damage to the overall effect of smartness. They formed up—in a manner of speaking—in a specially designated group accurately named the "Awkward Squad." After roll-call we would strut about like spastics, lampooning the disciplined formations elsewhere on parade. It was fun. The second best thing to surfing was the Awkward Squad.

My fellow-pupil who was the cadet officer commanding was a disciplined, tall, Olympic-standard backstroke swimmer, Stephen Mulholland. His involvement in my career was to be indelible. He was not only to be in charge when I was banished to the Awkward Squad. He was also destined to fire me from my job as editor more than thirty years later.

Mulholland was a stickler for smartness and discipline. He would get the whole field organized in tidy formations, masses of khaki-clad cadets turning, wheeling, at his command. This finger-tip control of people served him well in business life later when he headed a newspaper company and returned it to profitability. In a varied earlier career, he attended universities in the U.S., discovered Adam Smith and Milton Friedman, and was briefly a GI. On parade ground and in business he had a touch of General Patton about him.


It was in this atmosphere of sound colonial schooling and white privilege that we lived our lives in the first half of the fifties in Durban. All around us swarmed black South Africans, most of them doing heavy jobs for whites. Almost every household had its "boy" or "girl." Hordes of bare-handed or white-gloved servants would be employed in affluent white houses as cooks, maids, "houseboys," gardeners, drivers, "delivery boys." They served, they cleaned, they dug, they rinsed, they mopped, they polished, they carried, they delivered, they cared for white children. They seldom answered back.

An Israeli ambassador to South Africa once observed to me that he had found South Africa the "country of little bells"—the bells that summon blacks to work. Though never enslaved in the formal sense, local Africans knew what the sound of a bell meant.

Blacks did much of their work by bicycle. As it happened, a parked one figured in one of my elementary lessons in race relations. I had visited a shop not far from Durban High. A large, balloon-tired bike was being parked against a pillar outside the shop by a burly adult African. Irritated, I said to him: "Hey, boy! Move your bike."

I was about thirteen, in my school blazer and tie—all navy blue and gold. He was much older, dignified.

He turned hurt eyes on me, made room for both bikes, and announced: "I am a man, not a boy."

Wherever he is, I thank him.

Another incident occurred in bustling West Street, Durban's main thoroughfare. Mixed humanity would course its way past department stores like Greenacres and Payne Brothers and fashionable boutiques with posh names like Montclair Modes.

On this occasion a crowd had gathered. A white man was in the process of beating a black man with his fists.

A tall Durban High senior whom I admired and respected moved forward.

"Leave him alone," he rasped at the white man, placing himself between them.

That ended it. This was a brave thing to do in Durban in those days when whites in the streets tended axiomatically to be right.

That incident I never forgot either.

Growing up in South Africa—the country of critical choice— I found that, however cocooned from reality people were, they faced decisions they could not duck.

Not to decide was to decide.

49

The decisions were not about mundane but fundamental things—right and wrong, affluence and poverty, justice and tyranny, integration and segregation, domination and democracy . . . about beach co-workers who dare not swim; about "boys" who are men; about beatings and bravery in city streets.

## LONDON 1954–55

After matriculating in Durban in 1954, I spent six months in London. At that stage, my experience of other races was largely confined to being served by burly Zulus with housemaid's knee in Natal. Pitman's College in High Holborn, where I learned shorthand and typing, was an exclusively white assemblage of London "office girls" in their beehive hairstyles. The atmosphere was similarly white at the Ludgate Circus offices of the Methodist Youth Department at the foot of Fleet Street where I washed teacups and typed envelopes. That was the closest to Fleet Street that I could get.

In London I shared lodgings with a fellow beach boy from Durban who later became an active right winger in South Africa and worked for the police public relations department. We lived in Earls Court where "colonials" gathered at places like the "Snake Pit" in Trebovir Road and the Overseas Visitors' Club. Most were white, but we also met Pakistanis and Indians—and even a Nigerian or two. In those days South Africans did not require a permit to work in Britain (this changed after South Africa left the Commonwealth in 1961). So a large number of young whites would go over in the Union-Castle Line mailships, tasting the wine in Madeira en route, and try their hands at any job they could find. Example: One friend who wanted to be a Royal Navy admiral had to content himself with carving the crosses on the hot-cross buns at Lyons Corner House in the Strand. Work was menial, but life was good. London was eminently livable, less touristy and cheaper than in later years.

Race relations were not much discussed. It was before British tolerance was put to the test by large-scale black immigration—and indeed before right-wing politician Enoch Powell made an anti-immigration speech about the Thames foaming with blood like the Tiber of old. An acquaintance of mine, a tea-taster in the City of London, had seen his family dispossessed in Ceylon (later Sri Lanka) when tea estates were seized, and his view of people of colour was not complimentary. He warned me darkly that the same fate would befall white South Africans. When I was nagged by Britons about apartheid I responded defensively with the usual white South African excuses about blacks "not being ready" to share power, etc. I once went to a party in North London and heard the wife of a South African tenor going on shrilly about the influx into Britain of "these bleddy bleks, who give me the shits" [sic]. There were plenty more shocks in store for her, considering the wave of immigration to come.

Before returning to South Africa, I had begun reading the *News Chronicle,* the fine liberal daily that was later closed. Its South African correspondent, Stanley Uys, and other liberal journalists made an impression on me with their reports about the madness of apartheid. Moreover, I was intrigued by the freedom enjoyed by eloquent blacks in speeches urging colonial freedom at Hyde Park Corner.

# CHAPTER SIX

# MOTHER CITY, JUNE 1955

"We had everything before us, we had nothing before us."
*A Tale of Two Cities, 35*

The city of Cape Town, where I began my career in 1955, lies in the embrace of Table Mountain and spills away from its rock fastness to the sea. Suburbs ribbon along the footslopes and valleys, wedged between mountain and ocean. They form a racial and linguistic mosaic.

To the west, hard against the mountain slopes lie the well-heeled, largely English-speaking "Atlantic" suburbs. Sprinkled among them are pockets of poorer areas and the historic Cape Malay quarter of Scottsche Kloof. Suburbs close to the city are rich in Dutch/Afrikaans names like Tamboerskloof (literally, "valley of drums" and Vredehoek ("peaceful corner"). Houses are concentrated on the lower slopes of Lion's Head, Signal Hill, and the Twelve Apostles—running from Green Point to Sea Point, and on to Camps Bay. From here a winding, well-cambered coastal road favoured by motor-bike enthusiasts sweeps on to Llandudno then past Little Lion's Head down to the green valley of Hout Bay (this, the Vermont of Cape Town, was once declared a "republic" by locals as a half-serious joke). Just before Hout Bay lies a beach, inaccessible except by foot and four-wheeled-drive vehicle. Called Sandy Bay, it defies the conservative moral order with its bronzed naked bodies—and was on many occasions raided by over-enthusiastic police upholding Calvinist law.

To the south are high-density racially mixed areas like Observatory, Woodstock, and Mowbray. They lie in the shadow of Devil's Peak, which is part of the Table Mountain range. These became the "southern suburbs" which run through leafy areas like Rondebosch, Pinelands, Claremont, and Wynberg to the once wine-rich Constantia Valley and beyond. The southern suburbs, too, are mainly English-speaking strongholds, and the homes are handsome. At the end of that southern route lies Simon's Town, the naval base which was British until 1957. Then on to Cape Point nature reserve where Indian and Atlantic waters pound the shore, where baboons take to mugging when they are fed, and where "perlemeon" (like abalone) and crayfish are to be found in the rock caves of the swirling sea.

To the east are the Cape Flats—a poorer-class sprawl stretching far across the windy, silica-rich flatlands. There coloured people and Africans were positioned by apartheid in cramped townships bulldozed out of the sand and Port Jackson tree undergrowth. When the "pass laws" were abolished in 1986, and the black tide lapping the cities was made "legal," there was an explosion of African urbanization on the Cape Flats. A massive township, Khayelitsha, made an almost overnight appearance. An informal business sector—small *spaza* ("hidden") shops, chicken cook-outs, services, and black taxis—mushroomed. Workers would queue shivering at open fires at the roadside at dawn waiting to be loaded up by whites for casual work. Nearby were "coloured areas" such as Athlone, Retreat, and Grassy Park—augmented by massive new urban development like Mitchells Plain near the False Bay Coast and Blue Downs further inland near D.F. Malan Airport. The impoverished Cape Flats, situated across the railway line from the white southern suburbs, were regarded as the traditional "combat areas" for African and coloured revolt. That line was seen by many of the underprivileged as the "border." A world-known focal point on the Flats for many years was Crossroads, a squatter area with an indomitable spirit under threat of demolition . . . a shanty sprawl in the rough shape of a heart.

To the north and northeast of Cape Town lie the Afrikaner strongholds of the Tygerberg and beyond—newish areas which burgeoned commercially and residentially after 1948 as the mainly government-supporting residents reaped the fruits of political power. The Dutch Reformed Church (described as the "government at prayer") erected ultra-modernistic buildings which seemed at variance with the conservative traditions of the Afrikaners. This Bible Belt of Cape Town even has a church "rush hour" on Sunday mornings, and extempore grace is said at businessmen's lunches. In the 1950s in places like Parow there would be serious moral disputation about crushing matters like public be-bopping—disputes which I covered as a young reporter.

The northern municipalities lead on to pretty wine towns like Paarl, Stellenbosch, and Fransch Hoek, where white and "brown" (coloured) people live in neat racial compartments among the vines. To a great extent they share the same language, church, and culture, but apartheid had kept them artificially separated.

Then, beyond the pretty wine towns lie more mountains, sometimes snow-dusted, encasing the Cape Peninsula against the sea. The Boland, or upper country, starts at those mountains and spills over passes into huge vine valleys and hamlets to the north and northeast. This, in turn, gives way to the scrub, sheep-country of the Karoo. On those prairies the night sky is clearer than imagining, and astronomers take advantage of it to chart the heavens. The winds stroke the wiry grass and send "Karoo bush" spinning in balls across the roads.

Due north of Cape Town lies the arid, mysterious West Coast. There, and elsewhere in the region, the earliest inhabitants roamed aeons ago. The Western Cape, with its winter rainfall, did not attract Bantu-speaking settlement before whites arrived. This was at least partly because the Africans' crops suited the summer rainfall of the interior and not the winter rains of the Cape. The early inhabitants are known broadly as the Khoi-San people—an amalgam, but roughly divided in two: the earliest people, the Bushman (or San) hunters, and the Hottentot (Khoikhoi) herders. University archaeologists sieve the earth near the sea on digs at sites on the West Coast a hundred miles north of Cape Town. They scrounge for burial places, beads, and pottery to solve mysteries about these people's lives and habits. These earliest Cape dwellers shared a habitat with large mammals long gone from the area, such as lions and elephants. Cape leopards still occur, endangered, in the remote hills.

After the Dutch came to the Cape in 1652, Cape Town and its environs slowly became a thriving colonial centre. It was laid-back, rural, and charming in the early Dutch period. It provided victuals and lumber from the forests of Hout Bay (Wood Bay) for the tall ships. It acted as a post box for the Dutch East India Company. The Dutch settled the region, followed soon by the arrival of the French Huguenots with their wine culture. The Cape boomed economically, particularly after the British took hold in 1806, and the region gained better access to world markets.

The nineteenth-century Cape was an important dot on the British imperial map. It was a crossing-point of Empire. British figures including Lord Nelson, Charles Darwin, and Winston Churchill passed through. So, incidentally, did Mark Twain on a trip round the world. Cecil John Rhodes, the gold and diamond magnate who founded the Rhodes Scholarships at Oxford and dreamed of "Cape-to-Cairo" British control in Africa, was a controversial Cape premier around the turn of the century. For generations his money bolstered the English-speaking financial establishment.

The city I got to know in the mid-1950s still had much of its old flavour and grace. Narrow streets, built for Cape carts, were hostile to the motor car. Many of the smaller roads were still cobbled and rutted from the wheels of wagons. The number of cars and people in the city was a tolerable mix. But about to arrive were huge freeways, the most extensive network in South Africa, thanks to the indefatigable efforts of a city engineer who believed in them. These scythed through colonial charm, threatened historic buildings and gardens, swooped down from suburbs to city at the sea, separating city and people from what could be a charming dock frontage. More and more cars thudded down offramps into a city unable to take them. Citizens, fearing Los Angelization, managed to curb the freeways after much environmental loss.

It was not only freeways that radically changed my city.

For years, many members of the coloured population lived near whites, nestling in pockets in places like Tramway Road at Sea Point, in Newlands, in Observatory, and elsewhere. They lived close to the city in larger concentrations like District Six. This proximity ensured the city life and activity at nights and weekends. It thus ensured safety for all citizens. District Six, to be turned white by government decree in 1965, was a bustling, run-down, colourful, and commercially active place. It lay cheek by jowl with the city and was populated mainly by coloured people—though about half rented their houses from sometimes exploitative white landlords. Whites regarded it, even in the most rigorous apartheid years, as daringly chic to go to dinner at a "mixed" restaurant, such as the Naaz or the Crescent, in places like Woodstock and District Six. (For some people, food and drink tastes better under threat of arrest; for others it causes indigestion.) Racial mixing in the Cape, though not extensive, was a fairly common tradition.

Hansom cabs were operated from the centre of the main thoroughfare, Adderley Street. Fresh produce was offered from barrows. fish horns could be heard above the city noise as vendors hawked the ocean's wares in hilly suburbs. Flower sellers brightened many streetsides. The Grand Parade, where Britain's King Edward VII stood invariably with a sea gull on his head, was an open place of religious, commercial, and political activity—a "speaker's corner" in the centre of the city offering everything from God to the African National Congress. As a young reporter, I covered the latter. Queen Victoria presided with her sceptre and her orb outside the Houses of Parliament, and, although ardent Afrikaner republicans had gained power, she was likely to stay put.

Black and white would rub shoulders in the city. In those early 1950s there was considerable informal segregation, but nothing like the nightmare that was ahead. Buses—run profitably by private interests—were open to all, though there was a company that concentrated on predominantly black routes on the Cape Flats. All rail facilities were being rigorously segregated in the early 1950s by act of Parliament—though there had been considerable segregation on trains in the past. Most schools had been traditionally segregated in the Cape, but there had been some mixing, particularly in church and private schools. The beaches and other amenities were not segregated by law, but tended to be by custom. Coloured people sat on the Cape Town City Council and contributed greatly to the welfare of the city. At least one coloured leader, the respected Dr. A. Abdurahman, had served on the Cape provincial council in days gone by—though no person of colour had ever taken a seat in Parliament. The British act establishing the Union of South Africa in 1910, in a crass error, ordained that only whites could sit as members of the House of Assembly and the Senate (the upper house). Many old Cape families classified "white" had coloured blood flowing in their veins, and some were openly proud of it.

Any attempt systematically to segregate people was bound to founder in this melting-pot seaport. But this did not bother the government elected in 1948. It set about achieving the impossible with cruelty and zeal.

Though white attitudes were paternalistic, and many blacks subservient, there was an "open-endedness" about Cape Town which could have led to better things. That's about as far as one can go in defence of the Mother City's racial reputation. Notions that Cape Town was a haven of non-racial liberalism are as wrong as notions that it was a society segregated in cast-iron.

Up to 1956 coloured males of the Cape had enjoyed a century-old right to vote for Parliament on a common roll with whites, as long as they satisfied certain property qualifications. The exercise of that vote had its roots in a municipal non-racial franchise dating to the mid-1800s and for the old Cape Parliament. (This legislative assembly, which Mark Twain described on his visit in 1897, was a place "where they quarrelled in two languages . . . and agreed in none."[24]) The British Act, though locking "non-whites" out of the new South African Parliament as members, kept and entrenched the Cape non-racial franchise.

That same common-roll vote had also been exercised by Cape African men but was taken away in 1936 as part of a shoddy "compromise" among the main white parties. Its abolition followed what the constitution required for such a change: a two-thirds majority at third reading of the bill at a joint session of both houses. (As long ago as 1911 General J. B. M. Hertzog, later to become prime minister, had written that the "Cape Native franchise" was a crime toward the whites and for the "Natives" it was a "snare and a hypocrisy."[25]) A small band of members, including Jan Hofmeyr, dissented at the vote in 1936. The arrangements made in 1936 gave Africans more land, three (white) representatives in the House of Assembly, and four (also white) representatives in the Senate, plus an advisory Natives' Representative Council dominated by white officials. That council was derisively referred to as the "toy telephone" by leading blacks. Even these grossly inadequate arrangements were to be done away with in time, in the years of Dr. H. F. Verwoerd.

In Natal, there had been vestiges of a non-racial vote in the nineteenth century, but the reactionary whites dominating that colony saw to it that this was frustrated by Jim Crow–type arrangements. Indians were effectively excluded from voting as far back as 1894, and only a handful of Africans "exempt from native law" could vote—so political life for everyone except whites was negligible. By comparison, in the Cape Colony in 1909 about one in seven of the voters were not white—and this could, even then, tip the balance in a handful of seats. Yet the vote was watered down. Even before the 1936 (African) and 1956 (coloured) abolition steps, the voting power of Cape coloured and African communities was reduced in significance. For instance, when white women were given the franchise in 1930, black women remained voteless in the Cape. But the coloured vote was a significant democratic right in the Cape until eliminated in 1956.

The new government elected in 1948 on the platform of apartheid—and, ironically, also promising white bread after the brown bread of the Second World War—set about bleaching Cape Town in particular of its colour and charm.

The coloured people had shared many things culturally with the dominant Afrikaners. Liberal Nationalists called the coloured people "Brown Afrikaners." Yet they were rejected with a special vehemence by the Afrikaner Nationalist establishment because they were a living denial of the racial tidiness it sought to impose in all things. They were also an awkward reminder to white racists of an enthusiasm for dominance over, and often sexual encounter with, darker people. The coloured people's axiomatic support of parties opposed to the ruling National Party at election time made them special targets for discrimination by Nationalists. Indeed, this was a major reason why the government stripped them of the common-roll vote in 1956. (The other reason cited by Nationalists, that the coloured vote could be "bought," was an excuse for a massive act of treachery.)

Official discrimination gouged at the lives of the coloured people in the fifties and sixties. They were turned out of their homes by white rulers simply because they were not white. There was irony in the fact that sometimes the officials doing the ejecting, though technically classified as white, were of the same or darker hue than those being removed. Coloured families feared something virtually unknown to whites—a visit by officials from the "Group," the bureaucracy set up under the Group Areas Act which segregated living areas. Grim, busy little white men clutching precise little documents and evil little briefs. Generally, but not always, these civil servants of apartheid were Afrikaner Calvinists, avowedly Christian and civilized. Moreover, they were no strangers to repression themselves. Their families had been bullied by the British in South African history. Before that, in

60

Europe as non-conformists, their families had suffered religious intolerance. They were strangely impervious to the suffering of others. Their political vehicle, the National Party, had come to power by a slim margin in 1948. It promised Afrikaners power and a good white life. For many, this meant sheltered employment in the public service. Enforced apartheid secured their suburbs, jobs, schools, churches, and lifestyle against black encroachment and competition. There were lures of material benefit . . . a neat house, a "bakkie" (truck), even a boat and a shack at the segregated seaside. Apartheid could declare that a beach, as was the case at Kleinmond, a seaside town hardly an hour's drive from Cape Town, was specifically "reserved for the exclusive use of whites excluding servants who accompany white children."[26] Happily, such crudities were coming to an end as the 1990s opened.

And, of course, there were plenty of black servants. Only the far right would make a show of living their lives unsullied by black servants.

The dominant Afrikaners could look forward to all the things the better-heeled English-speaking South Africans had extracted from that rich land in earlier times. The price was twofold: repression of people of colour and ignoring the lessons of history. It proved to be costly, to whites and blacks.

A knock on the door by the "Group" could mean loss of a long-loved home and a tended garden, disruption, financial disadvantage, ruin. And lifelong anger. Under other racial laws, notably job reservation, coloured people were barred from white jobs. They could not enter employment of their choice. They were kept off beaches, parks, benches, and other "whites-only" amenities under the Separate Amenities Act of 1953. This was sometimes done with armed police and Alsatian dogs in attendance. As a "coloured" man once observed to me, at least the roads and the telephones remained non-racial; they could hardly be segregated even by the most zealous ideologues. But almost everything else became subject to racial taboo, and it bore down particularly heavily on the coloured people of the Cape who had been so central to that society. Once so close to whites, they were elbowed aside by apartheid.

It should have come as no surprise to the government that many of the coloured people would make common cause with black liberation. Coloured families produced some of the most dedicated sons and daughters of the revolution. They had seen their parents humiliated by apartheid. They had, in innocence as toddlers, asked their parents why they could not play on "white" swings and had seen the frozen helplessness on parental faces. They had answered the "Group's" knock on the door. They had helped their shattered fathers and mothers move house. They had, indeed, grown up exposed to their parents' frustration and suppressed anger. They did what could be expected. They sided with black liberation. In the late 1980s, from my home in the Gardens you could pick up the signs each day. Some time after the singing from mosques calling the faithful to prayer, you could hear the noise of police sirens on De Waal Drive. Some of the sons and daughters were being escorted to court in huge prison vans, with police outriders alongside and helicopters above. They faced political charges which could carry the death penalty. They sang freedom songs. Created by apartheid, they were the heroes of the Cape Flats.

Despite an underlying sense of tragedy and political gloom, there was lots of good-natured joking about skin colour in the multi-hued Cape. The adage was that the first coloured person had arrived at the Cape precisely nine months after the Dutch party under Jan van Riebeeck opened a refreshment station there in 1652. One early governor, Simon van der Stel, was reputedly a coloured man. Coloured people wryly noted how olive-skinned immigrants from places like Mozambique and Madeira could move, technically as whites, into their homes after they, the coloured families, had been displaced by the Group Areas Act. "I'm a good Protestant, with roots going back three hundred years in this land. And here come these dark-skinned Catholics to take over my home," was a remark heard more than once. No offence to the newcomers or their religion was intended. It was just that the preference given to immigrants, because they were "white," symbolized the injustice meted out to locals who were not.

Coloured lives were fraught with paradox and frustration. Those who were light of colour could easily "pass for white," particularly in the Transvaal province, where the mixed-blood population was small and where some racial mixing, plus the searing sun, had turned many whites dark. This was a severe embarrassment to some swarthy whites. Dark-looking members of the officially white Parliament, often among the strongest upholders of white supremacy, earned appropriate nicknames from the press. Occasionally genes with long memories would throw up a dark child in an otherwise "white" family—testimony to racial mixing in years past. The most celebrated case was that of Sandra Laing, who lived near Piet Retief in the eastern Transvaal with her white Afrikaner family. In 1966, aged eleven, Sandra started to turn darker. She was summarily reclassified "coloured" by the government and expelled from boarding school. She could not get a school place for nearly two years but then her parents got her into a private one. She was reclassified "white" at her parents' insistence. That was possible because the law had been changed in 1968 and "descent" had become more important than before in determining race (other lesser factors were "appearance" and "acceptance"). But that did not end her troubles as a dark girl in a white world. She eventually turned her back on whites and moved into an African community in a township near Springs in the Transvaal and raised a family. After turning twenty-one, she was classified "coloured" for a second time, this time at her own request. She effectively lost contact with her white family who moved to Natal province. She slowly forgot the white Afrikaner life. Journalists who traced her found her without bitterness, resigned.

The practice of "coloured" people from the Cape going north to the Transvaal and passing for white gave them the prospect of better jobs and no discrimination. But this usually meant the wrench of being cut adrift from family and friends in the Cape, for fear of being "found out" in the Transvaal. A domestic worker I knew in the Cape had not communicated with her daughter, living in the Transvaal, for twenty years for this reason. The frail, elderly woman wept when she related this. Her people were oppressed in the Cape, yet torn from family when they tried to "escape" north. It was an invidious choice. So was emigration abroad, which usually offered the chance to live in better racial and economic circumstances, but could mean heartbreak. Many coloured people were driven to it. But parts of families settled in Toronto, Sydney, San Diego, or Surrey pined for other relatives in Athlone or Retreat, Cape Town.

The government pressed on with removals despite strong criticism. More than fifty thousand people were removed from District Six alone. In an act of extreme cynicism, much of that district was totally cleared by bulldozers for "white" redevelopment. But it lay deserted for years, with a few churches and mosques that officials daren't destroy dotting the landscape. It looked like a bomb site. Despite financial incentives, few whites were willing to move in because of the coloured people's fate. A general property slump took its toll, too. The government tried desperately to develop the blighted area as a whites-only urban showpiece. A white technical college and a police barracks were among the few takers—and there was an insecure little row of subsidized white townhouses. An international oil company unwisely contemplated building a garage complex in District Six, but backed off rapidly after threats from the coloured community that they would boycott its products. The technical college found some of its business donors suspending donations.

District Six was the symbol of South African evil. The *Cape Times* called the removal an offence against humanity. The most dignified use for this area now would be as an open park—to stand for all time as a monument to white greed and as a spur to racial conciliation.

The coloured people displaced from District Six and elsewhere were packed off to the sandy, windy Cape Flats. There, urban middle-class people could find themselves dumped among former shanty dwellers in crime-ridden new areas with no sense of community or neighbourliness. The determining factor in where to live was race, not choice. This unleashed a generation of bitterness and, indeed, lawlessness. The alienated, brutal gangs of the Cape Flats terrorized whole communities. The centre-city, robbed of life and activity after dark, became empty, dangerous, and uninviting. It was a mugger's paradise, with crime rates worse than major U.S. cities. Down the years, numbers of people, including prominent residents and visitors, fell victim and were either killed or injured—including a guest of the mayor, mugged the day a new city pedestrian mall was opened.

A friend, a so-called "coloured man" who lived very close to the city centre in Stirling Street, moved under threat of the Group Areas Act and managed to find a new house a few miles away. He spent his life wondering if he might have to move yet again.

He was George Manuel. He had edited newspapers, managed a cinema, sold insurance, dug foundations, been a newspaper "messenger boy." He was employed on the *Cape Times* as a reporter—the only full-time "coloured" reporter on the staff—when I joined as a "cub" in June 1955.

## CAPE TIMES 1955

The *Cape Times* had a large newsroom with an all-white reporting staff except for George Manuel. A new "telephone reporter," Joe Forbes, who took dictated calls from country correspondents, later joined the newsroom and sat next to me in the middle of the stuffy, large floor. Joe spoke with a cultured Oxbridge accent. He was always a cheery voice on the line, and very popular with country correspondents. Some, never having seen him, would invite him and his wife Betty to dinner when they next came to Cape Town—not realizing that this would be a case of "Guess who's coming to dinner?" Even assuming the correspondent from the conservative country areas was happy to take a coloured man and his wife out to dinner at a restaurant (and, indeed, some were), apartheid made it illegal. Mixed dining could be a matter for arrest and prosecution.

Darting around the office all day were coloured clerks and messengers. They wore special *Cape Times* uniforms and were strictly drilled by Sergeant-Major Charlie Windrum, the bemedalled commissionaire who relived his war years every day. In those days, there was seldom more than one woman on the general news staff. (By the 1980s the mainstay of the editing operation was female.)

George Manuel took cub reporter Heard under his wing. He would tell me about the old Cape Town; what it was like before enforced apartheid and civic over-tidiness stripped it of much colour. He once was manager of the Avalon cinema in a dangerous part of District Six and confided that on some nights he would arm himself with an old bayonet hidden in a bunch of flowers and walk gingerly home—softly and carrying a lethal posy. He had finished with what he called his "firebrand" days, having previously edited a forthright newspaper called the *Cape Standard*. But he knew all the Communists, activists, and radicals around town, whom he would politely greet as we walked to the magistrates' courts each day. With age, George mellowed in his political outlook—though he was permanently bruised by apartheid. He told me how he resented being given a battered old mug to drink from when he was employed on a newspaper before he came to the *Cape Times*. Once in anger he told me his people did not want white "charity." They wanted, as full citizens, to live the lives of their own choosing, where and how they liked, and to be paid a living wage in order to do this. He deeply resented the uncertainties which racial removals and other apartheid measures had posed for his family. He told me how he had missed his carefully tended Stirling Street garden when he had been forced to move.

One of the Manuels' daughters (Rhoda) and their son (Gem) emigrated to England. Another daughter (Lorna) stayed on in Cape Town. George and his wife Kathleen were awarded an international visitor grant in 1960 to tour the United States as guests of the State Department. He wrote whimsically in articles and books about the old days of Cape Town and District Six—writings that are now collectors' items. In 1969 George won the Settler's Prize for outstanding journalism.

George, a diabetic, had enough to cope with in life without apartheid. He brought up a family, held down his job on newspapers, and worked hard at an extramural university degree. He and Kathleen grew visibly weary under the pressures and uncertainties. In any normal society they would have been pillars of the contented middle classes, and full citizens. But in South Africa they could not live where they wished, vote for whom they wished, dine where they wished—or even be buried where they wished. Both died within months of one another in 1981. By then George had become a familiar, subdued-looking figure, walking his small dog on De Waal Drive on the slopes of Devil's Peak above the city. A civic leader said of him in the *Cape Times,* October 24, 1981: "He had an ever-deeper awareness of the hurt that has been done to the black and brown people. . . . And yet there was never a sign of bitterness in anything George Manuel ever wrote or said; only a deep sadness in his eyes."

I owe George Manuel something special. The irony is that it was not a white Afrikaner but a coloured man who taught me to speak fluent Afrikaans, the language traceable to Dutch. Most coloured people in the Cape spoke Afrikaans, though they tended to prefer reading in English; and Afrikaans was overwhelmingly the language of the law courts. Afrikaans was a *sine qua non* for journalism.*

The Afrikaans I had acquired in Anglicized Natal was exceptionally dangerous to everyone within hearing distance. George set about teaching me, simply by using Afrikaans whenever we spoke.

*Though the mother-tongue of only 16 percent of South Africans—see *Uprooting Poverty,* 23—Afrikaans is very widely spoken by South Africans of all races. English is the mother-tongue of only 8 percent, but has a world and commercial significance way beyond that.

George used that language with facility. It was widely viewed as "the language of the oppressor" because of its close links with the rise of Afrikaner Nationalism and thus apartheid. Yet it was, and remains, the *lingua franca* of many parts of South Africa—and indeed even more so in Namibia (formerly South West Africa). Its aptness in describing things is not easily rivalled. It has beautiful literature and poetry. It may yet be rescued from being damned in history as an oppressor.

It was in this relatively relaxed Cape that I found myself in the 1950s—before the worst of enforced apartheid had taken hold. After Durban, with its arid white conservatism and strict segregation, I found Cape life liberating. Friendships could be made and kept across the colour line, despite legal inhibitions.

But the Cape was changing for the worse. Bus apartheid was soon to arrive. Job reservation, too. Entry by "non-white" students to the University of Cape Town was about to be prohibited, except by special permit, under a 1959 measure outrageously called the "Extension of University Education Act." The coloured voters were losing their century-old right to vote. The seven white representatives of Africans were about to be turfed out of the two houses of Parliament. The government had, indeed, embarked on the systematic segregation of white from "non-white" in every conceivable sphere—in jobs, living areas, blood, clinics, sex, marriage, lifts, taxis, beaches, swimming pools, cemeteries, ambulances, hospitals, schools . . . from crib to crypt.

Only those with guts or authority, or both—like a former judge-president of the Cape Supreme Court in the 1960s—could buck the tide. Andrew Beyers was always seen as a moderate Nationalist sympathizer, but he, too, had his bottom line. When Public Works Department officials got busy in the Supreme Court in Cape Town in October 1960 drawing offensive lines to enforce apartheid on spectators, Beyers threw them out and ruled that apartheid would not apply to his Supreme Court. It never was.

While South Africa intensified segregation, a world recovering from fighting Hitler's racism turned in the opposite direction. The United States saw troops ordered in by presidents

Eisenhower and Kennedy to break segregation. In South Africa they were used to enforce it. The London *Times* was to describe South Africa as a country marching resolutely out of step with humanity.

To be caught up in it was to live through a racial nightmare—for all.

Blacks suffered immeasurably more than whites—directly and physically—under what Wilson and Ramphele call apartheid's "assault on the poor" in their book *Uprooting Poverty*.[27] Millions of Africans were prosecuted under pass laws and removed forcibly from one place to another. But whites carried with them the subtle bruises of unjust privilege. They suffered in their souls. They lived in cities where the crime rate rose alarmingly; their currency shrivelled; alcoholism, mental disorder, suicide, and depression took their toll.

Almost all the people, black and white, were lessened, dehumanized.

# CHAPTER SEVEN

# CHOICES

Working on a newspaper in Cape Town in the 1950s and 1960s meant regular assignment with racial injustice. It was all part of the routine diary, covering apartheid as it scythed through communities. Apartheid, an ever-present phantom, could haunt anywhere: It could arise at a meeting of a local group areas board, dividing residential areas on a racial basis; of a hospital board, discussing divided medical services; or of a local road transportation board, grappling with the metaphysics of bus apartheid. (To understand bus apartheid required almost a doctoral thesis. It was introduced on April 16, 1956. On some routes there was no apartheid. On others there were separate buses. On others, with double-decker buses, it was all races upstairs and mainly whites downstairs. On yet others—like mine from Adderley Street to Camps Bay via Brighton Estate—there was one bus for all but movable $X$s and $Y$s demarcating where white and "non-white" must sit. Non-whites were confined aft of $X$ at the rear, whites fore of $Y$ at the front, and all races between $X$ and $Y$ in the middle. Some buses would begin with no apartheid in one suburb like

Wynberg, only to acquire it suddenly in the city centre, with X and Y boards unfurled en route to another suburb like Sea Point. That, roughly, was bus apartheid in Cape Town.)

Similarly, covering apartheid could take one to Wale Street to see the Cape Provincial Council dividing services like beaches and education, or to Parliament, dividing everything it could lay hands on—and ordering all authorities to do the same. These white-run bodies, of course, discussed other matters—the routine things of life which among ordinary mortals elsewhere in the world take up the full attention of authorities. Things like rates and taxes. But this was no ordinary country with ordinary problems. It was a country where the lunatic fringe was in the centre of politics. The overwhelming preoccupation was race. Some local authorities tried to hold out against the tide, such as the city council of Cape Town. It had a long non-racial tradition dating back to a municipal vote for all in 1837, and, until the government forced them out in the early 1970s, there were coloured city councillors who played an important role. The council objected to the unseating of coloured councillors, declined to put up beach apartheid signs (the Nationalist-run provincial government did so instead, then billed the city council), and it opposed racial group areas, notably District Six. But in many things it failed to stem the tide of apartheid.

In terms of interpersonal relationships, the Cape was a more relaxed society than Natal, and it was easier to make friends across the colour line. This was because of a history of some mixing. Yet the law conspired to make things difficult: South Africans were confined to their own racial living areas; ordinary social contact was bedevilled by an "immorality act" which prohibited sexual acts between white and "non-white"; it was a criminal offence to sit down at a public establishment and have a cup of tea or a meal with black friends (it was best to order take-outs, "to go"). A meal or "braai" (cook-out) at a private residence, at which people of colour were present could lead to white neighbours' complaints to the police. The police might even drive around in their Black Maria to check whether the "immorality act" was being contravened or "banned persons" (not allowed to attend a gathering of more than two people) were present. Some guests could get jumpy.

The law notwithstanding, there were many special people of colour whom one got to know. There was an array of people of all races available "on tap" in the Cape—people who strongly opposed the government, including M.P.s, newspaper people, clerics, playwrights, lawyers, academics, township-dwellers, educationists, and so on. Their political complexion, like their colour, was a rainbow. They included liberals, Africanists, black nationalists, Communists, ex-Communists, political priests, Christian fundamentalists, Social Democrats, free thinkers, radicals, anarchists, progressives. The human material was rich, varied.

Journalism, too, opened doors to meeting prominent people who believed in non-racialism. Far away in Africa, I met Dr. Julius Nyerere when Tanganyika became independent in December 1961. In the hot weather at the statehouse in Dar-es-Salaam the prime minister-designate momentarily bristled with anger in an otherwise relaxed interview. He declared that South Africa would never be at peace while Africans were seen as "hewers of wood and drawers of water."

Apartheid produced choices for people every day of their lives in Cape Town. That is, if they cared. My friend, Roland Darroll, faced a decision when he went to the Cape Town railway station, with its fresh-painted apartheid signs, in the late 1950s. Offended by being told thus where to enter, he strode in under NON-EUROPEANS. He was stopped by a policeman and informed that as a "European" he was required by law to use the *other* door. "But I am not a European," law student Darroll said with accuracy. (Though classified white, he was a native of South Africa, and not part of Europe.) Nor, indeed, was his hue all that white, considering the pink-grey colour which goes for "white" in South Africa. *"Toe maar,"* (Go on, then) said the policeman, not prepared at short notice to become an expert in the finer points of race. The same expert decisions faced bus conductors every day—e.g., whom to place in front of the $Y$ ("whites") or behind the $X$ ("non-whites") on segregated buses. Some conductors, having to adjudicate the racial claims of sunburnt whites and fair-skinned coloured people, openly betrayed mental strain. "Ag, man. I just want to sell the tickets," I heard one say in Sea Point on a memorable Brighton Estate-bound bus trip.

Darroll and I were members of the celebrated "Native Law I" class of 1958 at the University of Cape Town. It was highly politicized. We sat at the sandalled feet of Dr. Harry Jack Simons, a top Marxist theoretician and academic.

Simons, banned by the government and detained after Sharpeville, later moved to Lusaka, Zambia, and worked on ANC causes—to return home only in 1990 when he was eighty-three. His wife, Ray Alexander, was barred from Parliament in 1954 under the law outlawing the Communist Party. Both their daughters, Tanya, a librarian, and Mary, an academic, were at one stage banned and cruelly prohibited from doing their jobs at the university—victims of naked state vindictiveness aimed at a South African family.

Simons taught what was then called "Native Law and Administration"—the long title of a course later to drop the native and become "Comparative African Government and Law" and "African Studies." It was the closest thing to political science available at the university at that stage, and a superb course.

The native law classes produced pyrotechnic careers, including careers in prison. One student, Fikile Bam, spent ten years in Robben Island prison for joining a Maoist discussion group. Some of the students turned saboteur as members of the African Resistance Movement in the 1960s. That was a group of frustrated white liberals who wanted to "do something" dramatic to end apartheid. The youngsters involved were egged on by older people, including an expert in sabotage and guerilla warfare in Malaya. The ARM set about blowing up electric pylons, railway fuse boxes, and other installations, and stored what a judge described as "masses" of high explosives in the suburbs. Some older members of the group fled the country just as the police dragnet closed in. The student youngsters were caught and served time in prison, and—in a celebrated court case in Cape Town—one student turned state's evidence against close friends who went to jail. Future premier John Vorster, as minister of justice, would gloat over the success of his security police in breaking the ARM. He would enjoy relating, in private conversation, details of the state the police found these young men and women students in when conducting night raids. Vorster listened with unusual sympathy to the parents of certain white ARM prisoners and let them out early on the grounds that they had been "misled" and used by others. But he was not as forthcoming with blacks, who remained in prison long years. The escapade left students with careers shattered, in jail, on the run, or in exile.


## "PLATTELAND"

As a young journalist on the *Cape Times,* it was frequently necessary to visit the country in the vast Cape Province. And the country, or *platteland,* was definitely not Cape Town when it came to race. Our coloured and Malay drivers knew this too well. They would brace themselves for such trips. For instance, we had enormous difficulty finding a place for "non-white" members of the team to lay their heads at a hotel. In October 1957 Hadji Ismael Dawood drove a *Cape Times* team over the rutted Karoo roads to Upington to cover the floods on the Orange River in the northern Cape. The trip was memorable. The first reason was that there was a near-riot among down-river farmers when my dispatch in the *Cape Times* said the river had risen fifteen feet when it should have said fifteen inches. There had been confusion between the telephone reporter Joe Forbes and myself when I dictated the story. The newspaper had numerous inquiries and an immediate correction was required. The second and more important reason was the treatment of driver Dawood. He was told to go into the "black" section of the hotel, reserved for servants. Although we could obviously pay for a proper room, segregation was the iron rule in Upington. Dawood was a cultured man, a leader among the Moslems in the Wynberg area of Cape Town. He had, before it was taken away, enjoyed an equal vote with whites. He had been a lifelong supporter of General Smuts's United Party. Yet there was no room for Dawood in the hotel.

The "black" section of the hotel was an outside "barracks" which could only be called unlivable. Dawood complained bitterly, but we could do nothing about it. We felt like heels as we prepared for the comfort of the "white" section. I could not get myself to enjoy a "braai" with white guests only a few feet from where Dawood was billeted. Somehow he maintained his dignity and endured the night, hoping that we would pull out early next day. I was as anxious to leave as he. We did not feel welcome in the place. Moreover, I sensed uproar among Lower Orange River farmers expecting a fifteen-foot torrent to sweep them and their crops to the sea.

It is amazing to reflect on it now, but in those days there were hardly any hotels which would accommodate people of colour. Even in the cities it was a problem. There were a few "coloured only" hotels in coloured group areas, but the need was largely ignored. God knows where Africans went for hotel accommodation, outside of "Bantustans" such as the Transkei. It was no wonder that people of colour tended to camp out so much—it could be a form of self-defence against insult. This was the period before the government started allowing blacks to filter into the better-class hotels and eating establishments on an ideologically convoluted basis. (Racial mixing had, indeed, to wait for Premier John Vorster's notion that blacks and whites could mix socially—not as members of one community, but as coming from totally different Bantustan "nations," like Greeks, English, or Germans. In those circumstances, hotels, restaurants, and clubs could formally seek "international" status from Pretoria, which could be granted with a ban on mixed dancing and liquor consumption. Slowly, too, "multi-national" or "international" sport was allowed, after weighty debate in the National Party. Indeed, the issue split the party.)

So while the white reporters and photographers enjoyed first-world treatment, the drivers had to take their chances in platteland hotels. They were respected men of the community, and they were employed by an "establishment" newspaper. But they were subjected to second- and third-class treatment. They had no effective political rights, no means to demand a better deal—in

76

hotel accommodation or any other area of their lives. They paid the same taxes as whites but had no power. The dismal story was the same across the broad front of "non-whites," in the Cape and elsewhere. Unlike whites, they could not phone their local M.P. and raise Cain over inadequate services because they had no M.P.s. No wonder people of colour always saw the vote as crucial. And when the government did set up subservient and separate authorities for blacks, these impotent bodies had to bow and scrape and plead for services and goods, while whites demanded and received.

## SENATORIAL SIZE

The *Cape Times* under Victor Norton carried on a determined campaign against the loss of the coloured vote. Norton got into trouble with Parliament as an indirect consequence. The government had tried all manner of means in the early 1950s to get the two-thirds majority in Parliament required by the 1910 constitution to do away with the entrenched voting right of coloured people. It tried setting Parliament up as a "High Court" with power to override the courts in such matters. This trick was declared *ultra vires* by Chief Justice Albert van de Sandt Centlivres and his colleagues on the Appellate Division of the Supreme Court. Parliament, they ruled, was not a court. After various failed manoeuvres, the government hit on the device of simply doubling the size of the Senate by adding senators. The newcomers' sole purpose, and in most cases identifiable merit (apart from later on ensuring Senator H. F. Verwoerd a majority in the prime ministerial stakes in 1958), was to give the government the desired two-thirds majority.

The packed Senate was treated with derision, particularly by cartoonists and editorial writers; indeed, the Johannesburg *Star* was sued over a critical editorial and had to pay damages to a vast number of senators.

The *Cape Times* got into different trouble. J. Hamilton Russell, M.P., a prominent United Party member of those days, (whose son, David, was to be banned, then to become a bishop) went too far in castigating the Senate. That is, in terms of restrictively applied contempt rules. In a speech, Russell described the Senate as a house of ill repute peopled by gentlemen of easy virtue, which prompted powerful debate about whether this was not a contradiction in terms; but, in any case, his comment violated the restrictively applied, British-type contempt rules. It was a passing reference in the body of a lengthy report. (In those days inordinate length was given to important speakers—even to Josef Stalin, who was fondly remembered at the paper because the printers left out the first vowel in a stirring reference to the "countless" millions. Although in small print on an inside page, the item drew outraged public response. Norton swore blind that this proved *Cape Times* readers studied every line.)

When the report of the Russell speech appeared, there was immediate trouble. Premier Dr. Verwoerd, sitting at his green leather bench in Parliament, handed the *Cape Times* clipping to his Cape leader, a former lawyer-editor with a very crafty mind, Dr. Eben Dönges, who had devised the enlarged Senate scheme. He studied the clip and returned it to Verwoerd, nodding vigorously. I spotted this ominous exchange from the press gallery above, craning my neck to see. I alerted Norton. A select committee was appointed to investigate. The committee recommended that Norton be reprimanded at the bar of the Senate, and that Russell be thrown out of Parliament for a couple of weeks to teach him a lesson. The House thus struck a blow for its dignity.

I broke the news to Norton in his large, airy office in Burg Street. He put aside the paper he was reading and huffed: "If I had more respect for the enlarged Senate, I'd be worried." He went to Parliament to take his ticking off, which I reported from the Senate press gallery.

## POLECAT

All through the 1950s and 1960s the apartheid juggernaut plunged on. It created mass hardship, contradiction, anomaly—

*Family picture in 1944 (from left) Raymond, Vida, George, and Anthony.*

*Heard interviewing Oliver Tambo, London, October 1985. Courtesy of André de Wet.*

*Philip Kgosana (extreme right) parleys near Jutland Flyover Bridge, Cape Town, with aides, March 30, 1960, before marching down Roeland Street to Caledon Square. Heard on left.*

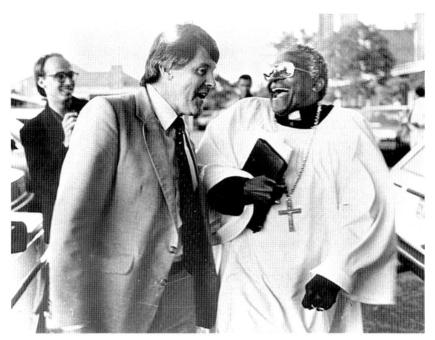

*Archbishop of Cape Town Desmond Tutu and Heard chat at Thanksgiving
Service, Bellville South, to mark release from detention of activist-theologian
Allan Boesak.*

*The march on Cape Town, March 30, 1960—scene outside Caledon Square Police Station.*

*Heard interviews Rhodesian rebel Premier Ian Smith 1970s in Salisbury.*

*Arrest: Heard being taken to court by Lieutenant Frans Mostert November 1985 after publishing Tambo interview. Also present (left) Marianne Thamm holding placard.*

*Robert Sobukwe surveys his new quarters on Robben Island after having prison term "extended," 1963.*

*Prime Minister B. J. Vorster in the gunport of a Ratel armoured personnel carrier during an official inspection of the vehicle, 1978. Courtesy of Richard Bell,* Cape Times.

and insecurity. It brought the wrath of the world down on Pretoria. A country that had been a popular Western ally fighting Hitler in the Second World War (even playing a part in restoring Emperor Haile Selassie in Ethiopia in the war years) became the "polecat of the world," as a Nationalist newspaper columnist admitted.

After the premierships of D. F. Malan (1948–54) and J. G. Strijdom (1954–58) came Dr. H. F. Verwoerd. Verwoerd promised the country apartheid with a new face—"separate freedoms." Before his election as prime minister in 1958, Verwoerd had for eight years been the minister of "native affairs" and had laid the foundations of his modernized apartheid system. He had seized control of all "Bantu" education, eliminated "black spots" in white areas, and set up tribal-based local authorities. The open universities were closed to blacks. The same year, 1959, Dr. Verwoerd had an important vision about autonomous Bantustans, and he duly informed Parliament and pressed ahead with the "Promotion of Bantu Self-Government Act," envisaging separate black statelets. They were promised autonomy, later even independence. Blacks elsewhere in the country were severely restricted. They were arrested if they did not carry passes. He explained that passes were a great benefit to them.

A vast bureaucracy set up under the 1950 Population Registration Act trundled on with the job of classifying all South Africans according to race from birth to death. Officials subjected countless individuals and families to humiliating tests as to race. They were questioned intimately about their families, their associations, and their habits, and even had to endure tests like the running of pencils through hair and checking nostril shapes.

Anomalies abounded. Chinese people, who numbered several thousand, generally fell into the category of "non-white," though some concessions were made to them. Japanese, fewer in number, were classed officially as "honorary whites" for all laws and purposes. Cynics concluded that this was because Japan bought so much South African pig-iron ore. Yet, at one stage, the government found time to stop a Japanese jockey from racing because he was not white. Papwa Sewgolum, an Indian golfer from Natal, because of racial restrictions on occupying premises under the Group Areas Act, once had to receive a trophy outside a clubhouse in the rain. One of the best all-rounder cricket players produced by South Africa, Basil D'Oliveira, who, as a "coloured," had been brought up in the shadow of Table Mountain, had to trek six thousand miles to Britain before he could play internationally—for England. And when he was chosen as a replacement at the last minute for an English tour of South Africa, Prime Minister Vorster angrily called off the tour. The world sports boycott of South Africa got under way with a vengeance. Within a few short years, South Africans were going down on bended knee to get people to play sport with them. They even manipulated the strict laws of apartheid to wangle their way back into world sport. Sport was the jugular, the vulnerable spot, in early international campaigns for pressure. White South Africans loved their cricket and rugby. Although "South African games" were organized amid fanfare and shows of patriotism, they were boring by comparison with pitting the nation's best against the world. Sports boycotts, in time, worked wonders.

At the height of the apartheid madness, all resistance to the ruling ideology was crushed. There was no appreciable right-wing breakaway from the National Party under Verwoerd—he *was* the right wing. Politicians, academics, church figures, and others who broke ranks to the left were ostracized by Afrikanerdom, harassed and spied upon by government, squeezed out of holy orders and jobs. Ostracism is hard to endure when you are part of a tightly knit tribe.

I saw Verwoerd sharply rebuke dissidents in his party, including journalists, who were toying with the idea of direct coloured representation in Parliament. He went to Swellendam in the Cape and, at a meeting at the showgrounds, pointedly reminded local Nationalists that it was *they* who had sought the disfranchisement of the coloured voters. He was warning against second thoughts. Nationalists had to keep the faith.

The English-language newspapers thundered away at enforced apartheid measures, but the government went ahead. It gained ever-increasing majorities at elections.

In one of countless exchanges with the *Cape Times* in 1971, the *Burger* dismissed racist incidents, which we had suggested both newspapers could jointly campaign against, as just the odd case of "administrative stupidity." Just the odd slip-up? Not a thoroughly evil ideology?

Things were to turn full circle years later when the person who had been editor of the *Burger* at the time, Dr. Piet Cillié, was to assert with cynical candour that apartheid had to be attempted to show that it could not work.[28] *That* was very comforting to the millions who had been moved; the thousands detained, prosecuted, investigated, and jailed; ordinary people who had seen their houses bulldozed, their families sundered, lost their jobs, suffered banishment, humiliation, financial loss, exile, and even death like Bantu Stephen Biko in 1977 . . . all in the great cause of something that could not work in the first place.


## IMMORALITY

Along with apartheid repression went powerful moral taboos.

The most vicious of all was Section 16 of the Immorality Act. That section banned sexual relations between white and "nonwhite,"* including "conspiring" to commit such offence. (Like kissing? *That* was a matter of learned legal debate in court in more than one case.) Suspicion and innuendo became the order of the day. Police spied on couples making love. They would break into premises and even feel bedding to see if it showed signs of sex. A newspaper said that a special police order detailed the use of binoculars, tape-recorders, cameras, two-way radios for "immorality" work.[29] Police in pursuit of offenders sat in trees, hid in cupboards, under beds, or in car boots. Wives suspected husbands and vice versa. Suburban husbands, taking a black "maid"

---

*Since 1927 it had been an offence for whites and Africans to have sex. From 1950 this was extended to cover sex between whites and all people of colour.

81

home, would frequently place her alone in the back of the car and drive on like a cab to the drab townships, hoping for the best. A breakdown, particularly at night, could bring the police with their torches, awkward questions, and handcuffs. Race relations were bedevilled.

When the government's new race laws were being debated in 1950, a Communist M.P., Sam Kahn, read out a letter which stunned the house. Indeed, so much so that it was expunged from the record by direction of the Speaker. Kahn had warned of racial "witch hunts" under measures like the Population Registration Act and the Immorality Act. He produced a letter he had received to prove his point—a letter which he said was a "scurrilous" and a "black-guarding letter," the truth of which he rejected. It read, as quoted in a previously unpublished dispatch by the domestic news agency, SAPA: "The House of Assembly is debating immorality. The Nationalists are so anxious. I would like to put it to them: who are pure Europeans and what is going to become of Mr. X's bastard child by one of his servants? This has been kept in the dark for fourteen years. The white men can never stay without coloured women." Sam Kahn added: "The letter has reference to a cabinet minister."[30] See also Hansard report of debates 1950, column 3114, showing suppression of the letter. No South African newspapers published the offending remarks; if they had, they would have been in serious trouble with Parliament.

There were several celebrated court cases too close to home for government comfort, cases involving Dutch Reformed Church clergymen, civil servants, and party officials. There was a sensational incident in 1971 in Excelsior in the Free State—an otherwise unspectacular little town with signs on the pavements urging "Keep your town clean." In 1971 there were fourteen hundred whites and twenty-five hundred blacks in the town; all of them, of course, neatly segregated into their own areas. Some whites were in the habit of picking up local black women for sex. Embarrassingly, five members or supporters of the ruling National Party were charged along with fourteen African women for contravening the Immorality Act. One National Party town councillor killed himself to avoid the ignominy. Shortly before court proceedings against the men were due to begin early in January 1971 in the full glare of international publicity, the authorities withdrew charges. They said prosecution witnesses were reluctant to testify. A more likely reason was that the political system just could not take the pressure. It was a moment of truth, I think, for Section 16. It lingered for some years, but police enthusiasm to trap and arrest people waned. In April 1985 it finally disappeared from the statute book it had stained for a full generation. Estimates put the tally of prosecutions at around twenty thousand. Numbers of people facing prosecution and family exposure committed suicide, or saw their jobs and reputations ruined, or they emigrated. Helen Suzman, M.P., said simply: "This law belongs to the days of witch burning."

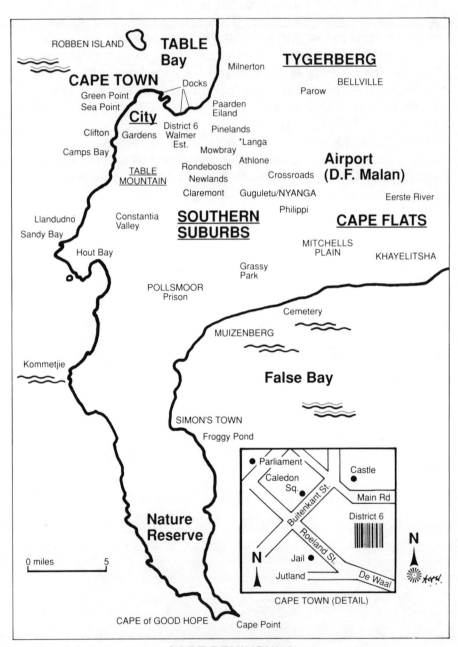

ROBBEN ISLAND

**TABLE Bay**

**TYGERBERG**

Milnerton

**CAPE TOWN**

Docks

BELLVILLE

Green Point

Parow

Sea Point

Paarden Eiland

**City**

Clifton

District 6

Pinelands

Gardens

Walmer Est.

*Langa

Camps Bay

Mowbray

Athlone

**Airport (D.F. Malan)**

**TABLE MOUNTAIN**

Rondebosch

Newlands

Crossroads

Claremont

Guguletu/NYANGA

Eerste River

Philippi

**SOUTHERN SUBURBS**

**CAPE FLATS**

Llandudno

Constantia Valley

Sandy Bay

MITCHELLS PLAIN

KHAYELITSHA

Hout Bay

Grassy Park

POLLSMOOR Prison

Cemetery

MUIZENBERG

Kommetjie

**False Bay**

SIMON'S TOWN

Froggy Pond

Parliament

Castle

Caledon Sq.

Main Rd

Buitenkant St.

District 6

Roeland St.

**Nature Reserve**

Jail

N

Jutland

De Waal

N

0 miles    5

CAPE TOWN (DETAIL)

CAPE of GOOD HOPE

Cape Point

**CAPE PENINSULA**

# CHAPTER EIGHT

# BETRAYAL, MARCH 30, 1960

"The murmuring of many voices, the upturning of many faces, the pressing on of many footsteps in the outskirts of the crowd, so that it swells forward in a mass, like one great heave of water."
*A Tale of Two Cities*, 413

Writer Gerald Shaw was far from happy with the headline or the report as published:
**PEACE IS AIM, NATIVE SAYS**.
The minuscule news report under this headline in the *Cape Argus* afternoon newspaper in Cape Town on March 30, 1960, had a dismissiveness which sums up white middle-class attitudes. Shaw's job as African affairs reporter on his newspaper was to cover life and politics in the overcrowded, restive black townships on the Cape Flats. This was primarily to enlighten the mainly white, middle-class readership of the paper. But his editor, Morris Broughton, clearly wished at the same time to make blacks feel a sense of belonging in that divided society so he stepped up cover-

age of their activities. Shaw was the vehicle, and he stumbled into history.

Shaw's story, as published, did little justice to the exhaustive interview he had conducted with an unknown young black politician. What neither knew was that before the day was out the politician, Philip Kgosana, was to be hailed, briefly, as a "black Messiah."

Shaw, a serious-minded young bachelor in his mid-twenties, had a solid background: Catholic schooling, politics degree at Pretoria University, voracious reading, and some travel and work abroad. He was to form a long and close association with me at the *Cape Times*—for sixteen years as my trusted deputy (1971–87).

In 1960 Shaw landed one of the first African affairs beats in South Africa, with the exception of those done on the *Rand Daily Mail* in Johannesburg. Shaw was given this task on the eve of a massive black revolt. That his editors still used the resented word "Native" in his copy instead of the preferred "African" (already in use at the pioneering *Rand Daily Mail* ) Shaw had to bear with fortitude. Kgosana could be interviewed, but not as an "African."

With the anti-pass campaign of the Pan-Africanist Congress (PAC) looming, Shaw spent time with Kgosana, a twenty-three-year-old University of Cape Town commerce student who was regional secretary of the PAC. Like Shaw, Kgosana came from Pretoria and was a stranger to the region.

It was important to Shaw, in the interests of maintaining his contacts in the black townships, to give a full account of Kgosana's views. Shaw's report sought to draw white attention to pressing black grievances. White society, shaken by the events at Sharpeville and Langa nine days previously, was not terribly concerned about blacks. Shaw's editors knew this. Kgosana had already been mildly critical of the *Cape Argus* and other papers in public, adding in a speech: "Let us close our ears to what the newspapers say and continue with our dynamic programme."[31] Shaw's published report was unlikely to impact on any programme, dynamic or otherwise. His original version was severely cut by the editors. Shaw wrote a background article, too, but by that time a state of emergency had been declared, and he was told apologetically that it could not be published for fear of breaking the strict provisions of the state of emergency.

It was always difficult to attract white readers' attention with news about blacks. Whites preferred to hear about "braaivleis, rugby, sunny skies and Chevrolets," as a banal advertisement in later years was to put it. They lived in relatively affluent white sub-urbs which were free of blacks except as servants. **PEACE IS AIM, NATIVE SAYS** would be about as riveting in these leafy surrounds as that headline penned by bored sub-editors in Fleet Street: **SMALL EARTHQUAKE IN PERU; NOT MANY INJURED.**

But other forces were massing.

The Sharpeville and Langa police shootings nine days before had gripped the country.

There had been earlier warning signs of African revolt. A massive treason trial droned on in Pretoria. In 1959 a number of ANC leaders had been banned or re-banned, like Oliver Tambo (June 12) and Chief Albert Luthuli (May 22), who was president-general. Luthuli had said in a speech on April 28: "We of the ANC do not wish to dominate others by virtue of our numerical superi-ority . . . we are prepared to extend the hand of friendship to white South Africans, who are our brothers and sisters." He was banned for his trouble. The tall, twitchy justice minister, C. R. Swart, swept me aside with his arm and barked irascibly "Ask Luthuli!" when I sought confirmation of the banning in the Parliamentary lobby.

Other things were happening. A trade unionist from Paarl near Cape Town, Elizabeth Mafekeng, forty-two, had in October 1959 been issued with a deportation order to Vryburg, a remote semi-desert area of the province seven hundred miles away. This sparked a riot and the stoning of cars owned by whites on the night of November 9. Mrs. Mafekeng fled to Basutoland.

The country was tense. The Cape was tense. And the PAC was making headway with its organizational work in the Cape.

There was no time for Shaw or Kgosana to give the matter a second thought. As the *Cape Argus* rolled off the presses at lunch-

87

time on March 30, 1960, a wave was breaking over Cape Town, threatening white power at its very base.

The peaceful young "native" was in its midst.

The other key figure in that day's events, Col. I. P. S. Terblanche of the South African Police, was also busy. He was on his knees praying for strength in a gamble with political authority. He was later wryly to recall that that very morning the pro-government newspaper, the *Burger,* had confidently proclaimed: **VIRTUAL CALM OVER WHOLE COUNTRY.**[32]

Something unbelievable was under way, and everyone in Cape Town knew about it.

The black townships around Cape Town were disgorging a multitude of men in a disciplined march almost to the gates of Parliament. There were hardly any women present. Black women were not welcome in Cape Town. Most of the marchers wore hats and workmen's clothes. It was a spontaneous denouement, after the Sharpeville and Langa shootings, to the Pan-Africanist Congress anti-pass campaign. This campaign, directed against the documents which Africans had to carry at all times in urban areas, was strictly non-violent. But it represented the most challenging resistance since thousands of people had been arrested in the Defiance Campaign against Unjust Laws of the early 1950s organized largely by the African National Congress—from which the Pan-Africanist Congress broke away in 1958. The fact that the campaign coincided with a rival campaign planned by the ANC gave it an added competitive edge.

The day before Sharpeville and Langa, that is, ten days before the Cape Town march, Kgosana had said:

> The PAC has made it clear that the first essential is a mental divorce from the pass laws. Our people have been so conditioned to the "dom" pass [a term used by police demanding passes, "dom" meaning stupid in Afrikaans] that they have been known to buy it for 15 pounds sterling or risk death in an attempt to salvage it from a burning building. In fact an African does not feel that he is himself if he does not feel the weight of the "dom" pass in his

88

pocket. What is necessary, then, is for every African to make up his mind that from to-morrow we will never carry the "dom" pass.[33]

The national leader of the PAC, soft-spoken Witwatersrand University lecturer Robert Sobukwe, had rejected violence in the following terms, as quoted by Kgosana in the same speech:

> I say quite positively, without fear of contradiction, that the only people who will benefit from violence are the government and the police. . . . After a few days, when we have buried our dead and made moving grave-side speeches and our emotions have settled again, the police will round up a few people and the rest will go back to the passes, having forgotten what our goal had been initially. In the process we shall have alienated the masses who will feel that we have made cannon fodder of them, for no significant purpose except for spectacular newspaper headlines.[34]

Sobukwe warned that anyone agitating for violence would be regarded as a paid agent of the government.

Kgosana, speaking prophetically about "to-morrow's country-wide uprising," elaborated: "We are not going to burn or damage any part of the pass book in any manner. [The ANC leader, Albert Luthuli, had burnt his pass publicly on March 26.] We are not going to fight or attempt to fight, insult or attempt to insult, provoke or attempt to provoke the police in their lawful duties. We are not going to throw stones at the police or do anything that is going to obstruct the police . . . nobody will carry money, knives or any dangerous weapon."[35]

He made it clear that a special PAC task force would police the campaign and see that no one acted against instructions. Though disciplined, the campaign was highly dangerous.

Kgosana explained that, if told to disperse by the police, the masses should "peacefully disperse" but refuse to go to work. "You go home, sit in your houses and paint the house or dig the garden or even play draughts." The PAC demands, he said, were:

Abolition of the pass laws.
Thirty five pounds sterling a month minimum wage.
No victimization of the leaders or the people.

The PAC set 1963 as the year of ultimate freedom. This date lingered in people's minds until it passed—like all other target dates had, without the advent of majority rule. The ANC, realistically, avoided setting dates. It was more of a long-distance runner—less reckless.

In the nine days that had gone by since the March 21 incidents, many Africans of the Cape Town townships, and also in some other parts of the country, had refused to go to work. Industry and commerce in Cape Town were suffering from a near-total strike in certain sectors. Food was running out in the townships, and courageous women of the liberal white Black Sash organization went in with supplies and blankets. The PAC task force saw to it that they were safe. (The Black Sash was established in the mid-1950s as the Women's Defence of the Constitution League to protest at the loss of the coloured vote and other apartheid measures. Mainly English speaking, it endured jibes from cabinet ministers, physical abuse, and attack from white right-wingers and the reserve of some husbands prominent in business. It outlasted many of its critics to celebrate its thirty-fifth anniversary in 1990.)

The police carried out regular raids on the black townships, attempting to get people to go to work, and arresting leaders. On March 22 police shot and wounded four protesting blacks. Crowds presented themselves for arrest outside police stations. Two thousand were led to Caledon Square police headquarters by Kgosana on March 25, but were led back again when police said there was no room in prison. That was miniscule compared with what was to hit Cape Town.

On March 30 when the police heard that numbers of Africans were moving toward the city, they thought at first that this was a sign that, hungry and penniless, the workers were returning to their jobs. The crowd left their homes in small groups, which gradually swelled. Some came by train and bus, but most were on foot. As the morning wore on, the numbers grew to a horde, divided into two sections. One took the high road to the city, along De Waal Drive, past Groote Schuur Hospital. This route dropped down the side of Devil's Peak toward the upper part of the city. The other sea of marchers took the low route, along the Main Road and straight into the heart of the city. It was eight miles to walk from Langa.

The police were soon aware that their first assessment was wrong and that they had a massive problem on their hands. Colonel Terblanche wrote:

> That afternoon about twelve noon the senior officer com-manding [at Caledon Square] telephoned me and said he could not cope with the situation. He did not know what to do. The black crowd was getting bigger. I walked over to my divisional criminal investigation officer, Col. J. A. C. Reay, and said: "Joe, let's go and have a look at what is going on at Caledon Square." When we arrived at the square, I immediately decided: Violence must not be used here today. It will be a disaster. Security measures, yes . . . but not violence. I immediately called for two Saracens and ordered the doors of Caledon Square closed. Inside were about two hun-dred [police] men, fully armed, but I ordered that not one should put his head out of the door. There was a powder keg in our midst and I did not want to bring a match near it.[36]

Meanwhile thousands of blacks were massed around the for-bidding red-brick police headquarters.

Earlier I had been detailed by my newspaper to follow the march. We spotted the one group, about fifteen thousand strong, just as it was leaving the Langa township. I got the shock of my life to see this great heave toward the city.

Like a modern-day people of Israel, unarmed men wearing modest clothes and hats moved over a railway track and filtered across a golf course. They skirted past coloured and racially mixed areas and headed down Klipfontein Road before going toward De Waal Drive, the main highway into the city.

Still close to Langa, as we moved beside the column in our car, we passed a suburban house where I spotted someone I knew well. He was standing at his front gate, smoking as usual and with a grave look on his face. It was Dr. A. C. Jordan, senior lecturer in Bantu languages at the University of Cape Town.

As this non-violent, dignified worker army with grievances to discuss with the rulers trudged past us, Dr. Jordan said: "I fear something terrible will happen today." He looked sad, worried.

A South African Air Force helicopter swirled overhead. Cape Town was in a state of severe shock. Word of the march had spread with amazing speed. Telephone switchboards were jammed because of the panic. Schools, businesses, and shops were closed. Some unsuspecting motorists drove along De Waal Drive to be confronted by a living sea filling the highway. Some did an instant U-turn and took their chances driving away on the wrong side of the road hooting loudly. Some who did not were graciously let through the throng. The newspapers noted an absence of hostility—and, from personal observation, this was so.

The police prepared themselves for a bloodbath. They were concentrated in the area of Caledon Square and Parliament, while army reinforcements were rushed from the stone-built castle a few blocks away.

Parliament was ringed with steel. Its precincts bristled with heavily armed troops and police, Saracens, military armoured cars, and guns. Just across from Parliament, civil servants in the Marks Building, where they worked in Cape Town during parliamentary sessions, debated whether to take their sandwiches into the Public Gardens for lunch among the strollers and squirrels. The Liberal Party, whose offices were in Parliament Street almost within touching distance of Parliament, was in a state of high excitement—particularly *Contact* editor Patrick Duncan, who had befriended Kgosana and had negotiated on his behalf with police. (The Liberals had for years ceremonially struck a propaganda blow against the apartheid government on the day Parliament opened. This was done by ostentatiously hanging their flag, showing white and black hands shaking, out of a window as the governor-general and other dignitaries passed immediately below.) Some M.P.s, including several of the newly formed Progressive Party, ventured out from Parliament, grim-faced, to see what the lunch-time disturbance was. They had been speaking themselves hoarse about black grievance . . . in fact, what was now at the very gates of Parliament. The M.P. for Nigel also walked out to watch. He was Deputy Minister John Vorster, later to become justice minister and prime minister and the person who set out to crush black opposition.

It was one of those historic moments never forgotten, like a presidential assassination, a nuclear bomb, or a moon walk. Few who were adults in Cape Town at the time would forget where they were and what they were doing as this stunning event unfolded.

Having failed to stop the march early on, the police found it had gone too far to check. This was particularly so once the marchers were in heavily built-up areas. There was a real danger of unleashing mayhem in the city if there was shooting. Moreover, there was a good man in charge of the police, Colonel Terblanche. Later, he recalled in his interview with the *Huisgenoot* magazine: "I am firmly of the opinion that all hell would have broken loose over Cape Town if we had used force that day. Murder, death, arson and rape would, in my opinion, have engulfed the city."[37]

It was the chemistry established between Kgosana and Colonel Terblanche which carved a niche in South African history.

Some reports suggested Kgosana had been caught off guard by the march, and was in bed when it began. He explained to Joseph Lelyveld, the *New York Times* man who wrote *Move Your Shadow,* that he was merely "evading arrest."[38] Already Sobukwe and other PAC leaders were in prison, having highly successfully presented themselves for arrest on March 21—but in the process losing initiative and control. Leadership was needed for the campaign. Indeed, a particularly harsh police raid on Langa that morning had triggered the march, and the chances were that, if Kgosana had been found then, he would have been arrested. Then the massed Cape Town body would have been headless. What would have happened then is anyone's guess. I think Cape Town would have been sacked.

It seems most likely that this march was not planned as part of the pass campaign—though it became in some ways its finest hour.[39] For days, Africans had been giving themselves up in smaller numbers for arrest, but no one expected anything as big as

93

this. The most likely reason for the march was the police raid on Langa earlier that day.

Whatever the reason for Kgosana's belated arrival on the march, the moment produced the man.

Kgosana, a young student in a society which respected age, an out-of-town stranger but regional secretary of the local movement behind the pass protest, grabbed some borrowed clothes, reportedly hitched a lift with an American news team, and took command of the most remarkable march in South African history to date.

When we first spotted him at the head of the column, moving agilely among the people, he looked a most unlikely man of destiny in his ill-fitting, borrowed clothes, short pants, no socks, and no hat. A penniless twenty-three-year-old student was heading a column of generally older men. But he was in total command. On more than one occasion he stopped the marchers and lectured them on non-violence.

Kgosana led the column which took De Waal Drive. He soon encountered a minor revolt. A dissident man had stomped off ahead of the marchers, maintaining, it seemed to us, that this was the moment to attack and sack Parliament and not be content with non-violent strategies. He was cutting across the Sobukwe dictum of non-violence, and his revolt could spread. Kgosana had to move quickly. Just as we passed Groote Schuur Hospital he asked us if he could have a lift in the *Cape Times* car which was moving along at the side of the crowd. He thus hitched his second press ride of the day. We drove him to the dissident. He hopped out and argued with the man while they walked ahead of the crowd. It was a remarkable and bizarre thing to witness. Fifteen thousand marchers behind, walking peacefully; and, in front, this young leader in shorts remonstrating with a man bent on violence. Kgosana succeeded, and the man grudgingly rejoined the main throng. The procession moved down De Waal Drive toward the built-up city area and the Roeland Street Jail. From all accounts, at that stage Kgosana planned to go to Parliament, but peacefully.[40]

Kgosana halted the march under some trees near the top of Roeland Street and discussed matters with his lieutenants and some white liberals who were present by design or accident. Colonel Terblanche had, meanwhile, sent a policeman, Sauerman, up Roeland Street as a sort of emissary.

After taking advice from people around him, Kgosana himself decided to keep well clear of Parliament. There was subsequent debate about the role of white liberals in that vital decision, specifically Patrick Duncan. I did not see Duncan in the informal parley that Kgosana called under the trees at the top of Roeland Street. At least one well-known liberal supporter, a journalist, was present. Kgosana told Lelyveld that his original plan had been to go to Parliament, but that he had decided on his own not to, because troops were drawn up in front of Parliament.[41]*

Prime Minister Verwoerd, his cabinet, and the full assembly of M.P.s and senior civil servants were present in the Parliament complex. Any approach by massed blacks would have led to dreadful loss of life and possibly sacking of the city.

White reprisal would be swift and bloody. What the consequences would have been for South Africa's history is a matter for conjecture.

When I detoured past Parliament on the way to Caledon Square from the top of Roeland Street, I saw the armoured cars, the helmeted troops, and the guns drawn up at the cockpit of white power, ready to shoot. The tension was broken momentarily when a drunk man climbed on a Saracen and slithered off amid laughter among the large crowd who had turned out to see what was going on. When Cape Town's traditional noonday gun went off on Signal Hill overlooking the city, many people thought the shooting had started, and jumped.

Kgosana decided to take a small group to Caledon Square, which lay a few blocks from Parliament. He left his massed followers

---

*"I thought that it was not wise to force my way to a Parliament surrounded by troops because otherwise we would have been presented to the racists to shoot, and that was not my purpose," he told Lelyveld twenty-four years later.

sitting in the shade under the trees. With a few companions he walked the several hundred yards down Roeland Street, past the jail, and turned right into Buitenkant Street.

That was the critical point.

If he had gone straight on he would have headed for Parliament and inevitable death. By the time he reached Caledon Square those who had taken the lower route to the city, the other fifteen thousand marchers, were gathered there in orderly fashion. But there was a loud din. Their voices hummed through the city, a sound I had never heard before. They jammed the road in front of Caledon Square, and side roads too. Shopkeepers boarded their stores, and people fled from that part of the city.

Colonel Terblanche, who had been called urgently to the scene, was staggered when he saw the size of the crowd. He fell to his knees in the police station and prayed before embarking on a daring quest for peace—which, without doubt, clashed with the views of the government. With all armed men confined inside Caledon Square, Terblanche led a small party of senior officers to seek out and talk to the leaders. He was unarmed. In his *Huisgenoot* article, Terblanche told how he almost had a fit when he saw a young constable walking in the midst of the crowd with a sten-gun, and he sent him inside.

I heard Terblanche's first remark when he was introduced to Kgosana: "Mr. Kgosana, I speak to you as one gentleman to another. Please would you ask the crowd to be quiet." Kgosana was given the use of a police loudhailer and, raised high on the shoulders of his lieutenants, said in a loud voice in English: "Let us be silent . . . just like people who are going to a graveyard." By then the fifteen thousand in the upper column had filtered down Roeland Street, adding their voices to the din.

Quiet descended abruptly on the scene. Kgosana said: "This morning the police came into Langa and threw the people out of their homes to force them to go to work. So we have come here to Cape Town to ask the police for protection." He said Terblanche had assured him that the people of Langa would not be molested in their homes. This said, Kgosana was let down from

96

his friends' shoulders. It was the most impressive silence I have ever known.

The fate of Cape Town, with its hundreds of thousands of lives, lay in the hands of two men: a seasoned police colonel who was the son of a bankrupt ostrich farmer and an African student from Pretoria in short pants. They negotiated.

I stood within earshot and could hear clearly what was discussed.

Kgosana asked for a meeting with Minister of Justice F. C. Erasmus to discuss their grievances. He complained about Africans being hurled from their hostel rooms in the townships by police trying to force them to go to work that day and earlier. The police, I thought rather resourcefully, pointed out that it was not possible for them all to see the minister. They said Erasmus was in any event "at lunch," which might have been true in a very technical sense. If he was, he was not enjoying it. Terblanche suggested that Kgosana return with his aides at 5 P.M., and undertook that an interview would then take place.

The atmosphere was tense for everyone. In mid-parley, I spotted a young, fair-haired woman—said to be representing an American news organization—being flung, protesting, into the Caledon Square building by police on the assumption no doubt that this was no place for a woman.

In journalism, the golden rule in a riot situation is check escape routes. I started thinking about personal safety, especially after glancing through slits in the big wooden doors of Caledon Square and having seen a disturbing sight. Row upon row of uniformed police, sten-guns at the ready, stood in the cobbled courtyard. If talks broke down a bloodbath would be upon us all. Without doubt the police would come out in formation, shooting. The crowd's peacefulness would evaporate. Anyone could die. Richard Lombard's death nine days before was fresh in memory. I earmarked a stormwater culvert at the side of the building as the safest place to leap the moment firing began. I discovered later that several other journalists had been eyeing the same spot . . . there would have been a sardine-like crush. Across the road, inside and on top of buildings, stood an army of spectators. There they stood, office workers, journalists, shopkeepers, etc., all gazing down at this silent sea of hatted heads. It was a lunch-time to remember. Brian Barrow, another *Cape Times* reporter covering the march, was on the roof of a building directly opposite me. I could see his small figure and balding head clearly against the blue sky.

In the unexpected cordiality of that day, Kgosana accepted the point that Erasmus was engaged at lunch. But he sought categorical confirmation that an interview would, in fact, take place with Erasmus later that day. Terblanche assured him of this as part of what was clearly a gentlemen's agreement. There is no room for doubt about this agreement. Kgosana addressed the crowd again by loudhailer, told them of the assurance, and asked them to disperse quietly. They did so.

That ended Kgosana's moment of power.

It was, in the words of Joseph Lelyveld, the hour "in which the Bastille might have been stormed in South Africa and wasn't."[42]

It could, indeed, have been the hour when "the living sea rose, wave on wave, depth on depth, and overflowed the city. . . ." *A Tale of Two Cities,* 245.

When the columns headed back to the townships, Kgosana was from that moment on at the mercy of the government he had challenged.

A lone police van accompanied the dignified procession to Langa. No shot had been fired. No baton used. No voice raised. The city returned to its normal life in abnormal times. The police and army reinforcements dispersed for the time being. The division bells rang in the Lobby of Parliament as usual at 2:10 P.M., calling members to their benches and debates. As the black protesters went back to their single hostels, the white Parliament began business after the speaker intoned the usual prayers.

Kgosana and the trusting thirty thousand were to be tricked.

As arranged, at 5 P.M. Kgosana and several of his lieutenants returned to Caledon Square. According to evidence given later to the judicial commission which inquired into the Langa riot, they were met by the tough Cape Town security police chief, Col. J. H. van der Westhuizen. (Later to become the government's chief black affairs administrator in the Cape when removals and pass law repression were at their height.) According to this evidence, Van der Westhuizen informed them that the minister, Erasmus, was not interested in seeing them, and that a state of emergency had been declared by the government. They were placed under arrest. Colonel Terblanche, obviously unhappy, later said that he had been ordered by "higher authority" to arrest the men. So they went to jail and were charged with incitement.

The government started wriggling. It was under immediate criticism for having broken its word. The excuse was offered that Terblanche had never promised an interview with the minister; he had undertaken simply to *try* to arrange it. That was a lie. The crowd would never have dispersed on that basis.

Erasmus, clearly already annoyed that Terblanche would not use force, let him down. In the process, he did irretrievable damage to the government's word. The available record leaves Terblanche an honourable man and condemns Erasmus. In subsequent talks after his retirement, Terblanche left me in no doubt about what in fact happened. He told me in 1983 that he had received a telephone call from Erasmus early on in the crisis, as the Africans were marching toward Cape Town, and that he had had a "difference of opinion" with the minister; they had a "flaming row." Terblanche even confided to me that he thought he might be demoted as a result. It can be asserted with confidence that Erasmus demanded that the strongest line be taken from the very beginning, i.e., force. That was the Verwoerd government's style. When I met Terblanche at a *Cape Times* occasion at Simon's Town on August 8, 1976, he confided: "If I had followed what the minister had wanted me to do, Cape Town would have been destroyed." Clearly, Terblanche, aware of what shooting could mean for Cape Town, resisted the very notion. No wonder he fell on his knees and prayed; he had more to contend with than the marchers.

Attorney-General W. M. van den Berg told the Langa riot

commission that there were no promises, which prompted me and a journalist colleague to make statements which we handed to Van den Berg confirming that there *was* a commitment. My statement, made on May 12, 1960, said in part:

> Kgosana's demands included a personal interview with the Minister of Justice immediately, and an assurance that the police would not continue beating Africans at Langa in their efforts to get them to go to work. Colonel Terblanche said the Minister was not available at the time (it was lunch time), and Colonel Reay remarked: "Come on, Kgosana, you can't see the Minister with all these people round you. Come back with a few of them." (or words to this effect).
>
> I then heard Colonel Terblanche clearly promise to arrange an interview later between Kgosana and the Minister of Justice. He gave his personal assurance that he would do this, and I heard no talk of his *trying* to arrange such an interview.
>
> After hearing this assurance, I saw a (Cape Times) photographer standing near the charge office door, and because I had been trying to locate our photographers earlier, I went over to him. Shortly after this Kgosana was lifted shoulder-high and he told the crowd that an assurance had been given that he could have an interview with the Minister. He then told the crowd to disperse quietly.
>
> I was convinced that if this assurance had not been given, Kgosana would not have been satisfied and would not have told the crowd to disperse. I felt great admiration for Colonel Terblanche because he had, I believe, avoided bloodshed that day.

Erasmus was defensive. Under attack from liberals in Parliament, he held to his denial and tried to explain away the arrest with the excuse that police had been out looking for Kgosana from early that morning. As the day wore on, they do not appear to have looked very hard, because Kgosana was a world story at local police headquarters, rubbing shoulders with the head of the Cape Town security police and all senior police who counted. He had even received a police van escort back to Langa.

But there was also a big Erasmus give-away. He did arrange for an early meeting between Kgosana and two others who were under arrest with him, and the secretary for justice, C. J. Greeff, the permanent head of his justice department. Why do this if he did not have a conscience about the assurance? A brief, meaning-less meeting took place, followed by a brief, meaningless state-ment. I recall jotting it down from Greeff on the telephone. It did not even say that the three were under arrest, nor where the meeting took place.

Greeff claimed that "Kgosana stated that the request [sic] to Colonel Terblanche for an interview with the minister of justice was to enable them to put a request for the release of their lead-ers and for no other purpose." Naturally Kgosana, in prison, was unable to comment on this subjective, truncated account of his wishes. It was a matter of jailer meeting jailed, and the former having a monopoly on information. The whole event was a face-saving charade.

The breach of faith was not lost on the black townships. It had profound consequences. There was no further inclination to accept the white government's assurances. Lelyveld described it as a turning point, the "moment at which black leaders were finally forced to see the inadequacy of non-violent tactics in the South African context."[43] It was Dr. Douglas Smit, himself a former sec-retary of justice and of "native affairs," who about a year later summed things up in Parliament in his rather paternalistic way. Referring to the broken assurance, Smit described it as a "grave breach of faith" which "brought the name of our police force and of the white man generally into further disrepute among the natives."[44]

And it was not long before radical offshoots from the PAC, after the organization's banning in 1960, would form themselves into the Poqo underground organization which attacked white civilians in gruesome fashion. Five were killed in caravans at Bashee River Bridge, Transkei, on February 5, 1963, after two youngsters had been hacked to death on the night of November 22, 1962, in the Cape wine town of Paarl. I was called to the Paarl scene at first light to see the blood-spattered streets, evidence of a 4 A.M. attempt by Africans to storm the police station—and to wit-ness the legacy of a broken promise I had heard being given.

Poqo (meaning "alone" in Xhosa) was beyond talking, beyond negotiation.

101

South Africa endured a state of emergency from March 30 to August 31, 1960. All-citizen force units were mobilized, the townships were ringed with steel, and two thousand people, from the mildest liberals to Stalinist Communists, were detained.

The pass laws were temporarily suspended from March 26 to April 6. That was little compensation for local Africans. I saw the "whip" come to Cape Town on April 4. Police lashed Africans on the streets in unprovoked and indiscriminate fashion. The *Cape Times* reported on April 5 that many (white) callers were overcome with horror and disgust at the attacks. It was said that the police action was aimed at keeping "intimidators and idlers" off the streets. The United Party opposition, true to its conservative image, criticized the suspension of the pass laws and supported the laws banning the ANC and PAC. Hard times saw a flight of capital and brains, and a property slump—followed, later on, by an economic boom.

The ANC and PAC were suppressed; they both went underground and turned to violence, with leaders in prison or exile. The ANC played the leading role in liberation.

"Headlong, mad and dangerous footsteps . . . not easily made clean again if once stained red. . . ."

*A Tale of Two Cities,* 243

"The sea of black and threatening waters, and of destructive upheaving of wave upon wave, whose depths were yet unfathomed and whose shapes, voices of vengeance, and faces hardened in the furnaces of suffering until the touch of pity could make no mark on them. . . ."

*A Tale of Two Cities,* 249

# CHAPTER NINE

# HENDRIK FRENSCH VERWOERD

## 'DOUBT WAS UNKNOWN TO HIM'

In 1958 I entered the Parliamentary press gallery to report debates for the *Cape Times*. I was still not twenty-one and too young to vote; the eligible age later was reduced to eighteen. Though voting for the politicians was out, reporting them was in order. And it was a busy time politically. There was an upwelling of unrest in the land as both white and black opposition politics took strain.

The group of dissidents that was to become the Pan-Africanist Congress was led out of the ANC by Robert Sobukwe in 1958. The PAC was formed on April 6, 1959. The break was caused by the PAC belief that the ANC was too much under the influence of white leftists. The PAC, with the credo "Africa for the Africans," sought to be an exclusively black organization—though at least one white, the liberal Patrick Duncan, joined. The son of a former governer-general, and editor of *Contact,* Duncan served the PAC in Algeria before he fell out with the organization and died of natural causes.[45] The ANC, which had been founded in 1912, soldiered on without the PAC.

White opposition politics, too, were developing fissures. The main vehicle was the United Party, now led by an urbane, but politically ineffectual country squire, Sir De Villiers Graaff. The U.P. spent most of its time ingratiating itself with white voters, and it was dismissed by liberals and blacks as offering no opposition worth talking about. It adopted various meaningless slogans like "white leadership with justice," which had a paternalist ring that enraged politically aware blacks. The U.P. floated complex constitutional schemes like a reform of the Senate, all of which obfuscated the Party's central objective: maintaining white control. It proposed "race federation" for South Africa, whatever that meant. The United Party's opportunism and old-school-tie racial paternalism embarrassed and irked its liberal wing, which broke away in 1959 to form the Progressive Party. (The U.P. later died, under an alias, the New Republic Party.)

As far back as 1953 a small group of liberals under the leadership of Alan Paton had formed the Liberal Party and had bravely faced the prospect of a one-person one-vote plan. The Progressives started by promoting the more cautious idea of a qualified franchise with economic or educational barriers. But inexorably the Progressives moved toward the Liberal position. They began to realize that self-respecting blacks would accept nothing less than one-person one-vote.

The Progressives found what the Liberals already knew. To be white and liberal in harsh South African conditions was becoming increasingly difficult. There was sustained mainstream white hostility. A generous black attitude of admiration of earlier years was giving way to rejection, rooted in growing frustration caused by apartheid repression. Blacks did not want liberals to do things for them, and they made this plain—particularly those who expounded black consciousness like Steve Biko. Liberals got used to being rebuffed, on all sides, although they managed to maintain some contact points among the fracturing races.

When the Liberal Party disbanded in the 1960s because of

an act of Parliament (the Improper Political Interference Act of 1968) which forced parties to segregate on racial lines, some joined the Progressives who had decided not to disband. With some big-business backing, the Progressives remained a factor in trying times. (They merged with other, generally more conservative, opposition groups and under the Democratic Party banner in 1989 showed some growth in the general election that year.)

As black and white groupings in the country split, the government of Verwoerd looked as stable and self-assured as ever.

Verwoerd was born in the Netherlands—a little-known fact till he became premier. Like the Corsican who became such a good Frenchman, or the Austrian who became a super-German, he was more of a nationalist than all the rest of South Africans. He had come with his missionary parents to South Africa when he was young, and did very well at school in South Africa and Bulawayo, Southern Rhodesia, and at university in Stellenbosch. A brilliant, misguided man, he became a professor of applied psychology at age twenty-six at Stellenbosch and later edited the northern National Party newspaper organ, the *Transvaler.* One of the most damning things ever said about him came from an ardent supporter, Professor A. N. Pelzer, who edited a collection of his speeches after he died and wrote in the introduction: "Doubt was unknown to him."[46] Another indication of Verwoerd's singlemindedness occurred during the Second World War. When Verwoerd was editor of the *Transvaler,* a Transvaal judge found (July 13, 1943) that he had allowed his newspaper to become a tool of the Nazis. In 1947 his newspaper totally ignored the Royal Family visit to South Africa.

Verwoerd had built his power base in the enlarged Senate and on the army of white officials who ordered blacks around, the Native Affairs Department which he had taken over as minister in 1950. He and his racial zealots set about drawing elaborate new racial boundaries, smashing homes, channelling blacks to menial work, banishing them to distant places as never before. Generally, blacks were treated as temporary sojourners in white cities—or as

105

"surplus appendages," as one celebrated remark by a deputy minister put it.

Verwoerd's thesis was simple: if the races mix, they fight. So they must be separated. Taking his views to their logical conclusion, Africa would have hundreds or even thousands of nations based on tribal and language affiliation. Under his "Bantustan" scheme South Africa alone was to have about ten "nations."

Verwoerd made no secret of his view that he would rather be white and poor than integrated (with blacks) and rich. This brought him into conflict with the white business lobby who wanted to be rich even if this meant some mixing at elite levels. I heard Verwoerd, in those persistent, professorial tones, speaking of standing like granite against world and local forces. When Harold Macmillan warned in Cape Town in 1960 of a "wind of change blowing through the continent" and explained why Britain could not support South Africa, Verwoerd maintained that the world did not really understand South Africa.

His self-assurance did not stop short of pig-headedness. As minister of native affairs in the mid-1950s, Verwoerd pointedly ignored the recommendations of a socioeconomic report which favoured "big apartheid"—massive consolidation of African land, the use of "white" initiative capital in the "black homelands" to stimulate development, and the setting up, independent of Verwoerd's Native Affairs Department, of a socioeconomic development council to monitor progress. Verwoerd was not yet minister of native affairs when Prof. F. R. Tomlinson of Pretoria University was chosen by others in the party to head the inquiry after the Nationalists' 1948 election win. Tomlinson's objective was to provide a socioeconomic basis for what was called grand apartheid. In effect, the report warned that if the recommendations were not implemented, the full implications of racial integration would have to be faced. Verwoerd, who obviously felt he and his bureaucratic minions could do better than Tomlinson, allowed him to finish his job—but then ignored key proposals. A major reason was pique. In Parliament, commenting on the report, he did not even thank Tomlinson, saying this would be done on another occasion. Grand apartheid was not even to be given a chance. The Tomlinson report recommended that 104 million sterling be spent on the "homelands" over ten years. Dr. Verwoerd was prepared to spend only three million sterling in the first year.

Verwoerd as premier redoubled the efforts of his predecessors, J. G. Strijdom and D. F. Malan, to segregate everything possible. He tried to give white "baasskap" a moral face by promising blacks full political rights—even autonomy and independence—but only in the fragmented reserves set aside for exclusive African settlement since 1913. Yet this land, much of it remote from cities and impoverished, constituted only 13 percent of the area of South Africa—and the Africans numbered about 75 percent of the population. This "Bantustan" scheme was impractical in conception, inadequate in scope, cruel in implementation, i.e., daft. It demanded massive movement of populations. But it was clung to by Nationalists for decades after Verwoerd because it seemed to offer them a morally defensible argument: "separate freedoms" for black and white. They could never find a better one.

I sat through the Verwoerd years, watching and reporting from the press gallery of Parliament where my father had sat in the 1930s. The press sat on benches beneath huge portraits in oils of the British Royals, King George V and Queen Mary. These reminders of the British monarchy we expected to fall at any minute and decapitate us. In 1961 when the country changed from monarchy to republic they were removed to a Parliamentary museum.

If Verwoerd's premise (that race mixing means conflict) was accepted his arguments for separation were flawless. But then, surely, the premise implied that the whole world was destined to end in racial conflagration. If one rejected his premise, what he was proposing for South Africa was delusion and disaster. That was the view of a minority of whites and most blacks.

Verwoerd impatiently shrugged off criticism and spent much of his time painstakingly lecturing his audiences, as if in class, telling them that they simply did not understand his objectives. In fact, the critics understood too well. What he was proposing was a powerful white South Africa with blacks divided on tribal lines, crammed into small corners of the country, and supposed to be content with *that*. It was an old colonial policy of divide and rule of the British, *divide et impera* of the Romans. Verwoerd tried to get away with it in postwar conditions in the twentieth century.

The government would come to Parliament each year seeking more power to keep the racial compartments intact. The Group Areas Act, providing for different racial living areas, was amended a score or more times. Double-talk was perfected. University education was "extended" when limited. Black self-government was "promoted" when made subservient. The pass laws were "repealed" when intensified. An act of 1952 was styled the "Natives (Abolition of Passes and Co-ordination of Documents) Act." Though this was described as a measure which would "restore freedom of movement" to blacks for the first time since 1867, it extended passes for the first time to the whole Cape Province and did away with exemptions for African clergy, clerks, etc.

The pass laws, indeed, provide one of the most instructive examples of double-talk. The government more than once announced that it was doing away with the pass laws. As early as May 30, 1952, Verwoerd, as minister of native affairs, told the Senate:

> The complete pass system as it has grown up through the years has become ineffective and troublesome to the Native, the administration of justice and the employer. I should like to put an end to this position. . . . My object is to provide every Native with a handy holder for his identification card in the form of a little pocket book in which the most important data concerning him will appear, as, for example, his employment contract and tax receipts. Persons in possession of this card will then be exempted from the pass laws, which will probably be repealed in the near future and the Native will also not have to carry further documents since everything that is necessary will be recorded there. . . . I also expect further that as a result of this measure there will be much less friction with the police.

How wrong he was. Friction grew. African women were soon to be issued passes—and jailed for not having them. Up to a thousand Africans were to be arrested by the police daily under his scheme to "repeal" the pass laws. That meant the creation of a whole generation of "criminals" who would be law-abiding citizens elsewhere in the world, but were locked up with common felons in South Africa. Sharpeville and Langa were to be a direct result of the "repealed" pass system. And still the government did not learn . . . until July 1, 1986, when President P. W. Botha really did repeal these laws.

Double-speak was prevalent everywhere: the government banned "improper political interference" by itself interfering with the right of parties to have as members whom they liked. The Natives (Settlement of Disputes) Act banned black strikes. The government blamed the world for interfering in South African sport when it did just that by insisting on sport apartheid—for instance banning Maori rugby players from New Zealand. New, soothing names were sought for the paraphernalia of apartheid. The newly named Bantu Administration Department did not seem a good idea because (not unlike the Coloured Affairs Department, C.A.D.) the acronym was unfortunately B.A.D. The name was changed to the Department of Co-operation and Development. Blacks being removed from their homes could now take heart that this was all part of "co-operation and development." (At one stage the department was called "Plural Relations," leading black wags to describe themselves as "plurals," and a gardener, for instance, as an "extra-mural plural.") The "black spots" in white areas were ruthlessly eliminated, and the land turned over to whites, sometimes with names dripping in insensitivity. When blacks in Sophiatown and elsewhere in the Western Areas near Johannesburg lost their home-ownership rights and were removed in the 1950s, Sophiatown became a white town called Triomf (Triumph).

For years, the amount spent on black education was pegged at an abysmal level. It was the Verwoerdian doctrine that blacks should pay for as much of their services and welfare as possible themselves. He would boast how cheaply he could build black dams. Blacks must not be educated as "Europeans" but only to serve their own people or to provide labour in white areas. Verwoerd put it this way: "The Bantu must be guided to serve his own community in all respects. There is no place for him in the European community above the level of certain forms of labour."[47] When he was minister of native affairs, Verwoerd took over church and private schools for Africans, centralized under "Bantu education," and administered by his bulging bureaucracy. He tried to ban blacks from churches in "white" areas but had to back down in the face of a church revolt. Critics had charged that under Verwoerd's scheme blacks could get down on their knees in church to clean floors, but not to pray.

There was an eccentric scheme to remove all Africans from the Western Cape, providing an African-free zone all the way up to some mythical "Eiselen line" (named after an apartheid ideologue, Prof. W. W. M. Eiselen). This line ran somewhere south of Port Elizabeth and right across the Cape province to the West Coast. The Western Cape removal target was 5 percent of its African inhabitants a year. It never even partially worked. A human flood of work-seekers cascaded in from impoverished Bantustans like the Transkei and Ciskei. In years to come, government officials monitored incoming traffic on mountain passes and realized that it was futile to try to stop the flow.

The objective of the removal policy was to turn the Western Cape into the white man's "region of last resort," a last-ditch area—an "Israel" or, more aptly, a Masada—which could be defended if the need arose. And not a black African in sight. The coloured population was to provide all the labour of the region. Before taking on an African worker it was necessary for employers to fill in encyclopaedic forms confirming that they could not obtain coloured labour for that job.

In Cape Town, coloured traffic officers were, by government edict, no longer recruited to work in "white" areas, and the same happened to ambulance drivers. National Party M.P.s, particularly those from northern parts where coloured people were few, came to Parliament each year and resented being directed by traffic officers who were not white; or, worse, they objected to the prospect of being taken to hospital by ambulance drivers of colour. The remedy was simple: they stopped the city council from hiring them except in coloured areas.

Blacks had nowhere to go to eat or to find recreation in many cities, yet they were essential to the smooth running of those cities. The good white life would collapse without them. If Verwoerd's schemes of whitening the cities had in fact worked, there would have been industrial and commercial chaos.

In the late 1950s when black acquaintances of mine organized "sit-ins" at classy shops and restaurants in Cape Town, they were hauled away and prosecuted for serious offences. (It would be thirty years before blacks would dare to do this again in a new campaign of defiance on white buses, beaches, hospitals, and elsewhere, when black protest—in Martin Luther King's tradition—was approaching the "Selma, Alabama" stage.)

Painting slogans on walls was regarded by the courts in a grave light. I covered a court case in Cape Town in the 1950s in which two coloured men were given stiff prison sentences for their mural art.

As things turned full circle and political expectations burgeoned in the 1980s, Cape Town's walls became alive with protest. Slogans were daubed by the political left and right, and local wags added bits by the day. One wall painting, referring to jailed ANC leader Nelson Mandela, said: NELSON IS NOT A SEAGULL, HE'S A JAILBIRD. Then someone added the words: HE'S AN ALBATROSS AROUND P.W. BOTHA'S NECK. The city council would attempt to paint over the daubings, but they would sprout anew overnight.

At the height of his power, Verwoerd was shot twice in the upper jaw and neck by a wealthy English farmer, David Pratt. It happened at the Union Exposition, or Rand Show, in Johannesburg, on April 9, 1960. Pratt used a small-calibre pistol which did not get deep enough to kill. Verwoerd staged a remarkable recovery, and his bodyguard an even quicker one. Having looked after nearly half a dozen premiers without incident, the bodyguard had fainted in a pool of Verwoerd's blood—leading people to think he, too, had been shot.

At his first public speech after the attempt, Verwoerd told a group of nurses that "the protection of Divine Providence was accorded me with a purpose—a purpose which concerns South Africa too."[48] Many white South Africans believed him. He was fit enough to open the celebrations of fifty years of the Union of South Africa on May 31, 1960, in Bloemfontein. The newspapers reported that before he made his speech he was handed a white pigeon, the "dove of peace," which he squeezed tightly, it seems in nervousness as cameras clicked.

Like a modern-day Noah, this tall man—with flowing white locks and, many thought, touched by God—released it. This was the signal for hundreds of racing pigeons to be freed. The report went on: "The pigeons wheeled above the crowd before finding their path and winging away. But Dr. Verwoerd's white pigeon fell to the ground and it was several minutes before it rose and flew after the others."[49]

Six years later Verwoerd sat at his usual seat in Parliament, his face draining of blood. He was dying from the powerful thrusts of two hunting-type sheath knives used by Demitrio Tsafendas, a mixed-blood illegal immigrant from Mozambique.

Both Pratt and Tsafendas were declared mentally unfit for trial and confined; Pratt committed suicide not long after his attack. Tsafendas languished in incarceration for years.

White South Africa managed to forget all this pretty quickly.

## AND ON

The years 1958 to 1976 were apartheid's "glacial" years. They were dominated by Verwoerd and, after his death, by his rigid thinking. His successors could not escape his warped notions, notably the Bantustan scheme. The government held all South Africans in an iron grip. Even when the 1960 emergency was lifted, the government sought to maintain strict control on every walk of life. Hundreds of acts of Parliament, and rules and

112

regulations framed in terms of those acts, imposed apartheid in every conceivable sphere. The right of the media to publish and to comment freely was restricted by act, with vast areas such as defence, police, prisons, oil supply, nuclear fuels, the statements of banned or listed persons placed out of bounds. Promoting "Communism" was a serious offence and widely defined.

Whites were fearful as the wind of change in Africa began to produce powerful regional pressures. These included the ex-Belgian Congo (Zaire) crumbling into civil war after independence in 1960; Rhodesia's white-settler unilateral declaration of independence from Britain in 1965, followed by world sanctions and guerilla conflict; a growing war in South West Africa (Namibia) from the early 1960s; and colonial then civil war in Mozambique and Angola after the Portuguese grip ended in the mid-1970s.

The fledgling Progressive Party was annihilated in 1961 in an election Verwoerd called two years early—partly to wipe them out before they could gain a foothold, and partly, some said, to avoid a scheduled election in 1963, in which year the PAC had boasted it would gain power. A sole M.P., Helen Suzman, a distinguished parliamentary liberal in the highest Western tradition, survived the electoral massacre. The madness went on: pass arrests; population removals; racial edicts. Not far from my own home, pathetic shanty dwellings were bulldozed (with the authorities choosing the wet of winter to do this, and a cabinet minister having the insensitivity to say that there were not bulldozers—merely "front-end loaders").

The Group Areas Act hit the coloured people of the Cape so hard that it even disgusted the once-hardened Ossewa-brandwag leader of the war years, Hans van Rensburg. He had, after patching things up with the National Party, taken a job on the Group Areas Board, whose job it was to divide residential areas on a racial basis. In this capacity he had to conduct on-the-spot inquiries before demarcating areas which were listed in the *Government Gazette*. But he resigned from the board in February 1962 amid much speculation. At the time it was reported that there were "serious differences of opinion" over the administration of the

Act. It was noted that Van Rensburg had held hearings in places including District Six, and that "he has often appeared to be disturbed when faced with evidence of the hardship, sadness and frustration that many of the racial zoning schemes have entailed—particularly among the coloured people of the Western Cape."[50] When he resigned he confided to one of the paper's reporters, Roger Williams, that he could not "with any conscience" go on doing the job. The interview was confidential, and Williams, a most dependable journalist in all circumstances, respected this. But when Van Rensburg died in March 1983, Williams disclosed the O.B. ex-leader's disenchantment.[51] And he recalled the full story to me thus:

> Van Rensburg specifically mentioned Simon's Town and Caledon when I saw him soon after his resignation. "You saw and heard what happened there," he said, "and having been at those hearings yourself I'm sure you will have no difficulty in seeing why I had to quit. All those people . . . you know what I mean."
> What Van Rensburg was referring to, of course, was "all those people" who stood before him pleading to be allowed to continue staying in areas they had grown up in, and where their families had been living for generations. I recall one Malay tailor witness at Simon's Town, tears streaming down his cheeks, telling Van Rensburg that he and his forebears had been tailoring the uniforms of Royal Navy admirals and other officers for generations—"and now you want to throw me out of my own home-town—why?" And much the same story at Caledon, where coloured and Malay traders had been doing business in the main street for donkeys' years and were now under threat of being herded into a "coloured" township on the outskirts of the town.[52]

Even a man with Van Rensburg's background was disgusted. Williams spent his early adult life fighting the Germans in the Second World War while Van Rensburg aided and abetted them. Of Van Rensburg, Williams said: "I got on very well with him. I found him a cultured, knowledgeable, and ever-courteous and sensitive person, and I found no difficulty in understanding why he could take no more of the Group Areas hearings, which were clearly disturbing and depressing him. As he put it: 'A man takes just so much. . . .'"53

But, as with the Immorality Act and other measures, the government did not let up. The whole mad scheme had an unstoppable momentum. It extended to idiotic lengths. A few examples (of which I bear some personal knowledge) will be described.

## TRAINS, TRAILS, CAVES

It is not widely known that a trail for hikers was once designed with such insensitivity that it required superhuman walkers. That is, if they were coloured. (No matter how superhuman, Africans were not welcome.)

Called the Outeniqua Hiking Trail, it was a hundred and fifty kilometres long. That would mean an average of about twenty kilometres each day over a seven-day walk.

The start was aptly named. Walkers set out from a spot called "Witfontein" (White fountain) at Blanco, near George, the political stronghold of P. W. Botha. Separate cabins were provided for white and coloured walkers, the "white" ones holding thirty hikers overnight, the "coloured" ones only twenty. Seven such cabins were provided for whites, but only three for coloured hikers. The whites would walk about twenty kilometres a day. The coloured hikers had to be made of sterner stuff. They had to walk nearly forty the first day, nearly fifty the next, then a quickie (of ten), then a long march of fifty to the end of the trail—and no doubt resuscitation. Judging from the official data on the guide map in 1976, Africans did not appear to be provided for at all. (Presumably, hiking was something Africans just did not do.)

It was well-nigh impossible for coloured people to walk the full trail, as required by apartheid, unless they sneaked into cabins demarcated for whites or slept in the open. For this reason few attempted it. Knowing their limits, they would settle for briefer walks, say for a day at a time. The whites could enjoy the full trail in the George/Knysna area, rich in trees, flora, and wildlife—a place of interest, mystery, and folklore. The southernmost elephants to be found on earth would roam the yellowwood forests near Knysna in dwindling numbers; and there were traces of a gold rush of the 1880s to explore at overgrown places like Millwood.

And how did the authorities know who was white and who was coloured when bookings were made? Simple. The Forestry Department booking office always asked for I.D., and this document carried by South Africans had a special number identifying race. I.D. documents were explicit. Africans had their own system of reference books. Others were given the following digits in their identity numbers to indicate race:

| Race Group | Identifying number |
| --- | --- |
| White | 00 |
| Cape Coloured | 01 |
| Malay | 02 |
| Griqua | 03 |
| Chinese | 04 |
| Indian | 05 |
| Other Asian | 06 |
| Other Coloured | 07 |

Later, I was told, the authorities reorganized the huts, and converted at least one to "general use," which gave coloured hikers some relief. In due course, apartheid on the trail withered with other excesses. Its legacy? A plethora of huts on the Outeniqua Trail—now surely one of the most hutted trails in the world!

Another attempt at imposing apartheid on nature was at the world-famous Cango Caves, near the ostrich farms of Oudtshoorn. At first white and "non-white" visitors were admitted at different times through the same entrance. But this was not good enough for the racial planners. They blasted a fifty-foot tunnel through the outer rock of this natural wonder to create a totally separate entrance for "non-whites." White and black thus gained entry simultaneously but separately, with the latter being admitted via a small cave leading to the main one at the start, called Van Zyl's cave. Then segregated parties would set out at different times, though the *Cape Times* noted ominously: "Even with different starting times it is probable that white and non-white parties will meet at certain points."[54] A separate "non-white" parking lot and a restaurant—which shared a kitchen with the white restaurant—were planned.

That crudity, too, was to wither with time, but only after nature had been permanently violated by explosives.

In those days even trains were shunted around to keep things racially tidy. This was to overcome the daunting problem that the railway stations in Cape Town and Johannesburg had the races at the wrong ends. Johannesburg had the section for blacks on the Cape Town side. And, a thousand miles to the south, the one in Cape Town, built with much fanfare for nearly twenty million rands in the Nationalist era, had the black section facing Johannesburg, i.e., the end farthest away from the commercial centre of the city, Adderley Street. A fool could see that as the trains headed for their destinations, there were the makings of an almighty Verwoerdian embarrassment . . . with the blacks and whites arriving at the "wrong ends." The solution was simple: coaches were disconnected and shunted around to the "correct" side of the train at a place called Touws River, in the boondocks of the Cape province. This was often done in the dead of night. The *Cape Times* was so intrigued by this story that we hired freelance writer Charles Bloomberg in the 1970s to get to the bottom of it. (Bloomberg's various distinctions included exposing the Broederbond secret Afrikaner society in South Africa when on the *Sunday Times* in the 1960s, and writing the section on the Holocaust in the Emmy Award–winning British television series, "The World at War," narrated by Sir Lawrence Olivier. Charles died in London after open-heart surgery.)

Bloomberg was intrigued by the thought that South Africa could in all seriousness shunt half a train around in the dead of night to satisfy apartheid. He was eager and determined to investigate. Duly commissioned, he embarked by train from Johannesburg and set his alarm clock to wake him just before Touws River. Lo, amid the clanking and hissing, he beheld it: racial shunting. When he got out of the train to take pictures of

117

the "non-white" passengers being shunted to the "right" end of the train, there were peals of laughter. They yelled to him: "You must be from the *Times*." *They* knew what was happening. His piece duly appeared in the newspaper, and the railways admitted to the practice. By the mid-1980s, it should be noted, South African trains were being integrated—slowly and tortuously, with a cabinet minister still proclaiming that whites had an "established right" to travel separately.

A bureaucratic notice, circular no. 12 of 1977, issued by the Department of Community Development and dated July 6 that year, illustrated the determination of the government. Directed to local authorities, it noted that a recent amendment to the Illegal Squatting Act of 1951 had "removed previous encumbrances like the compulsory serving of a notice and ready access to the courts on trivial grounds." This, in effect, meant that local authorities could act against hapless squatters without further ado or fear of court process. The *Cape Times* described the edict as "chillier than the bitterly cold wind that blew in the Peninsula" and said the "way for the bulldozer" was now completely open. The small protection given thousands of squatters had been removed, said the paper, adding: "How well the bureaucrats must sleep, content in the knowledge that no shack, no family, is beyond their lawful reach even for a day or two. As neat and tidy—and as inhumane—as any petty tyrant could wish for."[55]

And the squatters, like the "scarecrows" in *A Tale of Two Cities,* washed around the peninsula living a pathetic, makeshift life, their homes bulldozed in front of their eyes—in the middle of winter. Cape Town people opened their hearts to them. One Sunday morning a city councillor, Eulalie Stott, took two busloads of squatters to the suburban church in Cape Town where the state president was at divine service to show him the problem at first-hand. He did not respond, nor indeed was he moved. Some squatters were taken into suburban homes by middle-class white families, enjoying the instant comforts of crackling log fires and "white" cuisine. . . . Nuns, priests, charity workers, and others appeared as if from nowhere on the Cape flats to care for the

118

displaced people in churches, halls, and humble homes. I went with my family to bulldozed areas like Modderdam and Unibell to see the suffering. My teenage daughters Vicki and Janet had one of their first glimpses of apartheid in action, and I explained to them what was happening. I had taken them along with mixed feelings. Seeing such disgraceful events so early in life can radicalize people and bring them into conflict with the state. Indeed, when in 1982 both Vicki and Janet were arrested with other Rhodes University students in Grahamstown after a United Democratic Front anti-apartheid demonstration, I recall feeling a curious mixture of admiration and fear.

Apartheid produced its ironies and twists of fiat. A suburban train smash at Woodstock near Cape Town in April 1957 killed mainly white people (fifteen whites, three coloured people, and no Africans) simply because whites were concentrated in the impact area by official fate—segregation. When in January 1981 floods ravaged the sleepy town of Laingsburg a few hours' drive from Cape Town on the main Johannesburg road, the coloured populace escaped the worst. They had been settled, by apartheid, on higher ground—away from the torrent. In a selfless show of fellow feeling, many of them pitched in to help the white victims. I recall thinking: there's hope for South Africa yet.

And while blacks smarted under apartheid whites went to great lengths to thank the government for keeping things separate. The *Burger* reported in 1978 that the ratepayers of Eerste River near Cape Town had arranged a special "braai," or cookout, to honour favourite son of the area, Cabinet Minister Chris Heunis and his wife, "to show their thanks for the fact that their town would remain white."[56] A government wand had been waved to remove the prospect that Eerste River might be zoned for coloured people. Those with the vote had the influence, and they powerfully thanked ministers over chops and steak after having used the vote to their own ends.

In the "glacial" years of apartheid, some whites spoke out vigorously and consistently against government assaults on fellow-citizens. Two chief justices, Albert Centlivres and Henry Fagan, raised dignified voices against apartheid when they retired. The Progressives' Helen Suzman was a constant critic. She visited Nelson Mandela on Robben Island long before it became the fashion. Human rights activist Helen Joseph suffered more than almost any other white in a lifetime of opposition. Laurence Gandar, editor of the *Rand Daily Mail*, bravely ran his campaigning liberal paper and was eased out by the cautious owners who maintained, ludicrously, that "some of his writing was not in the national interest." Anthony Delius, a remarkably gifted writer and satirist who turned out the "Notes in the House" column on Parliament at the *Cape Times*, was another. He was thrown out of Parliament permanently for his writing.* There was the incredibly brave Beyers Naude, thrown up from the bosom of Afrikanerdom who spurned a leading position in the Dutch Reformed Church to dissent. After Sharpeville, he broke with his kinsmen and his church and went into full-scale opposition to apartheid. He started the Christian Institute, which was banned in 1977. He was also banned for years and later headed the South African Council of Churches. There was my close friend, Theo Kotze, a Methodist minister who escaped to Britain after being banned when he was Naude's lieutenant in the Cape—and who, with his wife Helen, yearned for home. There were bold Afrikaans writers like Breyten Breytenbach, Uys Krige, and André Brink. And there was the towering presence of Alan Paton, author of *Cry, the Beloved Country*, someone the government never dared to ban.

In United Party and English-speaking big-business circles, criticism of the ruling National Party was regarded as desirable and legitimate, as long as it did not go "too far." The cautious moguls with gimlet eyes who dominated the economy—and owned the English-language newspapers—had to keep on cordial

---

*For those interested in a pen that stood virtually alone against Verwoerd, see Delius's "Notes in the House" in the *Cape Times* under the pseudonym Adderley, especially those dated February 2, 1962, and June 11, 1964, which got him thrown out of Parliament.

terms with government because of their financial interests. There were deals to be done with Pretoria. They would say to editors, referring to Nationalist leaders: "But remember, he *is* the prime minister." The endless refrain was "Give him a chance." I lost count of the number of times I heard this.

There were Afrikaner Nationalists and intellectuals who had grave doubts, but—with some exceptions like Stellenbosch professors, one or two newspaper editors, and doubting cabinet ministers—they were forced to hold their peace, in those granite days.

Meanwhile apartheid plunged on, like Dickens's depiction of the carriage, with a "wild rattle and clatter," at frightful cost to the people and the national budget. Economists and others attempted to cost it out. One of the best such costings came from an enlightened businessman Len Abrahamse who early in 1977 estimated, on a very conservative approach over thirty years, that "it would not be unreasonable to assume that gross national product per capita would have been some 50 percent higher." That is, without apartheid.[57] A Cape Town academic, Prof. Michael Savage, was to point in 1986 to the appalling duplication of services in South Africa—for instance at least fourteen departments of education. He gave the direct *annual* cost of apartheid to the national budget alone as between 2,800 million and 5,700 million South African rands.[58]

121

# CHAPTER TEN

# LONDON OFFICE

During 1966 and 1967 I lived with my family in Surrey, England. I worked on secondment in the London bureau of the South African Morning Newspapers whose office in the Daily Telegraph Building overlooked Fleet Street.

The London office years were dominated by Rhodesia's rebellion against the British crown. The leader of the minority whites, Ian Smith, had unilaterally declared independence in the South African neighbour-country on November 11, 1965. Harold Wilson was at Number Ten Downing Street as Labour premier, and he kept the press busy with his attempts to end Ian Smith's rebellion. There were several attempts at a settlement during my time in London, including those on board the British warship *Tiger.* Wilson insisted on NIBMAR, No Independence Before Majority Rule, which Smith rejected time and again. As Smith turned down deal after deal, his manoeuvring room was whittled away, and he finally succumbed to guerilla war, sanctions, and powerful United States pressure in the fading years of the 1970s.

By holding out for so long against the world, Smith missed the chance of securing for whites arrangements more palatable than those finally forced on them. There were lessons for the white South African minority here.

I met Smith on two occasions, in Salisbury and Bulawayo, as the crisis ground on. He was wooden and evasive and probably on his guard because he knew I represented a "liberal" newspaper tradition, and he had destroyed press freedom in Rhodesia through censorship. He came across as a stubborn man overtaken by events, but unwilling or unable to see it. He did not seem to notice the harsh reality of black rule rushing toward Rhodesian whites across the African veld. During that time someone, I think in *Punch* magazine, described white Rhodesia as a suburb masquerading as a state. Indeed, the quarter million white Rhodesians could be tucked into one corner of South Africa without much trouble. The Cape Peninsula alone had more whites. To visit this quaint white tyranny, busily censoring the press, evading reality, conducting dirty tricks and military destabilization against opponents, hanging guerillas, and denouncing the Western world as "decadent" was like walking through the looking-glass into a colonial Africa that had been gone for years. In time, the white Rhodesians' delusions caught up with them and Robert Mugabe won an election and took over in 1980. It was riveting to sit in a Salisbury hotel, turn on the television, and be greeted by "Comrade Robert Mugabe." Ironically, it was Smith's state of emergency which was retained, to work against the whites for a change.

London, with at least one big Southern African story to cover, was professionally enriching, and England was lovely. We rented a cottage on the old A 25 Road on London's underbelly in the green belt near Oxted in Surrey. Wild foxes, horse riding, music societies, village-green cricket, and pheasant dishes on Sundays added colour to life in the North Downs. I travelled to work each day by train, via Victoria to Blackfriars, where I was disgorged with other Fleet Street journalists on the District and Circle Line. The bowler-hatted stockbrokers would be up in first class and would change for the City at East Croydon. In two years, immersed in everything from the conservative *Daily Telegraph* to the Communist *Morning Star,* I travelled the equivalent of twice around the world in reputedly the safest spot in Britain, a moving train.

However interesting and enjoyable the life, I yearned to get back to the political choices and excitements of South Africa.

But before I returned home I was briefly to inherit a Swazi.

A prominent politician who came from that landlocked state on South Africa's eastern flank had been kept in jail in Stockholm for a long time and was awaiting trial for a bouncing-cheque offence which he averred was committed by a companion whom he had met at the independence celebrations of Lesotho—a con man who had flitted to Finland. I was flown from London to investigate and write about the unhappy Swaziland politician.

A white South African reporter turning up in the court jolt-ed the Swedes into action. Their criticisms of South Africa and its justice were well known. There was a very rapid decision to release the man. The magistrate asked me if I knew him. I stood up in court and affirmed, with some poetic licence, that we were almost blood brothers. He was simply dumped into my cus-tody—one large, immensely relieved, and amiable Swazi politi-cian to look after in the crisp Scandinavian snow. My London editor, who had years of experience in extricating various people, usually journalists, out of trouble in Europe, arranged emergency funds, and the politician managed to get a flight back home on a German airline. He remained prominent, and very controversial, in public life for some time.

It was on Fleet Street that I heard Verwoerd had been stabbed to death. A colleague at the London office bumped into me at lunch-time on September 6, 1966, in the street. He looked shocked and said: "Have you heard about Verwoerd?" We rushed up to the Reuters office at 85 Fleet Street and riveted our eyes on the telex machine.

125

Ben Schoeman, the leader of the House of Assembly in Cape Town, was announcing that, as far as he knew, the prime minister was dead. The slow, staccato telex characters spelled it out. The second attempt to kill Verwoerd had succeeded. What he had called the "protection of Divine Providence" after the first assassination attempt was not extended this time. Having worked in such close proximity to Verwoerd for nearly a decade, and having interviewed this aloof man on more than one occasion, I found the news staggering. I was not used to British satire and was jolted to see *Private Eye,* the British satirical publication, run a cover announcing **SOUTH AFRICA MOURNS** with a picture underneath showing blacks doing a tribal dance. I met a former South African M.P. in Fleet Street and he said: "Good riddance!" Fleet Street gave the event huge coverage—the assassination of the great white chief at his bench in Parliament, the cockpit of white power.

Back in South Africa, my colleagues and friends in the press gallery, people like Stanley Uys, Stewart Carlyle, and Gerald Shaw, had witnessed the event in person—Shaw with an extra sense of shock because he had been served a pot of tea and a hamburger by Verwoerd's killer, Tsafendas, just before.* Carlyle, who was political correspondent of the *Natal Mercury* in Durban, later told me that, when Verwoerd lay slumped in his bench as M.P.s grappled with Tsafendas, he went white and "the blood drained away like water from a bath when the plug is pulled."

An extra shock was also in store for Helen Suzman. Immediately after the attack, the lone Progressive M.P. was confronted angrily by Cabinet Minister P. W. Botha. In her own words to me, "He came down the aisle of the House, stopped opposite the front bench on which I was sitting, wagged the famous finger at me and shouted: 'It's you liberals, now we will get you all; you did it' and went storming out of the house."[59] Mrs. Suzman reported the matter to the secretary of Parliament, R. J. McFarlane, who took it up with the Speaker, H. Klopper. Botha

---

*And incidentally, Shaw had been given wildly inaccurate and generous change by Tsafendas, whose mind was on other matters.

"most ungraciously" apologized to her in the presence of the Speaker, saying: "In terms of the rules of the House I apologize." This she later reluctantly accepted after consulting Progressive Party colleagues.[60]

That night I found myself appearing on the "Twenty-Four Hours" BBC television programme which was devoted to the assassination. A verbal tussle went on between two very different South Africans. The one was Albie Sachs, a one-time Marxist lawyer from Cape Town who had been detained before leaving South Africa and joining the ANC in exile. (John Vorster had a healthy respect for Sachs. He once told me the police could "never break" him in interrogation, unlike others on the Left. Years later, in the 1980s, suspected South African agents got close to killing Sachs in a horrific car bomb explosion in Maputo.) The other was a former government-supporting journalist in the press gallery, Carel Noffke, who was information counsellor at the South African embassy in London. They were poles apart politically. With the programme dominated by Sachs and Noffke arguing, all I was expected to do was venture a forecast as to who would take over as prime minister. I was confident that the strongman minister of justice, John Vorster, though only thirteenth in line in seniority, would get the job. I had gained his confidence as a parliamentary correspondent, and he had made plain his belief that the party would turn to him in a crisis. Discussing the succession, he had said once: "After all, look what I've done for the people of South Africa. I have smashed Communism and Poqo." That was in 1964. He was running hard for the job even then. In September 1966 he got his chance.

# CHAPTER ELEVEN

# BALTHAZAR JOHN VORSTER

## INTO AFRICA

Vorster's early years as prime minister were marked by a massive "détente" effort in Africa that failed. Not much travelled himself, and disliking air flights, he was an unenthusiastic starter. But, egged on by Information Minister Dr. Connie Mulder and Secretary for Information Dr. Eschel Rhoodie (who was later to confide that it took "a great deal of time and trouble" to get Vorster to go), Vorster set out to win influence deep in Africa, secretly visiting several black states. South Africa, despite apartheid, was a powerful country and was in a position to drive bargains in view of black Africa's dire economic needs. Apart from trade, there could be diplomatic prizes, too, if black African states could be made less universally hostile to South Africa. Many African countries traded with South Africa, some openly but most secretly. A problem was that Vorster could never decide whether to be the gentle giant or the bully in Africa. His personality and instinct tended to the latter. While visiting African states, he would be indulging in dirty tricks and destabilization against neighbouring countries. Moreover, his domestic policies were so repressive for blacks that there could be no deal abroad until there was one at home. (Some examples, taken at random from academic, sport, and music worlds: 1. Vorster's government, believing that "whites should teach whites" pressured the University of Cape Town into rescinding its decision to appoint a brilliant Cambridge-educated black researcher, Archie Mafeje, to a senior lectureship in social anthropology. Senator Jan de Klerk, minister of labour and father of F. W. de Klerk who was to become party leader one day, said Mafeje's appointment would have been "tantamount to flouting the accepted and traditional outlook of South Africa." The incident was marked by a student "sit-in" protest which I covered as a journalist in August 1968. 2. Indian golfer Papwa Sewgolum was banned from playing in the Natal Open in 1970, and was generally harassed by race laws. 3. The government-run South African Broadcasting Corporation banned "non-white" pianists from a Beethoven music competition, maintaining that "different races perform best in their own idiom.") That has always been the reality. So his outward movement was collapsing almost before it began.

The Angola civil war which began in 1975 soon embroiled him, when he supported the leader of the southern-based UNITA organization (Portuguese acronym for National Union for the Total Independence of Angola), Jonas Savimbi. The South Africans had to retreat early in 1976 in the face of heavy Cuban and Russian arms after United States and other Western help failed to materialize. And Vorster was forced to ditch the crumbling white regime in Rhodesia in the late 1970s, under pressure of the Americans and others. The black youth revolt of Soweto in June 1976 shook South Africa. Then, finally, came a massive "Information Scandal" in 1978 involving Mulder and Rhoodie that scuppered his premiership and gave P. W. Botha his chance for power. Vorster's dozen years in charge were to be unrelentingly turbulent.

130

Probably the most important regional event in the Vorster era, and the turning point for white South Africa, was the fall of the Portuguese empire in Africa in 1974. That changed the power equation in southern Africa virtually overnight, after more than four centuries of Portuguese presence. It removed white-ruled buffers which had shielded white South Africa from a hostile black continent. With Smith's Rhodesia finally falling in 1980, South Africa was exposed on most sides to black-run African states. I recall Vorster in 1975, slumping back in his leather seat in his high-ceilinged, airy office in Union Buildings, Pretoria, waving his hand to the east and remarking that "the communists" were now only a few hundred miles away (in Mozambique). But he felt he could get on with them—and even clear their harbour in Lourenco Marques (Maputo). He was more worried about Angola where civil war threatened.[61]

## TAKING THE PAPER: SEPTEMBER 1971

When Vorster was reaching the peak of his power, on September 1, 1971, Victor Norton handed over to me what he called the "bag of tricks." That was the editorship of the *Cape Times*. I was thirty-three, cocky, with a good contract. Both the tradition at the paper and that contract ensured about as much independence as any editor could expect. The arrangements were part of my letter of appointment (see Appendix 2, p. 245), and the key section read: "Provided they do not involve any departure from the established and recognized policy and practice of the *Cape Times*, you will conform to all instructions and directions from time to time given by the chairman of the board of directors on behalf of the company."

At first sight this was rather discouraging. But, put another way, it meant and was supposed to mean that the editor could resist attempts by the board to influence him if he felt it was acting contrary to the "recognized policy and practice" of the *Cape Times*. And it made the editor, in the first instance, the arbiter of this—though it would ultimately be a matter for the courts to resolve a dispute. When Norton was asked about his contract by the Press Commission (which took twelve years to investigate the press after its appointment in 1950), he said that this section guaranteed his freedom of decision in the direction of the editorial activities of the newspaper and the expression of opinion. "In addition, the traditions of the *Cape Times* establish very clearly and forcibly that the expression of opinion is the function of the editor. In more than 20 years' close association with the *Cape Times,* I have not known this requirement to be infringed or questioned, in the letter or the spirit, overtly or covertly, by any director of the *Cape Times* or by any officer of the *Cape Times.*"[62]

The section was of obvious value to an editor under unreasonable pressure from management or owners. Yet I had no illusions about the company's absolute say in the hiring or firing of the editor—unlike, for instance, in parts of Europe, where staff can play a decisive role in such matters. At most, it provided some security, as did the six months' notice of dismissal in the letter of appointment. Firing was the last thing I expected.

Sixteen years of editing—about six thousand days and nearly as many editorials—lay ahead of me. And it was a matter of "walking blindfold through a minefield"—to quote a remark in the 1950s by Horace Flather, former editor of the Johannesburg *Star* on the perils of editing in South Africa. It was worse than the 1950s. It was to be marked by restrictions, pressures, threats, charges in court, states of emergency, arrest. . . . It was to unfold hand-in-hand with lurching events in South Africa.

The *Cape Times* had always been independent of other newspaper groups. It was the oldest established daily in the country, having been started on March 27, 1876, by an Irish-born former Anglican clergyman turned diamond prospector, F. Y. St. Leger. It had never missed a day since then and was rich in history, tradition, and anecdote.

The *Cape Times* had been a paper of Empire, modelling itself on the London *Times*. Stories about Rudyard Kipling, Cecil

Rhodes, and other Imperial figures ran through its corridors.* But by the time I took over in 1971, this imperial reputation, thank God, was gone. We still strove for the same journalistic standards of reliability, accuracy, and non-sensationalism, but the times had driven us forward. We were thoroughly South African. In fact, every senior member of the staff was a South African citizen, which was a fact we had to point out publicly when wrongly accused of being staffed by foreigners.

For generations the *Cape Times* looked like the Rock of Gibraltar, backed by the financial establishment of Cape Town which traced its business origins to Cecil John Rhodes's money. It was also backed by a massive commercial printing works, Cape and Transvaal Printers. Work at the paper could be a bit "stuffy" but secure and professionally satisfying. The printing business fell victim to British take-over predators who wanted to strip off and sell its undervalued assets. In 1973 the *Cape Times* was bought by the South African Associated Newspapers group, based in Johannesburg, which had been an associate of the paper for years. We were given assurances of editorial independence, we remained profitable, and things went on very much as before. . . .

## TABLE TALK

As correspondent and editor, I had a good personal relationship with Vorster, despite our powerful differences. He shared many confidences with me and certain other journalists.

Unlike remote Verwoerd and bellicose Botha, the dour and cynical Vorster was not difficult to get on with personally. He was once urged to smile by our photographer for a picture. Looking grimmer than ever, with that hang-jaw expression, he said: "But I *am* smiling." To a flustered journalist at a press conference whose

*Kipling recommended its fourth editor, Sir Maitland Park, for his job in 1902; Rhodes invited then-editor Edumund Garrett to dinner on February 22, 1898, in a scrawled note thus: "Dear Garrett, Come to dinner. I will not bully but remember I am your host."

concealed tape-recorder had started whirring embarrassingly, he said: "Is that yours or is that mine?" He would sit up in his parliamentary office till late, ordering Frisco brand coffee for his guests, and would relive his life—discussing his days as an advocate at the bar, as registrar to a Cape judge-president, as an anti-war activist, and as a politician. At these sessions, a cross between "table talk" and "fireside chats," he got on pretty well even with sworn political enemies—like Donald Woods, who became editor of the *Daily Dispatch* in East London.

Vorster told me that he saw the press as a "necessary evil," and it is true that he never went to the comprehensive lengths of P. W. Botha to curb it. Even at the height of the black youth revolt in Soweto and elsewhere in 1976 he held back from declaring a state of emergency, though he did aim a death blow at one newspaper. By contrast, four of Botha's eleven years were marked by states of emergency. Botha calculated and planned. Vorster hit out instinctively. Vorster, as minister of justice in the early 1960s, was, however, absolutely ruthless in his suppression of dissent and in building his claim to the leadership of the National Party. This he did with measures such as the ninety-day and other detention laws, the Sabotage Act, providing a possible death penalty for sabotage, and "house arrest" and "extended prison term" measures aimed vindictively at individuals like Helen Joseph and Robert Sobukwe respectively.

Vorster would aver that he had changed only one major political principle in his life. As a member of the O.B. he had not believed in Parliament, but he had changed this view and now appreciated Parliament's role. That was not surprising, considering what the white Parliament did for him and his party. He confided, to my surprise, that he had once been a Wolf Cub, the youth organization which, together with the Scouts, was founded by a British arch-enemy of Afrikanerdom, Lord Baden-Powell, who fought the Boers and was hero of the siege of Mafeking. But Vorster added that he did not like the "British-orientated practices of the cubs, so I joined the Voortrekkers" (a parallel, Afrikaner youth organization).[63]

Vorster once gave me the nub of his political credo. He said he was prepared to make "big changes" in South Africa, but only if they did not violate the following principles:

1. There must be no threat to the identity of whites.
2. There must be no share by blacks in the white man's political power structure.[64]

With these non-negotiables it is clear why there was no chance of fundamental reform under Vorster. But he himself felt he was going a long way. He saw "multi-national" or "international" sport as a major reform, though it was rejected by most blacks as window dressing. He ordered the racial integration of an opera house in Cape Town, the Nico Malan, over the head of a conservative Cape administrator. But he was still basically racist in his approach. Vorster thought he had stumped a colleague of mine, John Scott, when he asked Scott defiantly if he would like his daughter to go to a school with blacks. Scott shot back: "Delighted." Vorster's inherent racism made him sensitive to criticism from the right wing, particularly when right-wingers festooned the hustings with pictures of him sitting at a banquet with Malawi's president, Hastings Banda, and his black woman hostess. He complained bitterly to me in private about this and also about the publicity given the event by English-language newspapers. Vorster was hostile toward critical bodies abroad like the International Commission of Jurists whom he described to me once as "bastards."

Despite Vorster's gruff humour, his popular golfing jokes, and a capacity to get on with people on a personal level, he had a smouldering hatred for South Africans who still regarded Britain as "home." I did not tell him that the *Cape Times* style book had, till Norton's time, instructed staff not to refer to England as "home." Vorster identified with President Paul Kruger of the South African Republic in the Transvaal and frequently quoted what Kruger had told the British in 1899 in Bloemfontein: "It's not the vote you want . . . it's my land." Kruger headed what Churchill called the "recalcitrant Dutch" who had denied the vote to British immigrants in the Transvaal who equalled the Boer numbers but paid all but one-twentieth of the taxes.[65]

Vorster had powerful likes and dislikes. He cherished an institutional hostility toward the English-language press, though not toward all its individuals. At a private meeting of English-language editors he declared: "Let us be candid about it. You hate me and I hate you. You have tried to bring me down at every turn."[66]

When his détente moves in Africa suffered setbacks, he became sullen and belligerent. He warned at the above occasion that if détente broke down, he would blame the press and take action against newspapers, "because it will mean war with Africa." He was bitter that newspapers dubbed him pro-German and pro-Nazi during the war. He summoned me specially to his parliamentary office once to deny such a charge, made in a letter to the editor by writer André Brink. He started the conversation, as I walked in: *"Hoekom belaster jy my?"* (which means: "Why are you defaming me?") He had been anti-British, not pro-Nazi. Considering the conditions of war, this seemed to me a distinction without a difference. He also deeply resented having once been reported as likening "Christian nationalism" to Nazism and fascism. He maintained that all he had said and meant, as an O.B. general, was that in Germany there was Nazism, in Italy facism, and in South Africa Afrikaners wanted Christian nationalism. Once again, an unenlightening distinction.

Vorster would bully. He enjoyed the smoke-filled rooms of political life. He would play with the press like a cat. On more than one occasion he used friendly Afrikaans journalists in the press gallery to pass on to people like Anthony Delius of the *Cape Times* warnings that "your book is full"—meaning that some action was likely against the individual. Such warnings were calculated to temper bold journalism. They were serious because Vorster had power to destroy lives. Delius himself simply ignored the pressure. Similarly, Vorster would tell me darkly how close the *Rand Daily Mail* was to the brink of closure or other government action, knowing I would run straight to Raymond Louw, its editor at the time, to tell him. Louw had some titanic run-ins with Vorster, but held firm—unlike some others.

Vorster's favourite cat-and-mouse game with the newspaper owners was to tell them to "put your house in order." That meant to control critical editors and journalists. He knew newspaper owners and managers scared easily. He kept notes on press lapses. He prepared elaborate newspaper legislation, but did not pass it. He pressed for the newspaper industry's voluntary watchdog body, the Press Council (later to become the Media Council), to be given more "teeth" so that it could punish newspapers more to his satisfaction. He did ban the successful black newspaper, the *World,* in 1977 (a successor, the *Post,* was effectively banned by Botha later). As far back as 1972 he tried to secure the compliance of the press in an "informal" state of emergency, involving self-censorship, which the public never knew about. Many editors opposed the idea, and that attempt failed. But Vorster held back from the comprehensive excesses of Botha; Vorster never tried anything as all-embracing as Botha's "media regulations" under the state of emergency. Neither Vorster nor Botha was a democrat. But, as party leader, Botha went marginally further along the road to repression. This is not to say that Vorster would not have got round to it.

There is reason to believe that Vorster was reserving his *Götterdämmerung* for a stage when he expected the country to be at war with Africa. This truth emerged in his blackest moments. I sat with him in his office in 1973. He was extremely worried about the effects of the oil crisis on the West's ability to act with resolve in world events. He spoke of the danger of "say, a thousand" whites being killed in Rhodesia, which would cause a war psychosis in South Africa. "Then I will close newspapers without hesitation." He sensed his African detente running into trouble. Black labour power was flexing its muscles in the South African townships. The world was growing more hostile. He said darkly: "If you and I can sit like this [meaning relatively peacefully] in three years' time, on November 27, 1976, we will be lucky."[67]

By that date Pretoria had suffered major setbacks in Africa, including getting bogged down in the Angola civil war. Smith was

137

losing in Rhodesia. Soweto had burst over the whole country. But Vorster would not see his *Götterdämmerung*. Botha would be bundling him out of public life by 1978, and he would be dead a few years later.

Yet Vorster's mood was not always black. Only two weeks before the above talk, he was meeting with newspaper editors and crowing. He brandished the agreement he had signed with Dr. Alfred Escher of the United Nations to establish an advisory authority for Namibia which Vorster said triumphantly he (Vorster) would chair—an agreement that later collapsed, with Vorster bitterly blaming U.N. Secretary-General Kurt Waldheim. On another occasion he joked with editors about the crocodiles kept in a lake by an African president he had visited. As Vorster and a party of white South Africans watched them, the crocs turned and swam toward the South Africans, who gasped and thought: "They're coming for us." He noted with amusement that his South African Airways Boeing had stood undetected for two full days on the runway of a major airport in the Ivory Coast while he made a secret visit. He told how black nationalists in Rhodesia—long before a settlement was achieved at the Lancaster House conference in London—had been flown for talks in Lusaka by South African planes on more than one occasion in absolute secrecy, and then locked up again on their return. The Africa travel bug had got to him. He confided: " Now I want to go to Kenya."[68]

In 1975 he made the incredible prediction to me that he would be addressing the Organization of African Unity by the end of that year. This was chutzpah-plus, and it was not to be. But he added an ominous rider, showing his irritation at the lack of support, as he saw it, from the country's English press: "If I do not make the O.A.U., it will be the fault of the English press and there will be war. I will have done what I could, and will say this to the youth of South Africa, and they can then fight with a clean conscience."[69]

138

# INFO SCANDAL 1976–78

The Information Scandal, which soured the last months of John Vorster's rule as prime minister, was exacting on sections of the press. Vorster's heir apparent, Dr. Connie Mulder, minister of information, and his stylish, slick secretary for information, Dr. Eschel Rhoodie, had from about 1974 set up an elaborate secret plan to use funds irregularly to try to sell the unsaleable, apartheid, to the world. Much of the money was voted by an unsuspecting Parliament in the belief that it was for the Defence Special Account (ironically of P. W. Botha's defence department). The Mulder/Rhoodie objective, with Vorster's knowledge and connivance, was to carry out an ambitious propaganda war at home and abroad. In essence, it involved starting up to 180 secret projects to buy political influence by undertaking covert activities to promote the government. Mulder made it clear that virtually any actions were justified in the cause of "South Africa," by which he meant the National Party. He said on November 3, 1978, that no rules applied when the existence of South Africa was at stake. It involved using prominent front men at home and abroad in the acquisition or starting of newspapers; seeking to upset the campaigns of overseas politicians critical of South Africa, like U.S. Senator Dick Clark; and spending lavishly in unorthodox directions to promote the government's image. Rhoodie would boast that editors and politicians could be easily bought. A major project at home was the secret funding of a new daily newspaper, the *Citizen*, launched in direct competition with the *Rand Daily Mail*. Thirty-two million South African rands were spent on the *Citizen*. The story has been chronicled in detail in the book *Muldergate* by two *Rand Daily Mail* reporters, Mervyn Rees and Chris Day. By playing the leading role exposing the scandal, they acted in the best traditions of crusading journalism. Eventually the whole edifice of malpractice, high spending, and influence buying collapsed. P. W. Botha, despite the fact that his own department had been used as the fictitious conduit for the Information Scandal funds, managed to arise from the ashes as the new National Party leader. Mulder wandered into the right-wing political wilderness and later died of cancer, and Rhoodie wrote a book and set up a business in Atlanta, Georgia. Vorster ran for cover after resigning as premier and became state president, then a purely ceremonial post. He soon resigned that post, too. The whole period was marked by shoddy manoeuvering and ducking and weaving.

The *Cape Times* was a player in the small coalition of press forces which exposed the scandal. The *Sunday Express* had got the ball rolling with some courageous reporting under editor Rex Gibson. But the main, and untiring, player throughout was the *Rand Daily Mail* under editor Allister Sparks. Qualities of determination-plus and intelligence fitted him for this exhausting campaign. It was one of the *Mail*'s greatest moments—and one of its last. It was to die (together with the *Sunday Express*) in 1985, at the hand of its own proprietors.

The high point of our newspaper's involvement came when Eschel Rhoodie had skipped the country in November 1978 because he was facing arrest and jail if caught. We had an elaborate system of secret phone calls among editors in the morning group which would summon them, at a moment's notice, to meetings in different parts of the country to discuss how things were going and pool information and resources. This joint investigation and funding of the operation by all the morning group papers (the *Mail*, the *Cape Times*, the *Eastern Province Herald* in Port Elizabeth, the *Daily Dispatch* in East London, and the *Natal Mercury* in Durban) gave the investigation sustenance which it would not have had if conducted solely by the *Mail*.

A reporter on the *Cape Times*, Ted Olsen, the son of U.S. missionaries, came into my office one day and said: "Do you want to know where Rhoodie is?" Who didn't.

I telephoned Sparks at the *Mail* in Johannesburg and asked if they had traced Rhoodie. "We're following up a few leads," he said rather vaguely. I asked him to book three air tickets from Johannesburg to Amsterdam as soon as possible, and we would make contact. Olsen, together with his "deep throat" from Cape Town and a *Mail* representative, flew to Europe, and the story unfolded from there. Communication was first established through front men by phone, then personally with a wary Rhoodie. He had the South African police after him and feared extradition as well as action against his wife, Katy, back home.

We traced Rhoodie to Quito, Ecuador. Other journalists got wind of his presence there, but by that time our morning group team had locked him into exclusive arrangements, and the others were severely scooped. Reporters Rees and Day spent many weeks with Rhoodie, and he poured his heart out, ranging over numerous matters which were sensational and enlightening. The morning group papers were able to publish the whole story of the Information Scandal. **IT'S ALL TRUE** said the headlines (March 17/18, 1979), complete with pictures of Rhoodie wearing sombrero in Quito. All five group papers carried the same lead story the same day. Rhoodie's confirmation of the scandal caused a sensation; he claimed the cabinet knew of the secret plan and said he had documentary evidence of money being paid to major political figures in the Western world to influence them. The disclosures were followed by government attempts in the courts to stop further disclosures. See Appendix 2, p. 247. Sparks was convicted and fined under the Commissions Act for anticipating the findings of a commission appointed to inquire into the scandal. He later won his appeal. It was nearly a case of hang the messenger.

The intrigue and camaraderie among morning group editors was exciting. At one briefing session, held in a run-down Johannesburg hotel, we thought we were goners.

The editors present were James McMillan of the *Natal Mercury*, a bronzed jogging enthusiast; George Farr, who had succeeded Donald Woods at the *Daily Dispatch* and won the Military Cross in North Africa in the war; Harry O'Connor, of the *Eastern Province Herald*, an "old pro" hard newsman who had covered the early years of the United Nations; Sparks and me.

We had closed the door of the room and were exchanging highly secret information. Things had become very tense as it was known that the government was trying to find out what we knew, and would do its best to stop us from making damaging disclosures. There were many in government who were, directly or indirectly, tainted by the scandal, and there was every reason for them to want us to stop publishing. There had also been the riveting event of the murder of Dr. Robert Smit, a brilliant government financial official, in November 1977. He was formerly South African representative to the International Monetary Fund. He and his wife Jean-Cora were brutally killed at their Pretoria home just when he was about to fight an election to enter Parliament as a National Party M.P. The word "RAU-TEM" was spray-painted on the wall, a reference which no one could fathom. There was talk of hired assassins, of scandals over foreign-exchange dealings among people in very high places.

The murders gave things an extra edge as we were embroiled in our discussions in the hotel room.

The door started to creak open.

This, we thought, was it. Following Smit, the headline would be **FIVE EDITORS FOUND MURDERED IN SEEDY HOTEL.** As we moved to scramble for safety, we realized it was simply the wind.

In the discussions with Rhoodie and various "deep throats" in the Muldergate scandal, the team of journalists learned much of a confidential nature which made their editors' hair stand on end: e.g., disclosures about the identity of an alleged government informer high up in the press—an editor. Someone, we were told, was keeping the government posted on exactly how much newspapers knew about a crucial investigation by the auditor-general's office into the Information Scandal. That probe begun in 1976 by this independent official answerable to Parliament played a key role in opening the whole affair up. Rhoodie threatened to unveil the informer. A *Cape Times* reporter happened to meet Rhoodie at the Supreme Court in Cape Town some time after he had been brought back to South Africa from abroad for trial (he got off on appeal). She sent me a memorandum which, in view of the talk of an informer, I found more than interesting. It read:

> I asked Rhoodie to enlarge on his statement that he would reveal in his next book details of the editor of a South African

142

English-language newspaper who was an informer at the time of the information scandal.

Still refusing to identify the editor further, Rhoodie recounted a conversation between Vorster and General Hendrik van den Bergh [head of Vorster's security apparatus called BOSS] just before the info scandal broke. The emergency meeting between the two, as well as Rhoodie and other unidentified officials, was apparently held at the Prime Minister's office or residence at the time of the investigation into the department by the auditor-general.

Van den Bergh told Vorster that he knew exactly what parts of the auditor-general's report had been leaked to the press.

Vorster asked him where he had got the information from. Van den Bergh replied: "From the horse's mouth." Expanding, he gave the informant's name, that of an editor of an English newspaper.

He told Vorster that the informer had not been paid for the information but had in return been given "assistance"—secret information.

Rhoodie then explained how BOSS operated. [That was the Bureau for State Security, as it was then called, before becoming the National Intelligence Service—no doubt because the acronym was revealingly embarrassing.] On the first rung were informers who received certain information in exchange for information or other assistance, then there were informers who were paid, then semi-agents who were paid a retainer, then full-time agents, followed by the professional staff in the agency.

I asked Rhoodie if the editor concerned was still an editor. He declined to comment, other than: "It's certainly not Anthony Heard."

Rhoodie's allegations buzzed around the journalistic world. When a former BOSS spy, Gordon Winter, produced a book called *Inside BOSS* he wrote: "In 1976 Van den Bergh told me that BOSS had 37 South African journalists on its payroll. Three of these were parliamentary correspondents, one was an editor in chief, and eight worked on news desks in one capacity or another."[70]

If such a senior spy existed—and it should be noted that Rhoodie and Ven den Bergh had their own axes to grind—that person was violating his profession and should be fired with the rest of them.

143

General Van den Bergh, who was a fellow internee with Vorster in Koffiefontein Camp in the Free State for his O.B. activities during the war, emerged from the whole scandal in the murkiest political light. His acknowledgment to the commission investigating the scandal that he "would stop at nothing" and, indeed, his men would even assassinate to achieve the state's aims, was regarded as so damning that, when the commission's report first appeared, some lines were omitted. Van den Bergh said: "I have good men. I don't have weak men. I have enough men to commit murder if I tell them [to] kill. I don't care who the prey is. . . . They are the types of men I have." [71]

The missing lines were spotted by the eagle-eyed lawyer friend of mine who was perusing the commission report. The remarks were later admitted to, after attention had been drawn to them in a *Cape Times* editorial.

# CHAPTER TWELVE

# PIETER WILLEM BOTHA

## EMERGENCY

The press won against Vorster over the Information Scandal. It lost to his successor P. W. Botha. After Muldergate, Botha was determined that the secret business of government should not be at the mercy of press disclosure again. Although Botha had been the political beneficiary of the scandal, denying involvement or knowledge and wangling himself into the leadership of the National Party over the battered corpses of Vorster and "crown prince" Mulder, he turned savagely on the press. In truth, he should have thanked them, notably the *Rand Daily Mail* and the morning group.

Botha wanted a free hand for the future. He passed legislation which regularized the use of public funds for secret projects—projects which could, in the future, escape the sort of awkward auditing and public discussion of the Information Scandal days. In fact, far from showing government remorse after

Muldergate, Botha declared open season for clandestine activities. He allowed some secret projects to continue—and thereby laid safe foundations for the activities of death squads. He set up the post of advocate-general, a senior judge who would investigate and report to parliament on allegations of corruption or malpractice by government. But this process was given the protection of the same strict contempt provisions as applied to a court of law. It was specifically an offence to "anticipate the proceedings at an inquiry or the findings of the advocate-general in a manner calculated to influence such proceedings or findings." It was also an offence to "insult, disparage or belittle" the advocate-general. So the simple answer, for the government, was to refer any embarrassing matter to the advocate-general. However industriously and impartially the advocate-general might do his job, the press was denied playing its role in uncovering abuse.

Botha leaned heavily on the defence establishment during his leadership, and he raised the status of the shadowy state security council to pre-eminence. The press got used to coping with a regular flow of unsolicited notices from defence which stopped or inhibited the flow of information. They were issued in terms of an agreement between the defence authorities and the owners of the press, the Newspaper Press Union, which was monitored by a special liaison committee made up of a hotch-potch of editors, newspaper managers, and bureaucratic brass. All this was supposed to ease the news flow, and lots of tea was cordially consumed. But in practice it was little more than a one-way mechanism to facilitate the flow of defence propaganda and whitewash to the unsuspecting public. The supposed communist onslaught facing the country was frequently used as justification for making "requests," but often this was a transparent excuse to browbeat the press and to stop it from delving into dark corners of government. A draconian Official Secrets Act (later called the "Protection of Information Act"), not unlike the British one in wording but far more severe in application, could be used against newspapers on the purported ground that they were giving away state secrets. Almost nothing could be said freely about defence and arms supply without authority, which is why the South African public was left in the dark about a matter as important as the 1975 South African invasion of Angola. Prisons and police matters were shrouded in secrecy because of onerous acts which made it an offence to publish any untrue or false material about them without taking "reasonable steps" to verify facts (Gandar's *Rand Daily Mail*, for instance, suffered a bruising court case in the late 1960s and conviction and a fine under the Prisons Act). Persons who were banned or listed by the government under the Internal Security Act could not be quoted. Promoting "communism," which could mean espousing anything marginally to the left of Attila the Hun, was a serious offence. The Inquests Act was used to check discussion of matters arising out of controversial deaths, such as Biko's and that of scores of other political detainees. The Commissions Act similarly shrouded matters being investigated by any state-appointed commission. The list of restrictions went on endlessly, and tomes were written by lawyers to guide editors, tomes that had to be updated frequently. *The Newspaperman's Guide to the Law* by lawyer Kelsey Stuart was the editor's bible.[72]

Under the burden of these acts and regulations an editorial slip-up could lead to a lengthy court case and the possibility of a heavy fine or even jail. Producing the equivalent of a medium-sized novel each day, newspapers could transgress with innocent intentions. Boards of directors, not roaringly liberal and concerned about newspaper assets and profits, were not keen on over-adventurous editing. They made this plain in private discussion with editors, though they openly gave lip service to their editors' independence. It was frequently, but not always, a case of "external" independence, but "internal" subservience to managerial or proprietorial pressure. Strong editors resisted; the weaker buckled. There were constant threats from the government, subtle and direct. To chronicle all events would be exhausting for writer and reader, but some might be instructive.

The National Key Points Act of 1980 gave the government power to declare certain "national key points" and provided for the "safeguarding thereof." These were strategic places, such as oil refineries, storage depots, explosives, or armaments manufac-

147

turing plants, etc. The state's object was that they should be made safe from sabotage and spying. But a problem facing the press was to know where the key points were. The government refused to supply any information to newspapers on this, which meant the newspapers could stumble into a contravention of the law by identifying a key point without knowing it was a key point. In terms of Section 10, anyone who without authority "furnishes in any manner whatsoever any information relating to the security measures applicable at or in respect of any national key point or in respect of an incident that occurred there" faced a fine of up to ten thousand rands or three years, or both. This, in practice, meant that any unauthorized news story about a security breach or incident at a "key point" could lead to heavy fine or prison for an editor. The act was rushed through Parliament in the last few days of the session in 1980, with the Newspaper Press Union, whose newspapers bore the brunt of Section 10, complaining behind the scenes that it was not given an opportunity to "make representations," which means make comments.[73] The government consulted the N.P.U. and editors only when it suited its book. The rest of the time it treated them in cavalier fashion. On one occasion when the editor of the *Burger*, W. D. Beukes, and I were appointed by the editors' body, the Conference of Editors, to see a then-powerful minister, Chris Heunis, about a press measure, he kept us waiting, then brushed aside our objections contemptuously. I had thought the reinforcing presence of Beukes would make a difference, but it did not. He was treated like a troublesome pet dog.

There was constant friction between the police and the press over security matters. The police wanted as little said as possible; the public interest required the opposite. Often police refused pointblank to supply information, as in this message from the directorate of public relations of the police to the *Cape Times* on September 26, 1980: "Security branch is not prepared to keep the media posted on releases of detainees as their immediate families already have knowledge of their releases." Sometimes when they felt like it the police were more forthcoming. But they had the monopoly of "security information" and did not share it readily.

148

In 1985, when the country was aflame with black unrest, Botha introduced a limited state of emergency in many magisterial areas which curbed the right of the press to report what was going on. This emergency was lifted early in 1986, but on June 12 that year a far more extensive, nationwide emergency was slapped on South Africa. It was reimposed annually all Botha's remaining years in power, in ever-repressive form. The editors of many South African newspapers were highly critical of the emergency. Some risked heavy penalties trying to evade its provisions to bring the public news of a vast, ongoing world story. They ingeniously managed to get round a provision which banned the naming of detainees except if the name had already been officially disclosed. A deputy minister stated in public that the police always informed families of detentions. Newspapers like the *Star,* the *Cape Times, Sowetan,* and *Weekly Mail* took the view that this amounted to "official disclosure" of the names—and took a chance and published lists of names and escaped prosecution. Newspapers like the *Cape Times* referred to "familiar yellow vans" or "men wielding sjamboks [whips]" when they were forbidden to identify police. On one occasion, the *Cape Times,* unable to identify police Alsatian dogs as such, spoke only of "Alsatians on leashes." When the report was referred to the police for their comment, the cryptic reply was: "Your telex re Alsatians on leashes is confusing and vague. What are you trying to say? If you are trying to make out that the Alsatians on leashes were police dogs, then refer the report to your legal advisers."

English-language newspapers daringly published advertisements, in the face of the emergency regulations banning such things, calling for the freeing of Nelson Mandela and the unbanning of the ANC. The company lawyers gave superb guidance on how to get round the emergency. The *Cape Times* regularly published the famous three monkeys—depicting see no evil, hear no evil, speak no evil—to alert the public to the emergency's draconian impact. Most newspapers published daily front-page warnings to readers that they were not getting the full picture of what was happening. Many strong editorials were written. Yet I well remember how it was not possible to get agreement in the

Conference of Editors, at a meeting in Durban, nor of the Newspaper Press Union, for a public declaration against the emergency. There was great fear of P. W. Botha—particularly from the quarter of the government-supporting press. In contrast, the Media Council came out with a forthright and lucid statement in defence of the right to publish, making the point that readers were even being deprived of the knowledge that they were being deprived of information. See Appendix 2, p. 249.

Editing under the emergency meant editing by *Government Gazette.* A myriad of taboos and rules locked the press out of reporting what was going on, in the realm of security and many other matters. The supreme insult to journalism was a provision which required that journalists immediately leave an area if unrest broke out. They could not even be "within sight." There were rules against publicizing boycotts or restricted meetings, promoting certain political causes, naming detainees, publishing "subversive statements," and so on. The iron clamp fastened itself round the necks of journalists, and when the Supreme Court intervened and found loopholes and weaknesses in the drafting of the emergency, the government cynically reimposed the curbs in revised, more watertight wording which was often more repressive.

The prime objective of the state of emergency was to shroud the security forces' actions in secrecy. There were occasions when incidents were not even mentioned in the regular bulletins issued by police or the government's propaganda clearing-house, the "Bureau for Information." A police spokesperson even admitted to omissions. For example, the *Argus* reported on July 25, 1989, that it had information that at least three incidents of vehicle stonings had occurred in Cape Town during the weekend, whereas only one had been reported in the unrest report. The spokesperson told the *Argus* that the official reports did not always contain all the incidents reported, even though they might be classified as "unrest."

The public's understanding of what was happening was distorted or blacked out. The taxpayers who paid the salaries of the security forces were not allowed to know how their money was being spent.

Meanwhile nearly two thousand people died in unrest from September 1984 to September 1986, and the deaths continued at varying degrees of intensity after that.

An order issued, in all seriousness, by Brigadier Christoffel Anthonie Swart, divisional commissioner of police for the Western Province, sums up the official mind. Dated January 29, 1986, it would even have had the effect of banning tee-shirt slogans. See Appendix 2, p. 250. Under other orders people were banned from lighting candles in the windows of houses to protest against the emergency, and specific campaigns such as "Christmas against the emergency" and "Christmas of Concern" were prohibited too. Funerals of dead activists were severely restricted. In one case, two full pages were devoted in the *Government Gazette* (No. 10644 of February 27, 1987) to restrictions placed on the funeral in Natal of one Msizeni Shadrack Mapumulo—right down to a limit of two hundred mourners and a three-hour duration. That the courts of South Africa frequently, in the early stages of the emergency, declared orders *ultra vires* and of no effect was a credit to independent-minded judges and not to the government. A Natal court, on September 4, 1986, ruled certain emergency regulations invalid, describing them as "so far-reaching and horrendous" that Parliament itself could never have intended them.

Relations between Botha and the opposition press were always bad. On February 4, 1982, at a meeting in Botha's parliamentary office called for general discussion, he sailed into South African Associated Newspapers editors. He said they were constantly denigrating South African leaders and were guilty of "vindictive and irresponsible" reporting and were playing into the hands of the communists. This was Botha's *"roskam"* (rough brush) treatment—well known to people even close to him who had felt the bristles. He tore into me over an editorial complaining about the "snail's pace of reform." He also objected to a story in the *Cape Times* that day giving details of his emoluments—which, after all, were public knowledge. He claimed this was published to "embarrass" him. Our political correspondent Michael

151

Acott, who had written the story, and I did our best to defend ourselves.

At one stage, Botha shouted at me: "Mr. Heard, this is my office; and you will leave if you will not listen to me."

He took it further. He later had a meeting with the chairman of the *Cape Times,* D. A. St. C. Hennessy, and complained that I had "belittled" him in the editors' meeting. I would have been so lucky; I could hardly get a word in edgeways. Hennessy sent him a terribly polite letter, saying: "We should like to place on record our view that, whatever differences might exist between the newspaper and the government on issues of the day, we have the highest respect for your person and for your office—as well as appreciation of what you are seeking to achieve as Prime Minister in trying circumstances. It is our hope that the difficulties in relations which led to our discussion can be speedily remedied."74

In November 1978 the *Cape Times* carried a front-page editorial suggesting that Vorster, who had by then become state president, should stand down from this high office in view of the commission investigating the Information Scandal.75 Prime Minister Botha exploded about it at a meeting with the Newspaper Press Union, and I received a midnight call from the head of South African Associated Newspapers, Clive Kinsley, saying the "PM" was "mad at us." The government referred the editorial to the attorney-general for prosecution on the grounds that we had injured the dignity of the president, a very serious offence under the constitution. Nothing came of it, but it was powerful pressure.

Only on one occasion did I see anyone put Botha in his place—and that was before he became premier. At a meeting in his office in Cape Town in December 1975 Botha, who was then minister of defence, and his senior defence staff briefed editors on the extent of the Angola invasion. He used the occasion to roast Raymond Louw, editor of the *Rand Daily Mail,* over a column by Donald Woods in the *Mail.* He angrily declared that Louw had published this article "by someone sitting at this table" and which betrayed a "sick mind." Woods, sitting next to me, jumped to his feet and said: "That was my article. It was meant for someone with a sense of humour." There was guarded laughter among the editors present.[76] Woods later disclosed (in his autobiography, *Asking for Trouble*, published by Anthenuem, New York, 1981, 255) that Botha threw this threat at him as we left: "Just you wait, Mr. Woods! I'm after you. . . ."

Less than a month before this incident, at a stage when the South African involvement in Angola was being flatly denied, I found myself in professional difficulty because of my close contact with Vorster. At a private talk in the Union Buildings, Pretoria, on November 19, 1975, Vorster—looking Bismarck-like, with a large map stretched out on his desk—had told me all about the invasion. South Africa had sent in forces to assist the avowedly "pro-Western" leader, Jonas Savimbi, in his attempt to take the capital Luanda and thereby win the civil war. My problem was that he spoke to me strictly on a confidential basis.

Vorster gave me a detailed account of the military actions and what encouragement the South Africans had received for the campaign from the United States and other Western countries.

South Africa was invading another country and I was sworn to silence. And we at the paper believed the military action to be folly. All we could do was campaign publicly against any involvement while knowing privately that there was already involvement. Having thus been alerted, we probably opposed it with more doggedness than usual. It was a memorable if awkward moment of my editorship. The *Cape Times* led the criticism in the press and faced unbridled hostility from the hawkish Defence Minister Botha. Deputy editor Shaw deserves praise for his persistence in his weekly political survey column in spite of bullying attacks on him, in private and public, by Botha. I had my share later, with Botha declaring in Parliament that I was "close to treason" and "not normal" for suggesting South Africa was destabilizing neighbour countries.

There were other occasions when our lips were sealed. We were given a detailed briefing on a joint South African–Israeli deal to do with missile boats, and we were told by Defence

Minister Botha in February 1975 that if anything came out he would simply deny it. The following story, received from our correspondent in Paris on April 3, 1978, was "killed" by the defence authorities under the wide censorship provisions of the Defence Act: "Paris. Sunday.—South Africa will be able to buy Israeli gunboats to replace the two frigates ordered from France but placed under a total arms embargo, the weekly magazine *Le Point* reported today. The magazine said that the gunboats will be smaller than the 1,200-ton French frigates, and probably more than two will be delivered. . . ."[77]

An indication of the frustration of staff over defence censorship can be gained from this overnight memorandum by a staffer to our news desk in the early stages of the Angola invasion: "A copy holder [printer] at the *Cape Times* on leave phoned late last night to say the B.B.C. reports that South African troops advanced 50 miles into Angolan territory—trucks supported by armoured cars. Checked with Cyrus Smith [defence department public relations officer] in Pretoria—true, but reminded of minister's instruction with regard to troop movements on S.W.A. borders. Pity we can't write damn good stories like this for a greater audience than the desk."[78]

Throughout South Africa's largely clandestine involvement in Angola on the side of Savimbi, which lasted well into the 1980s, the government kept up a barrage of confidential messages to editors, giving advice and guidance—or containing outright prohibitions on publication. Examples of how it went about this:

A notice was sent out in August 1977 to editors:

The confidential note sent to editors on Thursday July 28, 1977, concerning an expected propaganda campaign against government institutions in respect of the future of South Africa was discussed at a recent meeting of the joint N.P.U.-defence liaison committee. The intention of the confidential note was purely informative and was intended to warn editors about an anticipated increase in extravagant propaganda by South Africa's enemies. Nevertheless all accusations against the South African defence

154

force should be referred to the defence force. Other accusations may be referred to the authorities concerned.[79]

Another, on February 2, 1978, requested editors "in the national interest" to refrain from speculation regarding the length of the "call-up." It added that any speculation "or repetition of previous statements in this regard" might cause reaction "which will definitely not be in the national interest."

Another less than four months later said:

> A friendly request was conveyed to our media to refrain from publishing any more military details of the recent operation in Angola and accounts by individual participants. In spite of this request detailed stories about alleged action by paratroopers appeared in certain newspapers. Certain soldiers and officers were even named, while units concerned were also identified. This specific item was never cleared by defence headquarters . . . and constitutes a contravention of the defence act and of the press agreement. Defence headquarters wishes to repeat its earnest request that newspapers refrain from publishing any further military details or reports on the South African action in Angola. We have of course no reservations or request to make about the political consequences of this action.[80]

We got to know of arms shipments to other theatres of war in the world, but we had to keep quiet. On one occasion late in 1986 a decision by the Dutch Reformed Church reverently assembled in Cape Town was an immense and unexpected embarrassment far, far away. In conditions of high secrecy South African military men were training an Islam nation's forces in the operation of big G-5 cannons that had been exported to the Gulf. The "government-at-prayer" back home chose this very moment to pass a resolution violently attacking Islam.

## THREATS

It was the murky right wing in South Africa that was a more direct threat to liberal editors than Botha. The government would

155

huff and puff, even ban and restrict; but white supremacist thugs threatened life and limb. Unchecked by the otherwise extremely alert police (when it came to left-wing activity), these thugs carried on a constant process of harassment of journalists, churchmen, politicians, and others. In Cape Town this state of affairs went on through most of the 1970s, with a group called "Scorpio" wreaking suburban havoc. There were hammer-and-sickle daubings, threats, fire bombings, and more serious activities, including random shootings. I knew journalists who staked out their homes all night with heavy-calibre guns at the ready, waiting for an urban terrorist "Scorpio" to blow their heads off. The *Cape Times* published numerous editorials challenging the police to end this "terror in the suburbs." The police seemed, to me, more concerned to have open season to bug our phones, while ostensibly recording threats, than to bring the perpetrators to book. There was at least one case of a policeman who had pressing business abroad just when he could have testified conclusively against suspects.

Finally, a determined Supreme Court prosecutor put together a case based on incriminating letters and other factors and pressed charges in an atmosphere of police scepticism. I was there in court to see a respected judge send two men to jail for very long terms. But a man widely suspected as the ringleader of the right-wing urban terrorists was never arrested.

Right-wing terrorism was a scourge. In different parts of the country many left-wing activists were assassinated, at least forty-five between 1984 and 1989.[81] They included people I had known well. One was once a brilliant fellow philosophy student at the University of Cape Town, Dr. Rick Turner, who had later trained at the Sorbonne in Paris. He was living and teaching and banned in Durban—a "sitting duck"—when he was shot at his front door in a killing later claimed to be the work of a police death squad. Several people I knew had narrow escapes, including two leaders of the opposition Progressive Federal Party: Colin Eglin, whose apartment in the seaside suburb of Clifton was shot up in a rare case that was solved; and Frederik Van Zyl Slabbert whose library in his suburban home mysteriously exploded in flames one night.

So threats had to be taken seriously, and each was laboriously reported to the police—however seemingly pointless. The senior management of the *Cape Times* was exceptionally supportive. They put special security devices, fire extinguishers, floodlights, etc., in my home and in the homes of certain senior editorial staff. It was always worrying, particularly when my wife and I had small children, to go out at night at a time when threats were running high.*

The drapes would be pulled tight. Vicki and Janet would understand immediately and bravely ask: "Have there been more threats?" Vida Heard would often hold the fort, looking after the girls. In far-off years she had learnt to face threats and danger because of her husband's writings.

When I moved house to a different suburb, Hout Bay, I had a special security drill which I judged foolproof. A neighbour had a large revolver and he was in the habit of brandishing it if there were prowlers or disturbers of the peace outside. If there was prowling of any nature my alert ochre-coloured dogs (a cross between "ridgeback," collie, and labrador) would bark the alarm, and neighbour John would come out firing. I hoped.

One Friday night in the early 1970s an arsonist threw a petrol bomb in the foyer of the editorial office at the *Cape Times*. At work in my office, I heard a crackling noise—and found the well-oiled wood panelling blazing. Someone had run up the stairs from Burg Street and thrown the bomb. Our worthy doorman, Mr. Gallow, had to decide whether to go for the burly intruder or the fire extinguisher. He went for the latter and saved the building from severe damage. The man—of familiar build— got away.

Office security was pretty good, one reason being that we had a relatively small staff who would be quick to spot an intruder. In the daytime at the office we had the benefit of a group of enthusiastic body-builders on the staff. A special press on the office buzzer at my knee would produce an instant Mr. Universe

---

*Examples: 1. "Tell Anthony Heard not to be surprised to find his wife . . . family dead tonight. He'll die soon. . . . He's anti-white,"—Well-spoken English voice, 10:45 a.m., April 5, 1978, on the phone to the *Cape Times*. 2. "This is your death warrant, you pro-nigger pig. Kiss your family bye. They're going too, sincerely with haste. W.A.S.P."—Letter sent November 10, 1986.

parade, headed by Davids Isaacs, who was the Western Cape (coloured) champion, "Mr. Apollo."

## JAMBA

Yet it was least safe of all when a party of editors visited rebel leader Jonas Savimbi in his bush redoubt in southeastern Angola in the mid-1980s. flown in by a civilian aircraft at tree-top height over scampering elephants and MMBA (miles and miles of bloody Africa) we were told that the South African Air Force was monitoring the trip. This was because of the "valuable horsemeat" on board. We landed in the middle of nowhere and went through a crude passport rigmarole organized by Savimbi's rebel forces on the back of a truck. An aircraft emerged from the clear African sky and put down in front of us on the bush landing-strip. Out stepped an American, wearing Biggles-type headgear, and announced that he had just flown in from Zaire, one of Savimbi's major conduits for support. We were loaded on big Czechoslovakian trucks which had been captured from the Luanda forces by Savimbi in the war, and endured a bone- and organ-shaking trip to Savimbi's headquarters in Jamba which took nine hours. On the return trip, with tropical rain drenching us as we jangled around in the back of the open truck, I attempted sleep with my head resting on an AK-47 rifle and my foot in the mouth of the editor of the *Eastern Province Herald,* Koos Viviers (who was later to succeed me at the *Cape Times*). He had already cracked a rib while jumping down at the side of the the truck.

At Jamba there was evidence of South African aid everywhere, despite strong denials by Pretoria. Savimbi, an articulate but brutal fighter, saw nothing wrong with downing airliners and taking civilian hostages in the north, including nuns, and frog-marching them for nearly a month, sleeping by day and moving by night, across the length of Angola. One of the Czechoslovakian trucks had driven the hostages the last three-day leg to Jamba. Asked what was the worst thing they had to endure, the hostages were at one: the truck ride. The editors' visit, arranged through quarters friendly to Pretoria and Savimbi, turned into a propaganda triumph for Savimbi—once described to me by Vorster as "the man I want to run Angola." It was no mean PR achievement—almost all South African newspaper editors were as captive visitors in his bush headquarters to hear him speak and see his forces on the parade ground. It happened at a time when Savimbi was desperate to gain more world support for his war. I formed the impression of an intelligent man fighting a dirty war with dirty means—and "pro-Western" only for tactical reasons.* The dirty means included denuding the countryside of teak and ivory to earn foreign currency.

Far away in Hong Kong I had seen the results of uncontrolled ivory dealing . . . blood-stained tusks trundling through the streets piled high on trucks. Closer to home, visiting with desert-ranger friends in Namibia I had seen some of the effects of poaching (by others) of the famous "desert elephants." Because trees are few in that harsh terrain the elephants do not push them over. They feed carefully. Each leaf is taken tenderly with trunk-tip, making a gentle snapping sound as it breaks off. With their large, hardened feet the elephants can endure the hottest sand. They open the water holes so that other animals might live. In their droppings they spread seeds to keep birds alive. They are a critical lifeline of the area and no threat to humans, but the numbers were dwindling by 1980. There was one unforgettable visit to a wash near the dry Ombonde River. This is reputedly the oldest desert in the world—the Northern Namib where the unique, Gorgon's head-like Welwitschia plant grows for thousands of years.

Two elephants had been gunned down simultaneously in a poacher ambush. Their tusks had been chain-sawed off and removed. Once handsome, firm bodies had become grotesque cadavers of displaced skin and bone. They lay in the dust in a configuration which was immensely moving.

They had turned and faced each other as they died.

*He had once been supported by Communist China—and Donald Woods's humorous reference to this in a column had caused P. W. Botha to explode.

159

## SELF-CONTROL

After the National Party government came to power in 1948, the established press of South Africa fought off full-scale press control. The press achieved this by disciplining itself. It was done masochistically and in public.

Before 1948 there had been confrontations between press and government, but the former had managed to retain a large degree of independence, not unlike that enjoyed in the other British dominions. During the Second World War the newspapers were given a choice: government censorship or self-censorship. They chose the latter. The system worked pretty well, and the responsible minister was able to write to editors in the following terms after the war in a letter that I do not think has ever been published:

> The Information Bureau has informed you that all military and navy censorship restrictions have, in view of the cessation of hostilities, been suspended. I assume that the editors who signed the voluntary press censorship agreement will now agree that there is no further reason to continue with the agreement. On behalf of the Prime Minister and the government, I should like to express to you personally and to your colleagues the sincere thanks of the government for your co-operation in the implementation of this agreement. The government expresses its sincere appreciation for the manner in which that voluntary censorship has been applied, thus denying the enemy vital information during the war.[82]

Ritual public self-flagellation by the press after 1948 kept the government at bay—to a degree. A Press Board of Reference (later called the Press Council, then the Media Council) was set up in 1962 under government pressure by the employer body, the Newspaper Press Union. The N.P.U. denied "any suggestion of outside interference" or pressure at the time.[83] But pressure undoubtedly existed. The council was a voluntary body, chosen by the newspaper industry and in time established high standards and independence under the direction of ex-judges. They were fortunate to have the services of a respected journalist as registrar

(Bob Steyn, a former *Argus* political correspondent and Nieman fellow at Harvard University). The council had no formal government or statutory recognition, but a Sword of Damocles hung over its head for years: at any moment the government could use existing legislation to step in to "recognize," which means control, the media council. There was also a voluntary code of conduct, which newspaper members of the N.P.U. were enjoined to uphold. See Appendix 2, p. 251.

The N.P.U. or "established" newspapers were exempted from formal censorship under the Publications and Entertainments Act of 1963, which severely controlled what appeared in magazines, films, plays, etc. The self-flagellation had helped the N.P.U. escape. The council was, in time, given the controversial power to fine newspapers up to ten thousand rands for professional transgressions—a move opposed by many editors, including myself, in a public statement. The government was never satisfied with the council's performance. It wanted more "blood," more disciplining of erring or "hostile" journalists. What it could not achieve by informal pressure, it achieved by legislation. At one stage in the 1980s, in Botha's early years as premier, there were attempts to secure the agreement of the press for "guidelines" on the reporting of "terrorism." The self-discipline would have surrendered independent journalism. In a memorandum at the time, former *Cape Times* editor, Victor Norton, argued that if the guidelines were accepted, "The public will be deprived of information as drastically as in any authoritarian country." He pointed out that events such as the Information Scandal could have gone unreported, nothing would have been known of Steve Biko's death, bull-dozing of District Six and squatters' camps would have remained an official secret, news of strikes, boycotts, and lock-outs would have been suppressed, mixed marriage and group areas tragedies would have been known only to the victims and their friends, and so on. He added: "Officials would feel happier and politicians encouraged in the South African national pastime of self-deception. But any senior security officer or competent politician who believes that South Africa is being made stronger should have their heads read."[84] A member of

161

Parliament, David Dalling, got hold of a copy of the secret guide-lines and read them out in Parliament, to the outrage of Defence Minister Magnus Malan—and they were never proceeded with by the government.

Vorster had secretly tried, and failed, late in 1971 to get the press to observe an "informal state of emergency" on security matters. A much more serious effort by the government came late in 1986. The government's main target by then was the flurry of "alternative" newspapers which mushroomed as unrest in the country grew after 1984. These newspapers drew their strength from churches, university campuses, trade unions, and militant groups. They operated outside the clubby atmosphere of the N.P.U., with which the government would hold regular, confidential discussions. Botha set out to secure the support of the established newspapers in a strategy that would have destroyed alternative newspapers. It happened at a stage when the government was considering whether, and to what extent, to renew the state of emergency. It was toying with the idea of freeing the established (N.P.U.) newspapers from the provisions of the state of emergency. But if they had accepted the deal he offered they would have been in a worse position. Once again, the press would have to accept "guidelines." These amounted, in effect, to working under the same conditions as the state of emergency. For instance, journalists on the scene of unrest would have to leave immediately, a most resourceful form of news gathering. But it would be worse than the emergency—*the public would not even know about the arrangement.* By regulating themselves secretly under voluntary "guidelines," and not being openly coerced by state of emergency law, the participating newspapers would escape heavy fines, or jail, for their staffs. The price was treachery against others.

The "alternative" newspapers, significantly not part of this deal, would then be dealt with under the state of emergency by the government, and with a vengeance. The government would get what it always wanted: a "responsible" and "patriotic" (which means compliant) established press, with the rest bludgeoned into submission. Though Botha subsequently admitted to its existence, the government proposal was never published. It appears in full in Appendix 2, p. 252.

After much discussion, the English-language newspaper groups refused to go along with the Afrikaans groups in their acceptance of the guidelines. At one stage in discussions, which I attended, it looked touch and go, with lots of wavering, and the N.P.U. was unable to reach agreement. Botha withdrew his offer in an angry statement, and there were some recriminations between the newspaper groups. All the press remained under the same state of emergency provisions—preferable to one section being used to destroy the other.

Even the established newspapers had large numbers of black readers, amounting to half their circulation or more in some cases. This was not lost on them. The press would have risked losing many of those black readers if it were seen in a dirty deal with government. A black reader boycott was not impossible. The experience of the *Daily Dispatch*, Donald Woods's ex-newspaper in East London, was fresh in memory. The anti-apartheid mass movement, the United Democratic Front, had organized a wounding boycott of that paper because of what it perceived as a pro-apartheid stance. The matter was taken very seriously by the *Dispatch* and there were high-level attempts to get the boycott reversed—including at least one initiative in which I was involved. The *Dispatch* had always been between a rock and a hard place. It had a disparate readership: a large bloc in the nominally independent Transkei which could melt overnight (and on one occasion did) if the notorious Matanzima brothers who then ran the corrupt statelet decided to boycott it; another large bloc among anti-apartheid U.D.F.-supporting blacks in and around East London, militantly opposed to apartheid; and many reactionary white readers in East London and surrounding farming areas. Woods, because of his stout liberalism, faced hostility from the Transkei overlords and conservative whites. His successors, less liberal, faced problems with the U.D.F. The *Dispatch* resolved the boycott problem by publishing a remarkable statement in July 1985. It was evidence of mass black power, and a mind-exercizer to other newspapers. High up on the front page, it read:

163

**Statement by Daily Dispatch**

The *Daily Dispatch* concedes that certain references and terms used in some of its articles could have caused offence to a large section of its readership.

It further wishes to emphasize that although its editorial policy was assumed in some quarters to be pro-apartheid, it has no such intentions.

The *Daily Dispatch* now restates its total opposition to a policy that is abhorrent to all freedom-loving people, and re-affirms its intention to continue its proud tradition as an anti-apartheid newspaper, a tradition which it has followed for the past 37 years.

The *Daily Dispatch* recommits itself to a policy of fair-minded, objective reporting and to being a forum for various schools of thought.

**Statement by U.D.F. Border Region**

The U.D.F. withdraws its demand for the resignation of the editor. It thanks the people who have rallied to its call and declares that the boycott of the *Daily Dispatch* has been called off from 26.7.85.[85]

Alienating blacks had become, simply, bad business. Commercial firms were learning fast. An Eastern Cape activist, Gugile Nkwinti, told me how he had to be freed from detention, in effect, to appeal to his followers to stop the boycott of white stores which his detention and other repressive actions had sparked in Port Alfred.

# CAPE LIFE

Apart from the rigours of editing, there were the day-to-day experiences of living in a country in turmoil. When the Soweto upheaval hit the country in 1976, stoning was endemic on certain roads in the Cape. It was particularly bad in the area of Philippi, a rural spot near the city where my daughters went to riding lessons every Saturday. There was no way that they would be deterred from going there, in spite of warnings that half-bricks and stones could be hurled at passing cars. An informal "riot drill" was consequently devised for our protection. The carful of horsey girls in their early teens would keep their riding hats on—and would carry kitchen pots and pans for protection. I would sit as high as possible in the driving seat, pressing against the roof and door-strut of the car. We would move, but not too fast, down Wetton Road toward Philippi and the "combat area"—looking for hands with rocks in them. The middle of the road was filled with olean-der bushes, and on more than one occasion we saw men emerge from behind them. "Down!" I would yell. The girls would duck to the floor of the car. We were never stoned by anyone, but it made us very conscious of troubled times.

In 1980 my friend David Welsh of the University of Cape Town would fly frequently to Grahamstown on personal business. When stonings and tire-burnings on the airport road became seri-ous, he asked me not to take him to the airport because it was too dangerous. "I'll take the bus," he said. In the end, I took him by car—but only after the liberal editor-professor team had packed goose-down pillows in, and held them at the ready, as we drove gingerly across the Cape flats to the airport. There had been nasty rumours of stonings and tire-burnings, of bricks being hung by string from overhead bridges at windshield height. People had been injured and killed.

Dodging stones, crowds, police, tear gas, sjamboks, and suchlike was a routine part of the job for journalists. Sometimes the oldest and most battered cars were used for townships jobs so as not to draw police or crowd attention to the journalists. When a prominent Fleet Street editor was taken on a trip to the town-ships at the height of the turmoil, our transport manager said, "Better give him the battered Volkswagen." The *Cape Times* staff devised various ways to deal with danger. Cars would not race along the roads, for a rock crashing through a windshield of a car at speed could kill. The logos on the firm's cars saying "Keep up with the Times" were some insurance against stoning by the young lions, or "comrades," who virtually controlled the town-ships—though we were not popular with the police. The reporters found that a scarf dipped in lemon juice and wound round the face helped counteract the acrid tear gas. Some

165

reporters would arrive at work looking like irregular combat troops, wearing flack jackets, rough trousers and shirts, and even carrying a bedroll. That was in case they were obliged to stay overnight, sleeping rough, in a township after lengthy funerals or sustained unrest. One well-known local journalist from an international news network, George De'Ath, died when he was caught by an anti-comrade warring mob in a township. The *Cape Times,* which had already lost driver Lombard in 1960, was exceptionally lucky not to lose any journalists in the period 1976 to 1987—though close shaves, detentions by police, camera confiscations, and threats were commonplace. It was courageous journalism at its best. The newsroom covered the unrest with professionalism. They were caught between a government wanting to suppress news of its repressive actions and warring factions in the townships.

The newspaper was in a constant state of tension with authority. A front-page account on March 3, 1986, of a guerilla shoot-out in Guguletu caused an instant break in relations with the police. Our report, by Chris Bateman, suggested that two out of seven African urban guerillas who had been shot by police in Guguletu were killed in cold blood—one lying on the ground, the other trying to surrender. The commissioner, Gen. Johann Coetzee, ordered police not to have anything to do with the *Cape Times* as soon as this version appeared. This meant we could get no police news about even the most routine incidents of accident, fire, or crime, including the dangerous activities of a Table Mountain rapist who was terrorizing women in the suburbs. (This was the second time the police had broken off relations with the *Cape Times* during my editorship. An editorial in 1972 had referred to the police as "official law-breakers" after the police beat students on the steps of St. George's Cathedral in Cape Town.[86] The students had demonstrated peacefully and had been laid into in a vicious way. It was reminiscent of the day early in April 1960, when the "whip" came to Cape Town's streets in fierce police action against alleged idlers and intimidators after Sharpeville and Langa. The difference, this time, was that the victims were white not black. Immediately after the editorial com-

166

ment appeared in 1972, the *Cape Times* had all police news cut off. We managed to restore relations by explaining in an editorial that our reference to official law-breakers did not mean all police, but the "excesses of certain individuals.")

After the Coetzee news ban, the *Cape Times* formally complained at a meeting in Pretoria that the police had broken its liaison agreement with the press, whereby police were obliged to give certain items of hard news to newspapers. General Coetzee sat with his generals on one side of the table. Several colleagues and I, members of the Conference of Editors and the Newspaper Press Union, sat on the other.

The start was brittle. Coetzee rose and charged that I had accused his men of "murder." Our argument was that we had given both versions of the incident—the police version and the story related by witnesses we had interviewed. The upshot of the meeting was that the news flow was restored at some levels, while we all awaited the results of court proceedings.

An inquest on November 14, 1986, found that "no blame" attached to the police. The authorities charged the deputy news editor of the *Cape Times,* Tony Weaver, with publishing false information about the police because he related the essence of the Bateman story to the BBC in London. (Because of his fearless reporting in South Africa and Namibia, Weaver was on the police black list; they wanted to nail him.) He was acquitted after the defence produced exhaustive evidence, including the accounts of some dairy workers who were witnesses, backing up the *Cape Times* story. The defence hired a ballistics expert who shot bullets into dead animals to check trajectories, etc. In acquitting Weaver, the magistrate said that although he could not say what the truth was, medical evidence had revealed that the two could not have been shot as the police said.[87] The failed prosecution against Weaver was to vindicate the *Cape Times.* The immediate confrontation with the police came to an end, though relations remained tense.

The paper lurched from crisis to crisis, at any given moment facing half-a-dozen or more serious criminal charges in court. Reporters were detained and harassed by police—including one held for days after being arrested with a whole congregation at a church service. That was the most eventful church service mild-spoken André Koopman ever attended. He was released as the paper moved to bring an interdict in court seeking his freedom.

Meanwhile some whites grew hostile to our handling of the countrywide unrest.

CHAPTER THIRTEEN

# SKELETONS

By the 1980s about half the readers of the *Cape Times* were
not white. Yet the newspaper operated mainly in a white, middle-
class world. We had liberal convictions and some credibility
among blacks. But the centre of gravity had always been white
and "establishment." There were serious efforts to recruit
Africans to the full-time staff, but for years this was well-nigh possible because of severe restrictions on employing Africans in the
Western Cape. The Cape was regarded as a "coloured labour preference area." That meant Africans could not easily get jobs, which
were reserved for local coloured people. We ran into problems
when we tried to import gifted African trainees from the S.A.A.N.
group in Johannesburg to Cape Town, people of the calibre of
Zwelakhe Sisulu, later to become a Nieman fellow at Harvard and
editor of the Catholic-backed *New Nation* of Johannesburg. The
African townships around Cape Town, moreover, had few established families which could provide a pool of journalistic tal-
ent—unlike, say, Soweto in Johannesburg. This was because of

government policies limiting the numbers of women and children and the lowly status of blacks as "temporary sojourners" in the Western Cape. Another factor that worked against our hiring Africans was the system of "Bantu education" which was unashamedly designed to train most Africans for manual work. Generally speaking, we found many aspiring journalism recruits from the African community in Cape Town were simply not proficient in a writing world. We persisted, however, and gradually education improved (private schools, for instance, became integrated and provided better teaching for those blacks who could get in), and the ideological controls became less onerous. Some progress was made, but employing Africans was not the finest claim we at the *Cape Times* could make. Africans we did consider for employment tended to be so bitter about apartheid that it was difficult for them to maintain anything approaching objectivity in their writing. And some of the most promising Africans moved on.

A lanky, handsome man, Ray ka Msengana, who came from an old established family in Langa, did inspired work on the paper, for instance exposing the sausage-machine justice in the "pass" courts where hundreds of blacks were summarily convicted each week. His presence on our behalf in those courts was resented by officials, but newspapers had the right to report the proceedings, though few exercized it. Once I asked Ray what job he wanted to do most. He grinned, looked over my desk, and said, "Yours." For the time being, at least, he settled for an acting career in the United States.

With coloured staff, the story was different. By the 1980s the *Cape Times* had coloured staffers in fairly senior positions—a night news editor and senior-level reporters—and, at any time, up to a quarter or a third of the newsroom was made up of coloured workers. In comparison with some big papers in the U.S. South I visited, this was not bad at all. These staff members handled any stories that came up and were not confined to special-interest "black stories." Pay rates were equal for all. Relations among staff were good.

170

Yet, in attitude, those running the paper, including myself, had a "white" outlook—indeed, were captives of history, of generations of lingering prejudice. The paper operated in a commercial advertising market which, until about the 1970s or 1980s, was mainly interested in whites because they had the major buying power. Later as mass black buying power approached that of whites in South Africa—and overtook it in some sectors, such as clothing—the situation changed. Economic forces played their role in altering white attitudes—at least in jobs and the economy generally, if not in terms of political power.

The management of the paper in my day was white, too. The newspaper was a business, not essentially different from other businesses in Cape Town. These reflected a spectrum of white attitudes. So, as we launched into our liberal criticisms of enforced apartheid, the odd skeleton would rattle around in our cupboard.

The worst embarrassment was the Cape Times Fresh Air Camp. The problem was simple. The camp was for whites. Set up in the early part of the twentieth century, it was a seaside camp of painted wooden bungalows at Froggy Pond, a beautiful spot on the False Bay Coast just beyond the Simon's Town naval base. Each year schools in the poorer areas of the city and the country would send kids to camps at Froggy Pond. They could enjoy a healthy break at the sea instead of staying at home for the full holidays and being neglected, deprived, or even beaten by parent or sibling. In the old days, schools were fairly racially mixed in some areas, and the intake at the camps would reflect this—as old photographs confirm.

When the National Party government came to power, it did several things which affected the camp. It made school segregation stricter, and it used the Group Areas and Separate Amenities Acts to demarcate living areas and amenities for different races. Froggy Pond was in a white group area, and the beach nearby was also white by law. Moreover, we leased the camp land for a nominal amount from the Department of Lands, which was unlikely to

171

allow non-racial occupation at a time when the government was trying to segregate everything.

So the camp was run, essentially, as a white camp. Visits *Cape Times* executives made there revealed a number of youngsters who were dark in colour. This was because the Cape had such a mixture of colours and cultures that not even the apartheid school system could be racially watertight. In our minds this compensated a bit for our double standards. Although the camp had a public committee in charge (with representatives from white local authorities, such as medical officers of health, prominent among them), the editor was *ex officio* on the committee; it was chaired by the managing director; and the newspaper administered the camp. The fund raising was done through the newspaper's columns. Many people in the multi-racial readership of the *Cape Times* would leave money to the camp in their wills—some no doubt thinking that it was a non-racial camp. To his credit, Managing Director Walter Judge faced this awkwardness in public head on, and, in his speeches accepting funds (for instance from white Post Office employees each year), he would regularly stress the racial status of the camp. We discussed opening the camp at many committee meetings and briefed the company attorneys to find out what was legally possible. The answer was simple: the law made it impossible to have mixed camps. It must also be said that there was no major enthusiasm on the committee for a pioneering effort in mixed camps, particularly at a time when everything in the country was going in the reverse direction. As it happened, the poorer white areas from which the children came tended to be the most racially conservative. The matter of integration was viewed as delicate. There was a general feeling on the committee, I think, that the camp would gradually become mixed at some stage in the future. But not now. Though smarting somewhat, I lived with this.

We considered applying for a permit from the government to allow in people of colour. But seeking a permit to do things that are natural was strongly resented in the black community.

Pressure built up. Coloured readers wrote in, wanting to know what we were going to do about putting our liberal principles

172

into practice. Short of abolishing the camps or defying the law, we had little choice but to soldier on. We gave money each year to a well-endowed "coloured" camp, the John Power Camp at Muizenberg. The gesture only marginally eased the growing feeling of discomfort—particularly over the tricky question of bequests in wills made in the belief that the camp was open.

Three things happened.

The government, committed to a "reform" of apartheid, slowly allowed mixing in socioeconomic spheres, such as carnivals, some hotels, buses, beaches, and restaurants—with Cape Town in the vanguard. At first this was generally done by permit, with applicants having to go to the most ridiculous lengths to secure Pretoria's permission. (Clubs at one stage had to phone Pretoria for permission every time a person of colour was about to enter, for instance, the Cape Town Press Club in Church Street. No wonder blacks would boycott it in those days. See Appendix 2, p.254). The second thing that happened was a steady advance of non-racialism in churches and other groups which paid nominally for use of the camp when regular camps were not in session. These groups appealed to us to open the Fresh Air Camp.

Some of us wondered whether we would get away with unilaterally opening the camp to all, but this could backlash against young black children if they went for a dip at Froggy Pond beach and were chased off by armed police and Alsatian dogs after white complaints. The M.P. for the area, John Wiley, was a very conservative English-speaking politician who had joined the government and become a cabinet minister, after leaving the United Party. He disliked the English-language press with the venom of a Cape cobra. We feared that he would complicate any moves to open the camp and the beach. We were wrong. When the time came to open the camp (some time before he died in 1987) Wiley caused us no problem at all.

The third thing happened at a day at the races.

Walter Judge and his wife Pam attended a charity day at the races at the Cape Turf Club at Milnerton. Some of the proceeds were to go to the Fresh Air Camp. He blushed and Pam glanced at him inquiringly when the chairman of the club, Abe

173

Bloomberg, announced the various charity grants. Bloomberg was a city lawyer and former mayor. As such he had hosted the king and queen of England at a royal ball in the Cape Town City Hall in 1947. He had much clout in the city. He went out of his way to praise the Fresh Air Camp for being "open to all." Bloomberg just assumed that a camp run by the *Cape Times* would be non-racial—particularly in the changing times society was going through despite government policies. He did us a favour. Judge weathered the moment and went directly to my office and said: "Tony, I don't know how, but we are going to open that camp."

We did not apply for a permit. They were falling into disuse in any event. We just resolved that the camp would, from then on, be open. We touched a few bases in the ruling political establishment and satisfied ourselves that John Wiley or others would not kick up a fuss. Beach apartheid was crumbling, so no police Alsatians could be expected to chase dark kids having a swim at the beach. The Group Areas Act remained, but there was talk of "open," or free settlement, areas being established as part of a "reform" of the measure. It looked to be plain sailing.

The religious groups that used the camp were delighted. Some problems remained—for example, as long as state schooling was segregated, individual schools sending children to camp would do so on a racial basis. But there was nothing to stop our drawing people from different schools of our choice to Froggy Pond. The breakthrough had been made.

I had been engaged in (for me) very taxing correspondence with a coloured reader who, persistently and quite correctly, was accusing the *Cape Times* of hypocrisy by not opening the camp. In mid-fray, I was able—thanks to Bloomberg's unintended master stroke—to write to this reader and honestly say the camp was now open to all. Thank God.

Other skeletons rattled around.

One point of awkwardness had its roots deep in the community from which the paper drew strength, the English-speaking establishment. They were not keen on Jews. There was an effective ban on Jews in some select social circles in Cape Town, notably in one of its clubs.* Anti-Semitism never reared its head at the *Cape Times* in any overt way during my time with the paper. But the Cape English-speaking establishment was sensitive on the "Jewish" question, and there were major controversies over Jewish immigration in the 1930s—with parts of that establishment not emerging smelling like roses.

A "Jewish" issue once brought me a very mild rebuke at a bankers' lunch . . . not more than a gently raised finger and the exclamation "Naughty." It came from the non-executive chairman of the *Cape Times,* Clive Sinclair Corder. An editorial of mine had criticized the well-known Rand Club in Johannesburg for making it unnecessarily difficult for a Jewish M.P., Harry Schwarz, to join. It said: "Ordinary people who do not belong to these august institutions will be justifiably puzzled by what they have read [the deferring of Schwarz's application]. They should be reassured that clubs which play such an influential role behind the scenes in moulding opinion are not still heavily mortgaged to prejudices and emotions that should have disappeared years ago."[88] For this rather mild criticism of the English establishment, Corder's cautionary finger wagged at his editor.

There were some commercial sacred cows in the editorial offices when I took over the *Cape Times.* A certain kid-glove treatment was reserved for Syfrets Trust Company, the City Tramways Company, and the Aerial Cableway on Table Mountain. Needless to say, our chairman was their chairman.

We did not publish "non-white" weddings or social occasions as a rule on the special pages for social events until the early 1970s. On the other hand, we gradually turned to discouraging racial identification in news stories, except when race was the whole point of the story.

We tried the idea of running separate racial editions aimed exclusively at the coloured people of the Cape Flats. Even though they were not labelled "coloured," everyone knew what the

* An American ambassador told me that as a newcomer to Cape Town he had arranged a party to celebrate a national occasion at the Kelvin Grove club and wondered why there were no Jewish takers. Checking whether it was a special holiday or something, he was put the wiser by informed locals about Cape tribal life and changed the venue.

EXTRA or CAPE FLATS labels meant. We rationalized it with the argument that, however much we wanted to publish a general edition for all, news about people of colour would not make it, in volume, into a general edition. Thus a geographically based (obviously race-targeted) edition was justified; so the argument went. But the coloured community resented the racial innuendo. The opposition on an intellectual level was so vehement that, in time, we dropped these "ghetto" editions and did not lose circulation as a result.

There were also many questions about the conditions in which young "non-white" newspaper sellers, many of whom were children, operated. Many lacked protective clothing, were underage, and there was exploitation by older men who would own, body and soul, whole teams of young "newspaper boys." It was out of Dickens. There was criticism from the public, including questions in Parliament by Dr. Alex Boraine, then M.P. for Pinelands. The public would regularly see tiny urchins curled up in cold cinema foyers or elsewhere on rainy days or nights, clutching consignments of newspapers—including liberal newspapers. The newspaper managements said, strictly correctly, it was the responsibility of the "separate" distributing company, and the latter said they did not employ minors. There was too much buck passing and raising of Nelson's telescope to the blind eye. A particularly horrible newspaper van smash at Paarden Eiland, Cape Town, followed by fire which killed a number of urchin sellers—a misfortune which befell the *Burger* but could as easily have hit us—was sobering. It focused attention on this subject of newspaper vendors. Slowly, too slowly, conditions were improved, with proper, enforced age limits and protective and safety-illuminated clothing and proper employment conditions and better pay. The advent of trade unionism among blacks, notably the media workers, did much to improve things.

We had our better moments. In a board decision we suspended, for a time, our donation to the technical college which insisted, most insensitively, on building in District Six.

We refused to sponsor a segregated big walk. Increasingly, we tried to adopt non-racial attitudes, as a leading institution in

176

Cape society. We began calling Africans "Mr." or "Mrs."—even unconvicted accused in court cases, which brought an angry white backlash from conservative quarters. How could a black accused of murder be a "Mr."! We generally used the term "guerilla" instead of the government's favoured term, "terrorist."

There were plenty of opportunities to make significant editorial choices—indeed, almost daily. Some we handled better than others. We were a human, flawed institution in an abnormally flawed society. Our record, at best, was well intentioned but patchy.

Was working for the established press, with its privilege and hypocrisy in a sea of "poverty people,"* worth the candle? Undoubtedly. Despite the skeletons rattling behind the thudding presses, it provided the chance to challenge enforced apartheid . . . to challenge the law.

## BACKTRACK

It began to dawn on government thinkers that apartheid was leading nowhere. It is difficult to put a date on it, but as the 1970s unfolded there was a growing realization of this in all but far-right quarters. There was the tiniest hint of self-doubt among Nationalists in 1960 after Sharpeville and David Pratt's assassination attempt on Verwoerd. Paul Sauer, a "moderate" Cape Nationalist and chairman of the cabinet in the absence of Verwoerd, made a speech in his Humansdorp constituency saying that the "old book" in relations with blacks had been closed, and he called for modest reforms—for instance, allowing blacks to buy liquor—and, generally, a new attitude by whites. But soon Verwoerd was on the mend, Sauer was repudiated by hard-line ministers like Eric Louw, and the country continued on its path to racial disaster. When Laurence Gandar of the *Rand Daily Mail*, in the 1960s, wrote a series of prophetic columns about a nation that had "lost its way," it seemed that no one in government was listen-

* An apt term frequently used by Dr. Dick van der Ross, former principal of the University of the Western Cape.

177

ing. Nor were many white citizens. But things turned full circle, and Gandar, in his retirement on the Natal south coast, saw vindication of his position.

The grim, orderly men trying to reverse history came up against powerful local and world pressure. Blacks never gave up their opposition, despite repression. White liberals kept up a barrage of verbal criticism, too, though they shrank from militant activism. Powerful black trade unions organized strikes and won recognition under the law. Black consumer boycotts shook whites. The government's confidence level began to slip. The politicians who would assure whites that they could sleep safely in their beds at night no longer sounded convincing. The notion that South Africa was a haven of peace in a turbulent Africa wore thin. Rightwing groups broke away—a ripple under Vorster, a torrent under Botha, and a major threat to his successor, F. W. de Klerk—as the National Party sought to "reform" apartheid.

Ironically, it was often a hostile opposition press to whom the government turned in its reform efforts. "You boys must help us, man!" was not an uncommon appeal made in private to newspaper editors as ministers prepared the way for cautious changes in racial policy.

It was well into the 1970s when Vorster, shaken by regional African events and Soweto, began edging away from some of apartheid's excesses. The white-dominated South Africa of the 1950s and 1960s, the era of the great white chief Verwoerd, was melting into history like snowflakes on a warm highway. Blacks, as the 1980s approached, were outnumbering whites by about twenty-five million to less than five million. In 1960 Philip Kgosana had proudly talked of the power of eleven million Africans—when the white figure was about three million. Verwoerd, so meticulous in other matters, had greatly miscalculated the African growth rate. He had expected nineteen million Africans in total by the year 2000, but in reality it was likely to be about twice that number. He had seen 1978 as the "turning point" when blacks would flow back to the reserves—a prediction that totally failed to materialize.

Industry and commerce were creaking under the effects of

government racial policies which kept blacks out of certain jobs, duplicated services, and swamped managers in seas of ideological paperwork.

The scene was set for inevitable reform of the South African system, not so much because the government wanted this but because it could not avoid it. By sheer numbers, and their active and indispensable involvement in almost every sphere of South African life in a mixed economy, blacks were making their presence and their demands felt. Liberals had to step back. Blacks were seizing their own future. Perceptive whites knew that apartheid's time was running out. The security forces could hold the line for a time but not indefinitely. This eventually dawned on the white Nationalist establishment. They started confiding this belief in private. International sanctions and pressures undeniably helped to change things.

As the crumbling proceeded, Botha took the bull by the horns and abolished the pass laws, Section 16 of the Immorality Act, the Mixed Marriages Act, and other measures. He recognized black trade unions and—for the first time—blacks' right to strike without their risking prison. But he left "hearth and home," like state schooling and most living areas, firmly segregated. The central political system still locked blacks out, and all South Africans remained subject to classification under the cornerstone apartheid measure, the Population Registration Act of 1950. Under "reformist" Botha, the Land Act of 1913, allocating land on a racial and unfair basis, remained. But in many spheres of life there was relaxation. Hesitantly, without an overall plan, and not in good grace, Botha groped his way out of some of the dead ends of apartheid. The security forces maintained, indeed tightened, their grip. They showed themselves ruthlessly prepared to kill large numbers of protesters.

It was in this atmosphere of loosening up that the English-language newspapers—and the *Cape Times* in particular—did their thankless bit for "reform" in ways previously not revealed. In these matters, our assessment was that as long as the move was to a more integrated society, whatever official gobbledegook was used to describe it, we would help . . . as long as it did not conflict with our essential news function and the public interest.

The privately run bus company in Cape Town had been forced to introduce bus apartheid by the government. Because of the losses that the company would sustain, the government paid, through the Cape provincial administration, a special subsidy each year—running into hundreds of thousands of rands.

In time the bus company, weary of apartheid's anomalies, impracticability, and financial drawbacks, its insulting *Xs* and *Ys* telling people of different races where to sit, turned to the local newspapers for help. In July 1977, top management of the Tramways Company visited Shaw and myself at the *Cape Times* and disclosed that the green light for bus integration had been given by the government, "As long as it happened with no fuss or bother." My contemporaneous note on the discussion went:

> They asked us to go easy in the handling of the matter [integration of the buses]; particularly, we should not expect them to comment on matters as they came up. We agreed not to press them for comment on the record for the approximately six weeks they felt it would need to break the horse in, as it were, before seeking and obtaining official government permission to continue running buses on a non-racial basis. They had instructed all staff to remove racial barriers and not to take action if 'non-whites' sat in white seats. A special white bus would continue to run on some routes, but this would be at rather infrequent intervals, so any whites wishing to travel in it would have to wait a long time.[89]

That was what the bus company proposed. We saw no problem helping Cape Town get back to what was, after all, normal. Instead of seeking statements from the company itself (which we knew we would not get), the *Cape Times* monitored the desegregation process carefully and did its own surveys of commuter opinion. We carried reports, prominent but inside the paper, announcing that a quiet transformation was taking place on the city's buses. We also published statements by city councillors in favour of the move. Only one reader wrote in to complain about

180

the dropping of apartheid. We published the letter on July 20, 1977.

And there was a spin-off benefit for whites which was totally unexpected. They scrambled for the cheaper "clipcards" traditionally intended for "non-whites" only. As the *Cape Times* reported in July 1979:

> White commuters have discovered that scrapping bus apartheid works in their favour, even if they are possibly committing an offence.
>
> Since the introduction of higher fares a few days ago, hundreds of white users of City Tramways' buses have been making use of the clipcard system, originally introduced to help thousands of black workers to commute more cheaply.
>
> For the clipcard system, employers are levied at the rate of twenty cents for each coloured or African employee. This levy (in addition to that from the government) helps to subsidize bus fares and makes it possible for City Tramways to charge discount fares. The cash fare, for instance, from Mowbray to Cape Town is twenty five cents whereas the clipcard fare is only eleven cents.
>
> While apartheid was still being rigidly enforced on racially separated buses, the clipcard system was easy to control. However, since segregation on buses had been phased out, it had become almost impossible for City Tramways conductors to refuse clipcard payment.
>
> It would mean the onus was again on the conductor to decide whether a person was white or not. This was the conductors' biggest headache in the days of racial segregation on buses. They complained they had to act as race classifiers and enforcers of race legislation. This often led to friction between passengers and bus drivers and conductors.
>
> Yesterday spokesmen for both City Tramways and the Department of Transport declined to comment on the question whether it was an offence or otherwise for whites to use clipcards.[90]

The next day a Pretoria official described the clipcard dodge as "highly undesirable." Clipcards were to keep African and coloured fares low and were definitely not meant for the "casual passenger."

The quiet revolution had been successful—even profitable,

for some quick-witted whites. The special whites-only buses were discontinued in due course. A little bit of sanity returned to the city. That was way back in Vorster's time, years before desegregation of buses in other South African cities.

In May 1976 the minister of sport, Dr. Piet Koornhof, secured the co-operation of the Cape Town newspapers over the delicate question of the resumption of the traditional intervarsity rugby game between the universities of Cape Town and Stellenbosch. Intervarsity had been discontinued some years before because Cape Town University would have no truck with apartheid at the game, whereas at that stage apartheid was the norm at Stellenbosch—and, of course, the rigid policy of the government, with which Stellenbosch was closely identified. Koornhof explained that the game was to go ahead, and that apartheid would not be enforced. But if the press "made a big thing of it," there would be controversy and the Vorster cabinet would not accept the arrangements. A major stumbling block was that—South Africa being a small country—the prime minister was also chancellor of Stellenbosch University. As such, he could face severe attack from the Nationalist right wing for upholding apartheid as head of government but undermining it as university chancellor.

A senior representative of the *Argus* and I were present at the discussion with Koornhof, together with Sir Richard Luyt, principal of the University of Cape Town. While warning Koornhof that any "hard news" that broke about the resumption would be reported, we agreed not to blow things up unnecessarily. We warned that politicians and others might well comment on this "hot" subject, and said we would publish these comments in the normal course. Only later did we hear that the Stellenbosch campus had been considered for the game, at its Coetzenberg ground, but a sticking-point had been toilets. Some bright sparks even considered having portable toilets which could be used by the mixed University of Cape Town spectators outside their section of the stadium, so that blacks would not have to use Stellenbosch's. But, as it happened, the "easier" Cape Town venue of Newlands was chosen, which did not run the same risk of complaints about toilets, etc.

The following statement was issued by the university heads: "Agreement has been reached between the Universities of Cape Town and Stellenbosch to resume the traditional Intervarsity rugby game in 1976 within the previously stated policies of each university on Intervarsity, having regard to the factual position within the respective rugby clubs at the present time. The situation will be reviewed for future games in the light of the 1976 experience and prevailing circumstances. The game will take place on May 31, 1976."[91]

The game went ahead and there were no racial incidents—just some mauling of the drum majorettes by inebriated white louts. Most black students at the University of Cape Town were unenthusiastic about playing or watching normal sport in an abnormal society in any event, and none qualified then for the UCT team.

Over the years, the South African press made a number of "arrangements" to help the government out of its self-made difficulties. Bus desegregation and the resumption of intervarsity sport are just two local Cape Town examples. It certainly did not change the hostile attitude of government toward liberal papers. Our journalists were detained, charged in court, harassed, and threatened. Newspapers like the *World* and *Post* were closed. We were still seen by many in government as enemies of the country.

Indeed, as the reform process progressed, government hostility toward newspapers and dissidents did not lessen. The political pressure-cooker, which was so hesitantly being opened by Vorster and Botha, threatened to blow its lid off in their faces. They were under constant right-wing attack for being "Kafferboeties" (nigger-lovers). This made them jumpy. The reform moves brought out their worst instincts of repression.

# CHAPTER FOURTEEN

# ROAD TO TAMBO

Any person who without the consent of the minister prints, publishes or disseminates any speech, utterance, writing or statement made or produced or purporting to have been made or produced anywhere at any time by any person listed under Section 23 (1) of the Internal Security Act, is guilty of an offence. The penalty: a period of imprisonment [with no provision for an option of a fine] not exceeding three years.—Summary of the "no-quoting" provision under the Internal Security Act, 1982, as amended.

The controversy over quoting banned people had a long history. On several occasions newspapers had published statements by banned or "listed" people and got away with it. As far back as 1962, there was a row over the publication in a pro-government newspaper, the *Vaderland* of Johannesburg, of a United Press report quoting Oliver Tambo, head of the ANC, in exile.[92]

When Oliver Tambo, ANC leader, and David Sibeko, of the Pan-Africanist Congress, addressed the United Nations in 1976, the newspapers in South Africa faced the decision of whether to publish. Both Tambo and Sibeko were "listed" persons, thus unquotable. But some editors recalled a dispensation, extended by a former justice minister, Peet Pelser, that statements at the United Nations would be exempt from the no-quoting law. As editors prepared to publish, there was a problem. An urgent message was sent from the new minister of justice, Jimmy Kruger, to newspapers: "I have not given my permission for publication and people must look to the situation in their country before they publish this stuff."[93] The message made it plain enough: in view of the situation in the country caused by the Soweto upheaval, Tambo and Sibeko should not be quoted. Kruger's predecessor Pelser had not changed the law but just arranged that newspapers would not be prosecuted if statements made at the UN were published. The receipt of Kruger's message complicated the situation. We had been planning to go ahead when it arrived at that very late hour. There was some agonizing in the office, and hasty consultation with our brother morning group newspapers in other centres of the country (newspapers acting in a group were generally emboldened). Despite Kruger's message, the *Cape Times* took the chance, and published.[94] We got away with it, and there was no prosecution. Kruger remained unfriendly toward the paper, however. When our political correspondent Tom Copeland sent him a note in Parliament to ask whether the *Burger* had been given permission to quote the banned exile Donald Woods, who had been involved in a clash with a South African lawyer at a U.S. congressional hearing in Washington, Kruger scribbled on Copeland's note: "You tell your editor that is an impertinent question which has nothing to do with him."[95]

Then there was the confusing saga of Zollie Malindi, a Cape Town black activist who was banned and therefore unquotable. He spoke at a United Democratic Front press conference on November 23, 1984, in Cape Town. Representing the Western Cape Civic Association, he supported a two-day boycott of the City Tramways bus company because of a fare increase. The published quotation in the *Cape Times* was but four lines: his saying that the government transportation board and the City Tramways had shown no understanding of the plight of the commuters, and "they just rode roughshod over our appeals and objections to a fare increase." We published without realizing Malindi was on the list. It could happen in the rush to publication. Checking lists before publication was a hit-and-miss affair. South African editors would keep special tickler boxes in their offices containing white, pink, and green cards giving the names of people banned or listed and who were therefore unquotable. The boxes were kept up to date by a law firm, and the government regularly published updated lists in the *Government Gazette*. But it was easy to lose or miss a card, to misfile one, or even misspell a name. That was no excuse in terms of the law. Papers had been successfully prosecuted for making mistakes.

In the Malindi case, reporter Anthony Johnson and I were charged in court with quoting a banned person. We appeared first thing in the morning on May 10, 1985. The hearing was in court number thirteen in the Cape Town Magistrate's Court, a forbidding red-brick complex next to Caledon Square police headquarters, with huge vans drawn up outside carrying prisoners. We took our places in the dock and were ordered to stand up. In our dark suits we were conspicuous among the Hogarthian crowd of pimps, prostitutes, drug addicts, and other criminals picked up by the police overnight in the seaport (Cape Town) called the "Tavern of the Seas." The case was remanded to June 19 for plea and trial. The magistrate warned us that if we did not turn up then we "would be arrested." Presumably he thought we might flee or something.

An aspect of our defence was to be novel. Johnson, an otherwise meticulous fellow who was doing a U.S. doctorate on the Zimbabwe press, had made a most fortunate mistake in spelling Malindi. He wrote Malindini, and it appeared thus in the *Cape Times*. We were not over-confident about it, but one line of our defence would be to tell the magistrate that this was obviously not Malindi but another person . . . or we could at least be forgiven for thinking he was another person. That is, the well-known Malindini not Malindi. But the charge was dropped before we could launch this unique defence on South African justice. The afternoon newspaper, the *Argus*, had also quoted Malindi—namely, his appeal to the police to keep a low profile. The *Argus* also managed a misspelling of his name. They named him Malinidi. Misspelling his name is clearly endemic. They were not prosecuted in court. As things turned out, no one was convicted, and Malindi saw his banned words in print for the first time in years.

There were also incidents involving Donald Woods. This happened both before and after his whole family's escape to England by way of Lesotho in 1978. Woods provided us with "test runs" for our Big One which was to come in 1985.

When Woods was banned on October 19, 1977, I wrote an appreciation for the *Cape Times,* taking a chance and quoting him directly. It was an inconsequential remark to me on the phone, probably intended more for the security police than me: "Well, I have always wanted to concentrate on my music composition."[96] Woods, by the way, was no mean composer. With the indispensable help of his pianist wife Wendy, he had composed an impressive piece, "African Overture," which had gone on tour with the state-funded Cape Performing Arts Board in 1976. In my article, I also quoted previous statements by Woods, technically an offence, too. For instance, I cited his remark to Botha about having a sense of humour (when the latter was incensed about one of Woods's columns), and I described an incident when he jumped up at a press conference in 1962 at which the then Justice Minister Vorster was explaining his draconian sabotage act. "Mr. Vorster," he said, "how do you square this bill with democracy?" Also quoted was the "thought" Woods had when presented with his banning order by security police: "Now I know for sure you ban people for doing nothing." This was a direct quote from Woods, put as a "thought." Would quoting a *thought,* I wondered, be a criminal offence?

Nothing happened, even after Woods had on British TV drawn attention to the quotes. The authorities let me be.

The real close shave came a few years later, in December 1984.

Woods had appeared on a platform with the South African ambassador to London, Dr. Denis Worrall, at a debate organized by the Cambridge University debating society to discuss sanctions against Pretoria. As a banned person Woods could not be quoted in South Africa without government permission. Newspapers applied to the responsible minister, Louis le Grange, to publish Woods. Le Grange said he had not had time to study the transcript—and in any event he was not prepared to give Woods a "platform in South Africa." So the answer was no. The rest of the press observed this, publishing Worrall or nothing. But we at the *Cape Times* thought differently. We felt it terribly one-sided to quote just Worrall. We pounced on a remark made by Worrall in the debate to the effect that the editors of South Africa would all agree South Africa had a free press. As the *Financial Mail* noted afterwards, "Heard appears to have taken him seriously."[97]

The *Cape Times* went ahead and published both sides of the debate. In a rather prudent and tactical move, we edited out some of Woods's remarks which could have run us foul of the Defence Act; we preferred to break one act at a time. We added a note that both sides of the debate were being published in the confident belief that Worrall's remarks about a free press could be taken at face value.

My lawyer friend, who dispensed *pro amico* advice all my professional life, had advised against publication. I browsed around his bookshelf in chambers as he checked the Internal Security Act to assess the damage to me and the paper if I went ahead. I came across the *Apologia Pro Vita Sua* by John Henry Newman, on whom I had done my honours work at university. I flipped through the familiar pages. At page eighty-one I spotted this comment by the nineteenth-century poet-theologian-philosopher:

> I should have thought myself less than a man if I did not bring it out.

Publication caused a political stir, the equivalent of a small earthquake in Peru, and a police prosecution was started. But it never got to court. Presumably someone decided it was preferable to drop what could be an embarrassing trial—embarassing for both the government and its ambassador to London.

We were emboldened. . . .

We had already noted that Chief Mangosuthu Buthelezi of the KwaZulu "national state" in Natal province had quoted Oliver Tambo at length with impunity. He did so in an article in *Clarion Call*, published by his KwaZulu government in February 1984. On a later occasion Buthelezi read from a Tambo radio broadcast made from Addis Ababa,[98] when he (Buthelezi) addressed the South African Federated Chamber of Industries of Natal at the Royal Hotel, Durban.[99] Nothing happened to Buthelezi. Admittedly, unlike editors, he had several million Zulus behind him.

There had been successful prosecutions. In October 1980 the pro-government newspaper the *Transvaler* had been fined seventy-five rands for quoting ANC official Thabo Mbeki, who was banned. The editor of the *Star* of Johannesburg, Harvey Tyson, had been acquitted in court in 1984 after publishing a brief remark by Tambo, the court holding that Tyson was not personally responsible.[100] "It was a workshop situation where responsible people had to edit a large volume of overnight articles," said magistrate F. Strydom. He admitted the law "cast a wide net" and was difficult to comply with in the running of a daily newspaper. The Argus company, owner of the *Star*, was, however, deemed vicariously responsible for the illegal report, and fined a hundred rands. And what was the cause of all this? The report quoted Tambo as saying he was banned and could not be quoted! Even that was an offence in Pretoria's eyes. Tyson commented that it was impossible to edit an honest newspaper without coming into conflict with the law. "That is why numbers of law-abiding newspaper editors, including those of Afrikaans newspapers supporting the government, have criminal records."[101]

The government had perfected the art of quoting selectively from, or freeing for publication, statements of banned or listed people, but only when it suited Pretoria. President Botha quoted Tambo when it suited him; so did Law and Order Minister Louis le Grange.[102] For example, Le Grange gave permission to newspapers to publish a statement to Agence France-Presse, the French news agency, by Thabo Mbeki. This statement highlighted a rift between the ANC and the grouping of black-ruled states in southern and central Africa. This was like manna from heaven to the Botha government and eminently quotable. In February 1985 SAPA, the domestic South African news agency, was permitted to send out an interview Tambo gave to a local newspaper in Harare, Zimbabwe, in which he said there was no alternative to armed struggle against Pretoria. In this case, Le Grange cleared the full report, which came through from Reuters. The editor of SAPA later reported to his management board: "The request was granted, since Tambo lived up to his local image."

A message sent out to newspapers in 1987 said: "Please note that the minister of law and order has not given *carte blanche* permission to quote Oliver Tambo. He has given permission to quote freely from three particular newspaper articles which appeared in the *New York Times, New York Post* and the *Wall Street Journal.*"[103] That meant newspapers could not quote anything else Tambo might have said.

Another message reveals the government's selective intentions: "The law and order ministry has prohibited publication of anything, including comment, on American television Nightline interview with Oliver Tambo until minister Louis le Grange will have had opportunity to examine a transcript. . . ."[104] The significance of that edict was twofold. It showed that Le Grange wanted to manage the news; otherwise, why would he first want to "examine" it? But it went further: It contained a ban that, even in the conditions of a widely defined state of emergency in South Africa, was of no validity. There was no power to prohibit, in advance of publication, "comment" by newspapers. If papers commented in a way that could run foul of the emergency laws, or the many other laws, that was a chance *they* took. They could face charges or even seizure. But no law gave the minister power to instruct newspapers not to "comment." It was an example of how the government sought to extend already onerous laws by telex to editors.

Often permission to quote people was refused outright. For instance, a law and order department message to the *Cape Times* in mid-1985 said bluntly: "Your telex, requesting permission to publish an interview with Oliver Tambo, was referred to the minister of law and order. The minister has refused permission."[105] This was one of countless refusals.

The selective scraps that were allowed through were aimed to conjure up a picture of bloodthirsty terrorist-communists ordering and condoning the necklacing of people in townships with flaming tires, planning civilian deaths, and leaning increasingly on Moscow. The opposite was true. The ANC leadership condemned necklacing, sought to avoid civilian targets where possible, and tilted diplomatically closer to the West. Moscow, too, was changing. The new Gorbachev approach from 1985 on was very different from that of his predecessors. If anything, there was growing Soviet pressure on the ANC to negotiate with rather than fight white power. Yet the caricature of a bloodthirsty ANC was carefully nurtured by the South African government and its faithful media, the pro-Nationalist press and the South African Broadcasting Corporation. What a problem for the future, when inevitably white South Africans would deal with the ANC.

There was growing exasperation in the newspaper industry and elsewhere. Not only newspapers were affected. For instance, the *Oxford History of South Africa Vol.2: South Africa, 1870–1966* appeared in the country with a whole chapter on African nationalism in South Africa by Leo Kuper left blank—fifty pages. And at least one international newsmagazine appeared with a page blank, with an explanation that the emergency made this necessary. Over a wide front, South Africans were denied vital information. For example, the *Cape Times*'s architectural correspondent, Jack Barnett, was technically "unpublishable" because he was listed. His pieces appeared unsigned. The situation was untenable.

This all happened against the background of a growing clamour for the government to talk with the ANC. Circles close to the government took up the refrain. In 1980 Ton Vosloo, *verligte* editor of the Johannesburg newspaper *Beeld* and later to become managing director of that paper's owners, the southern-based publishing empire Nasionale Pers, predicted this. He said the day would arrive when a South African government would sit down at the negotiating table with the ANC.[106] In September 1985 the representatives of big business in South Africa, led by the head of the Anglo-American Corporation, Gavin Relly, met with Tambo and other ANC leaders in Lusaka, risking government displeasure in the process. Tambo, in a symbolic move, asked the whites and blacks to sit alternately at the table side by side—thus stressing the ANC's commitment to working with and not against whites.

It was known by newspaper insiders by the mid-1980s that Minister Le Grange was considering dropping or modifying the law on quoting banned or listed persons, an admission that the arrangements were unsatisfactory. For instance, he conceded privately, the press could get round the law by not naming the person being quoted, but referring to a "spokesman" of an organization like the ANC. Frequently, he said, spouses or friends of banned persons would be quoted—and they would convey the views of that person. Le Grange, in his contacts with the newspaper industry, actually said something enlightened. In May 1985 he told newspaper chiefs that the government did not want a repetition of the Rhodesian experience "where the public was kept uninformed."[107] He accepted that the opinion-forming public should be given a "balanced view" of events. For the spokesman of a government about to introduce a state of emergency, shackling the press, these were memorable remarks. In retrospect, they drip with irony. He even admitted that the law, as it was then applied, could prevent the press from giving a "balanced view."

Le Grange secretly offered to give the newspapers a list of names of people who could be quoted on a six-month trial basis—but he warned against newspapers committing other offences, such as advancing the objectives of a banned organization. The dispensation would apply only to members of the N.P.U. (and, of course, the government-controlled broadcasting corporation), which would leave members of the "alternative press" out in the cold. And he even explained that he would still have to get formal approval from the powerful State Security Council, the influential body chaired by State President Botha and bristling with security chiefs, before anyone on that list could be quoted.

It transpired that Le Grange had in mind banned persons

living abroad, or some of them. The matter was referred to the newspaper editors through their conference, which met on February 5, 1986. They did not want to get involved in deciding, with the minister or anyone, who should be free for quoting and who not. They took a professionally correct position. No one should be gagged. A list of quotables was as bad as a list of unquotables. The matter rumbled on inconclusively in the minister's court. Nothing came of it.

Soon came the state of emergency. The question would become academic—until the De Klerk era in 1989 saw major relaxations on the media.

# CHAPTER FIFTEEN

# MUSWELL HILL, LONDON
# OCTOBER 1985

The double-storey Victorian house in North London, England, looked like any other in the area, except that it had thick velvet curtains at the windows. They were tightly drawn when our party turned up on the evening of October 30, 1985.

A guard, burly but unarmed, stood at the gate of the house to welcome us.

"You have come to see the president?" he asked. Yes we had.

We exchanged pleasantries, and I inquired where he was from. "Natal."

"Me too," I said, realizing our different circumstances in years past. He had been one of the mass of unprivileged in the city where I went to school. Yet I wondered. Was it just possible that we had brushed shoulders somewhere, sometime—in busy West Street, or at the Indian market, or on the Esplanade? In pure theory he could have been the man with the bicycle who taught me the difference between boys and men.

In London in 1985 we were equals.

"But more recently, Dar-es-Salaam," he said.

War had taken him from Durban. He and other African National Congress cadres had gone to places like Tanzania. In exile, they had trained for guerilla conflict to be launched against the South African government from African soil.

"Please come this way," said the guard in a friendly way.

Inside the house was Oliver Tambo, the ANC leader-in-exile, and his wife Adelaide.

I had a tingling feeling. It was like treading on history.

Far from South African soil, in Muswell Hill, North London, an unusual interview was about to begin. It was planned to be the first published interview with a silenced ANC leader by a South African newspaper since the organization was suppressed twenty-five years before. It had brought a newspaper editor six-thousand miles to London to do it.

I clutched the sheet of paper with my jotted questions, and we went inside. I was technically on leave from work and yet could not be harder at it; this was the biggest story I had ever handled.

John Battersby, then London bureau chief of the South African morning newspaper group, had attended the Commonwealth heads of governments meeting in the Bahamas earlier that year, and he had made the necessary contacts which led to the interview in London. No other channels, or influence, were used to set it up. I acted on my own, representing my newspaper and profession. It had nothing to do with big business figures who had taken initiatives to meet Tambo earlier that year. It had nothing to do with opposition figures or anyone else.

It had to do with journalism. No one in South Africa, up to that point, had been able to know what the ANC stood for. *That* was the job of journalism to put right, to shed light on dark corners.

We went in. Also present was André de Wet, a photographer living and working in London, who had been on the *Cape Times*. I respected his work and trusted him. One hint of the interview given to South African sources, and it would be frustrated by seizure or other action when I returned home.

Tambo was on his second visit to London in a month. As usual—at that stage—he was getting the cold shoulder at the official level from the conservative Thatcher and Reagan governments in Britain and the U.S., something that was to change in coming months and years. At other levels, however, the thaw in relations between the western community and the ANC was dramatic. On his earlier visit to London, after which he had gone to Nassau in the Bahamas for the Commonwealth conference, Tambo was described by correspondent Nicholas Ashford in the London *Times* as "the star attraction at the Labour Party conference and journalists queued up to interview him."[108] He had also been to the United States, where he was "feted on Wall Street and Capitol Hill."[109] Not bad for someone portrayed by South African officials as a bloodthirsty communist-terrorist. He made the second visit to London to give evidence to the House of Commons Select Committee on Foreign Affairs, to address influential business leaders, and to unveil a bust of his old friend and colleague, Nelson Rolihlala Mandela, outside the Royal Festival Hall on the bank of the Thames River.

Tambo and Mandela had a long association in South Africa. They studied at Fort Hare University together during the Second World War and were founder members of the militant ANC youth league. They opened a law firm, Tambo and Mandela, in Johannesburg in 1952. They went through the "no bail, no fine" defiance campaign together, and they were among the 156 accused in the famous treason trial which began in 1957 and ended with the acquittal of all accused. After the events at Sharpeville and Langa and the declaration of a state of emergency on March 30, 1960, the police had struck at dawn and detained hundreds of people. In the nick of time, Tambo escaped abroad through Botswana in the company of Ronald Segal, editor of the left-wing magazine *Africa South*. Before long he was addressing the United Nations, touring the world, and beginning a life in exile—as "roving ambassador" and leader-in-exile of the ANC—with homes in London and Lusaka, Zambia. In 1962

197

Mandela went to prison for his marathon term. Apart from earlier charges, he was in 1964 given a life sentence for sabotage he had planned but did not execute—unlike the O.B. during the war years, several of whose saboteur members were released from "life imprisonment" after the National Party government came to power in 1948. Tambo, meanwhile, continued the struggle abroad. By the mid-1980s he was wooing the Western world with considerable success. That is when I arrived.

The ANC leader-in-exile greeted us with courtly warmth. I noted faint signs of the initiation rites of his youth scratched on the side of his face; a reminder of his boyhood in Bizana in the Eastern Cape near the Natal border. He was born the son of peasant farmers in 1917 in this area near the Wild Coast, a lovely place of hut-dotted hills, trees, seaside crags, and petrified forests. On many occasions, I had driven down that rough and exquisite coast, calling at coves where Portuguese ships were wrecked in days gone by, and I had watched the sea where a massive and notorious wave (the Mallory wave), swept on by tide and wind, can bury unsuspecting ships at sea. After the interview, I was to ask Tambo, "Do you personally miss being in South Africa?" And he was to ask in reply: "Who would not miss being at home?" Asked, further, if he would rest his bones there, he said: "I hope so."

Tambo waved me over to a sofa, and Battersby and De Wet to easy chairs, and he came and sat down beside me. Adelaide Tambo came in and out a few times during the interview. Her demeanour was warm and easy. It was nice to be among fellow South Africans so far from home.

I had taken the precaution of bringing along two tape recorders in case one malfunctioned. I did not want to take any chances. These I placed between Tambo and myself on the couch, and we began the interview, with those thick purple drapes just behind us. They were obviously there for the Tambos' security.

Tambo was courtesy itself, conveying an old-world charm. He reminded me vaguely of my deputy of so many years, Gerald

Shaw. Both were at home in conservative dress—e.g., braces, dark suit, and black shoes. Both had thick-lensed glasses. Both were churchmen. At sixteen Tambo went to an Anglican mission school in Johannesburg and became friendly with Father (later Bishop) Trevor Huddleston who wrote *Naught For Your Comfort*. I was told later by an ex-colleague in the Tambo and Mandela law firm that it was sometimes difficult to find Oliver Tambo—"he was always praying." Tambo planned at one stage to enter the Anglican priesthood. He and Adelaide had three children, and there was a picture of their daughter's wedding in St. Paul's Cathedral on the mantelpiece. Tambo looked more like a British banker than the leader of a guerilla movement. As the London *Observer* had noted three days before, he "looks far too gentle and grandfatherly to fill the role of revolutionary."[110] Here, for sure, was no Gaddaffi of Libya, and someone very different from a Castro or an Arafat. Yet he was portrayed in South Africa as an ogre. It was important to present an accurate picture of him and his views to South African readers.

An experienced lawyer, Tambo started off the discussion with a joke about the Internal Security Act. He observed that it was I, not he, who could be jailed as a result of this episode. He knew the law: up to three years in prison and no option of a fine for quoting a banned or listed person. He chuckled at the thought as we began the interview.

Tambo spoke in slow, measured tones, and he never got a word or thought misplaced. He knew exactly what his attitude was on the many subjects I raised, and the result was a comprehensive outline of his position on violence, the economy, a future South Africa's diplomatic stance, and so on.

His message was moderate but firm. He urged the South African government to create a climate for talks with his organization, something he said he would "welcome." He spoke of the possibility of a "truce" with the government and was of the view that serious negotiations could start at short notice, even before violence had ended. But he felt that the government of P. W. Botha was not ready to talk at that stage. He denied that the ANC was Communist-led, though admitted that it had some Communists in its membership and had worked with the South African Communist Party since 1921. He said that when the ANC was banned it had been gaining acceptance among whites, but the contact forged by people like ex-Chief Albert Luthuli had then been broken. He said the ANC was gaining more support from the West as interest in South Africa grew.

On the vexed question of guerilla attacks on civilian targets, he said "soft targets" would never be sought out but could be hit in crossfire as the ANC stepped up its attacks on military, police, etc. As a matter of policy, it would not go into bars and cinemas to attack. It was fighting a system, not whites. He disowned what he termed "excesses" in the townships (clearly a reference to practices like "necklacing" informers and others with burning tires).

On economic philosophy—worrying to the West and to whites who feared large-scale nationalization under an ANC government—he said his organization favoured the idea of a mixed economy, with a debate among the people about the extent of nationalization. "Some" industries would be nationalized, but there would be room for levels of private enterprise and private ownership. He wanted to see South Africa back in the Commonwealth, which it left because of apartheid in 1961.

Whites he saw as "fellow South Africans." He added: "They are as good as black." They were seen as "Africans."

Tambo's statement deserved space in South Africa—and, I believe, in history. The interview appears in full in Appendix 1.

I wondered what I would have done had he come out powerfully *for* violence against civilians; had he, for instance, condoned the "necklace." But, even had Tambo done that, the interview would have been published. This, too, would have been journalism. It would have contributed to a debate that so far had been one-sided.

Near the end of the interview Tambo was called to take a telephone call from the statehouse in Dar-es-Salaam, probably with Tanzanian leader Julius Nyerere on the line. It was a reminder of his standing throughout black Africa.

The interview over, he excused himself to attend another

200

appointment in London, and his wife Adelaide gave us tea and cake.

The cassettes firmly in my luggage, I visited Cornwall where Vida had settled. I had to pick her up because she was coming to South Africa. Most of the way from Portscatho, Cornwall, to London, England, the measured voice of Oliver Tambo played from the tape deck of the hired car. Tambo's demand for justice seemed remote from this world of pasties and Celtic culture. Vida's hair rose higher on her head as she realized what lay ahead in Cape Town—a big political fuss; she never tried to talk me out of it.

I tipped off a friend at the *Guardian* in London. Over a drink in the Black Friar pub just around the corner from Fleet Street and Ludgate Circus, I told him what was going to happen and arranged for the *Guardian* to have a transcript once the interview was published. In view of the possible repercussions in South Africa, including arrest and seizure, I thought a famous liberal newspaper might as well have the facts.

Then it was off to Heathrow airport and home.

The rest was straightforward. Arriving in Cape Town, I walked through the "green" customs barrier with the tapes in my hold-all bag, and no one challenged me. Here was a scrum of government officials intent on unearthing subversion and me sailing through with Public Enemy Number One in my hold-all.

The political atmosphere was markedly different from the one I had left. The state of emergency had been made even tougher the weekend I arrived, November 2–3. New clamps impacted heavily on the media, which was locked out of the townships, and visual material was banned. It was now an offence to make a recording (sound or visual) of any riot situation. This restriction aimed at television coverage followed, among others, the urgings of the South African embassy, which was on the defensive in Britain because of the nightly depictions of government violence on television. As early as March 1985 the embassy had noted in reports to an investigating judge, Mr. Justice Kannemeyer, in South Africa that the television cameras were a

201

catalyst and a factor in the unrest.[111] The media curbs had created an even more tense atmosphere in the country. It was certainly an adverse one when it came to risking publishing a full-page interview with a person officially regarded by government as a major reason for the emergency, Oliver Tambo. On the way to Cape Town from the airport we drove past nests of troops and police at strategic spots like exits and overhead bridges; they were positioned there to watch for stone-throwers. This was new. They had not been there when I had left. The climate was immeasurably more brittle.

But there was no turning back. I had to get the interview quickly into the paper, certainly before anyone tipped off the authorities. If alerted, the police could seize the interview, or even the whole newspaper—and charge me without the public's having the benefit of reading it. I could be portrayed as some subversive or other, caught in possession of an incriminating interview. Or worse, I could be seen as planning to promote the aims of the ANC. I would be damned without hesitation by fearful whites who would say: no smoke without fire.

I resolved not to consult with the management of the paper, notably Managing Director Walter Judge, which was a difficult decision because I liked him and we trusted one another. It was, after all, a weekend, I thought to myself. Moreover, I judged that publication, though enraging the government, would not threaten the institution of the *Cape Times.* Judge and I had a working understanding that if anything was likely to threaten the paper, we would consult. That permitted him to sleep at night. My letter of appointment said: "Both the editor and the general manager [managing director] of the paper are equally and independently responsible to the board, but it is important that a relationship of close co-operation should be maintained in all matters affecting the interests of the paper. Matters in respect of which there may be disagreement should be referred to the chairman."[112] My view was that a threat to the paper did not, and would not, arise. My contract, moreover, gave me wide editorial freedom to decide what to publish, as already explained. Non-consultation also provided protection for the institution in case my judgment was wrong—if publication did, in fact, threaten the paper. In that case, to save the paper from serious action by the government, the management could jettison me as editor on the self-evident grounds that I had not consulted them. I could be fired and the paper would live. I had worked for the *Cape Times* for most of my life, and its future as an institution for the public good meant a lot to me. (Later, in belatedly offering apologies to Judge after the event at a meeting of the local management board of the *Cape Times,* I underlined these points.) Consultation, moreover, would mean weighty consideration, calling in lawyers, threats to confidentiality, etc. It had to be a charge of the Light Brigade. Otherwise Tambo would not make it into the paper.

There was no point in my going to lawyers, either. Lawyers would have to advise against breaking the law, any law. They could tell me nothing new or helpful. I knew too well what the consequences were. I was breaking the law, a rotten law. I thought of James Thurber's remark: "Don't get it right, just get it written."[113]

Having arrived back in Cape Town on Saturday, November 2, Monday was the obvious time to publish; indeed, it was the first available day. Weekends were always excellent times to challenge authority. Many of the security forces made a habit of going away and enjoying themselves, relaxing, indulging in the South African outdoor ritual of the "braai." It was no coincidence that a person so knowledgeable in these matters, Donald Woods, the banned editor of the *Daily Dispatch,* chose the New Year holiday period to skip the country in 1978 and evade the East London security police whose guard was down.

All Sunday was spent alone in my office, inputting the interview into the electronic editing system. At first my tape-recorder would not work; I never was good at such things. (I later found that I had the "pause" button on.) I rushed to the Tamboerskloof area of Cape Town near the newspaper office and managed to borrow another recorder from my trusted secretary, Lynne Clement.

It took eight hours getting the whole interview captured and edited in the system. My touch-typing, learned in 1955 at Pitman's College in High Holborn, London, was a Godsend.

Gerald Shaw, who had been alerted in great secrecy and had come to the office, sat quietly in his office, reading the full interview on his computer screen. Toward evening he walked through to my office, looking graver than usual.

He planted his stocky frame in front of me, and I wondered what he was going to say. Would he argue against? Though determined to go ahead, I should have to listen and at least discuss his reservations. We had always respected one another's views and had taken thousands of decisions by consensus.

"Tony," he said, in measured tones, "even if I wished to stop you, I know you will go ahead, so GOOD-NIGHT." He walked out and went home, happy.

As the page was prepared for production it was necessary for some senior editorial staffers to know what was in the works. It had to be a very limited group, on a strict need-to-know basis, because there was real danger that the security police would hear about the plan and stop the presses or seize consignments of the paper. The police had wide power under the state of emergency and other laws and had stopped publication before in South Africa. Police spies were as routine as typewriters in newspaper offices. We had been told that it was the boast of the police in days gone by that the typed news menu produced every evening for the editorial conference got to Caledon Square police headquarters before it reached editor Norton.

About 5 P.M. I told the chief sub-editor, Welma Odendaal, about the plan to publish Tambo. It was she who would have to lay out the page. Her face beamed. Here was some real news in the desert of the emergency. A gifted writer, she had had her brushes with authority, having once edited a publication which fell foul of the censors. The night news editor, Yazeed Fakier, was also told about the secret plan. His wide-eyed comment: "Do you know what you are doing?" I reassured him. He walked off with a spring in his step.

The page was prepared. The interview overran the space available, so a small, unimportant section had to be left out. Otherwise the published interview was faithful to the record. A front-page story was done as a cross-reference to it. Though a big headline would have been apt, we purposely did not make the story the main "lead" so as not to draw over-much attention as it hit the streets. Once again, this was to evade the eyes of the security authorities until it was too late to stop consignments of the paper. Nothing was sent to the domestic news agency, the South African Press Association, or to our partner newspapers elsewhere in the country. That would have been too dangerous. We had to go with the story on our own. Satisfied that all was done and in good order, I went home late that Sunday night.

The next morning, very early, I heard the newspaper being delivered by buzz-bike at my front gate in Hout Bay. It was there—the world according to the *Cape Times* on November 4, 1985: A big front-page lead announcing the curbs on TV and the press, a story about a boxer who had died in a match at the Bantustan gambling resort, Sun City, news about Mandela's having an operation in Cape Town, the inevitable page one story about Prince Charles and Lady Di . . . and, crisply in column 9: **TAMBO URGES: CREATE CLIMATE FOR TALKS**. The real surprise was inside. The whole of page 9 was devoted to "A conversation with Oliver Tambo of the ANC." The explanatory note read:

> There has been a flurry of talks with the African National Congress recently, including the leaders of big business and the Progressive Federal Party. These contacts have raised questions about where the ANC stands on critical issues. So far, everyone's view but that of the ANC has been given in South Africa. The editor of the *Cape Times,* Anthony Heard, met the 68-year-old ANC leader Oliver Tambo in his North London home last week and conducted an interview with what came across as an essentially moderate black leader. The *Cape Times* publishes the full interview as a contribution to peaceful solutions in South Africa in a matter of overwhelming public importance.[114]

205

# CHAPTER SIXTEEN

# TAMBO SPEAKS
# NOVEMBER 4, 1985

Attention editors and publishers. CAPE TOWN, Nov 4 (UPI). The opposition *Cape Times* newspaper Monday defied security laws and courted prosecution by quoting Oliver Tambo, leader of the outlawed African National Congress, in a full-page interview.

The *Cape Times* editor, Anthony Heard, who conducted the interview in London recently, declined to say whether he had official permission to quote Tambo.

"You will have to draw your own conclusions about that," he said.

Tambo, who leads the ANC guerilla movement's 25-year-old armed struggle against white rule in South Africa, is "banned" in terms of internal security laws and may not be quoted in the country without official permission.

Local newspapers last month castigated President Pieter Botha for quoting Tambo during campaign speeches leading up to by-elections in which the government faced a strong right-wing challenge. Botha repeatedly has blamed the ANC for a 14-month-old black uprising in which at least 934 people have died. . . .

That report nearly knocked my daughter Vicki off her chair when it arrived on the wires at Global TV in Barber Greene Road, Toronto. There was interest elsewhere, too.

It is difficult to describe the response.

First, there was what can best be called an audible official silence. This ensued no doubt while ministers and officials scurried about trying to find out who on earth could have given the *Cape Times* permission to run a full-page interview with the chief "terrorist" leader.

The phone started ringing at my home at 7 A.M. It was Reuters, checking on a story that we had broken the law and quoted Tambo. Then the editor of the South African Press Association, Edwin Linington, phoned from Johannesburg to ask for a transcript. The phone rang solidly for two weeks. Vida, crippled with a bad hip, set herself up at my Hout Bay home as fielder of the calls from all over. Calls came from, among others, the Voice of America, Associated Press, Agence France-Presse, Columbia Broadcasting System, World Television News, Australian Broadcasting Corporation, United Press International, Independent Television News, Global TV Toronto, B.B.C., newspapers in Britain, the U.S., Israel, and elsewhere; Netherlands, Australian, German, Irish, Scottish, and U.S. radio stations (among others); Z.D.F. German TV, Reuters, McNeil-Lehrer News Hour . . . and the rest. A polite offer from Sergei Borisov, Harare-based chief correspondent for Southern Africa of the Soviet Novosti Press Agency, for me to contribute to Novosti's international Round Table project that year was declined with thanks. I was in enough trouble. . . .

Mandela had just had a prostate operation in Gardens nursing home. His wife, Winnie, told me later that as he awoke he made a wild grab for the paper when he heard nurses saying: "Oliver Tambo's all over the *Cape Times*." I like to think he concluded that the surgeon's knife had slipped and he had been transported to another plane. About ten miles away, over at Robben Island, where hundreds of political prisoners were still held, the *Cape Times* did not turn up as usual. A prisoner who was there told me later that this was a sure sign that there was something "hot" in the paper. Eventually it did arrive, and was only available for a short time—while prisoners scrambled to write down as much of the interview as possible before it was whisked away. At Paarl's Victor Verster prison detainees, I heard later first-hand, were greatly encouraged when they heard of the interview.

The page was torn out, copied, pasted on walls, mailed. Wags wrote "Let Tambo be Heard" on walls in Cape Town.

The official silence was short-lived. The rumble of Authority was heard the next day, Tuesday (which happened to be Guy Fawkes, November 5, the traditional day when fireworks were let off). Minister of Law and Order Louis le Grange was quoted in the *Burger* as saying no permission had been given, adding: "I can confirm that the police have opened a docket with a view to the possible prosecution of the editor of the *Cape Times*."[115]

Up to that point, when approached by the media, I had declined to say anything. Let the government find out everything itself.

The same day, Tuesday, a lieutenant called at my office to advise that charges were being investigated in terms of Section 56 (1) (p) of the Internal Security Act—quoting a banned or listed person. He had a police docket. A routine form regarding a suspected crime had to be signed. After checking with our company lawyer, Tim McIntosh, I declined to make a statement. Seconds later Sir Robin Day of the B.B.C. telephoned from London for an interview on the "World at One" programme, and he could almost hear the receding police footsteps as I told him of their visit.

Later in the week there was a visit from security police who took away the tape. No fewer than four big men were sent to take away one small cassette.

The world media made much of the story. Our London office reported "massive coverage," from the *Morning Star* to the *Daily Telegraph*. The story went everywhere from Bolivia to Iceland. The *Western Morning News* in Plymouth, England, wrongly thinking I was a local because my mother lived there, declared with a Churchillian ring: "Cornish editor defies Botha." The *International Herald Tribune* headline said: "Paper prints interview with rebel." The editorial page of the British *Guardian* carried extracts from the interview, as arranged; as did the *New York Times* and other newspapers. Tambo's peace call got world publicity.

Messages flooded in. In a few weeks there were three thousand, including those from my daughters. Janet, with her friends at Grahamstown where they were studying, telegraphed *inter alia,* "Get your surfboard ready"—a reference to a family joke that, if I ever was banned, I would try to escape by surfboard. My former wife, Val, a music teacher, aptly sent me Beethoven's Fifth Symphony. A school class in California wrote me letters of encouragement.

The messages were overwhelmingly supportive, though one anonymous critic placed a clip of my arrest in the post box, with "ABOUT TIME" scribbled above it.

And there were some other critical ones. A caller to the "Teleletters" phone-in service run by the newspaper, A. van der Walt of Knysna said: "Mr. Heard must be a very simple man when he believes what a terrorist tells him." Costa Lainis of Green Point, Cape Town, said: "Your editor Mr. Heard has been duped by the ANC. The ANC is a tool of the Soviet imperialism. . . ." A. Parker of Cravenby Estate said: "When the ANC takes over, Mr. Heard will be the first one to leave the country."

J. O'Brien of Fresnaye took issue with Tambo's remarks about "soft targets" not being sought out and his admission that they could be hit in "cross-fire." He said: "Isn't this exactly what happens when police react to petrol-bombers, etc., and innocent bystanders are hurt? But then it's made to look like unprovoked police action." M. Johnson, of Sea Point, smelled a rat: "The Chinese philosopher Sun Tzu said: 'The basis of war is to deceive your adversary'. This applies to Oliver Tambo—a deliberate ploy along those lines of deception."

Those critical comments apart, the flood was favourable. A major theme was thanks from readers for being treated like adults and for being allowed to make up their own minds.

Mrs. E. Duff of Diep River Village said: "That article is the best thing that has happened to us for many months. . . ."

Excerpts from others. Miss B. Kelly: "It is refreshing to be able to form one's own opinion." P. Roberts, of Rondebosch: "Mr.

Oliver Tambo is a very enlightened man. It is a great pity we haven't been allowed to listen to his beliefs before." H. Wood of Mowbray: "It is reassuring that the ANC is so pragmatic in providing a vision for peace and social justice. This is quite contrary to the destructive politics of this government." P. J. Coxon of Rondebosch: "I hope the average South African will now see the ANC as people and not just as some fearful mass out there somewhere. I hope people will now sit down and talk." Mohammed Ahmed of Steenberg: "At least now we can see the ANC's side of things."

The messages ranged from the Anglican archbishop of Cape Town, then the Most Rev. Philip Russell, to the Western Cape Traders' Association, a group of mainly Muslim shopkeepers.

Then there was the most moving message of all. A group of Africans from the townships passed word to me that if I were threatened by the white right wing, they would organize a protection squad. This, coming from the dispossessed and displaced of society, was passed on in dignity and friendship. Once again, I thought: there's hope yet for South Africa.

The support made me realize that, beneath the repression of South Africa, lay a yearning to be free.


On Friday, November 9, the police came for me.

I received a phone call from Lt. Frans Mostert, a well-known character among the left-wing activists whom he had pursued.

He was very civilized. He wanted to know when I would prefer to be arrested and make my appearance in court; before or after lunch?

I had a pre-arranged lunch which Barclays Bank was giving for *Cape Times* senior staff at their Adderley Street address. I felt it best to get the arrest over with. I told Mostert: "Before."

Stockily built, taciturn Mostert, and a polite, tall, athletic fellow called Lieutenant Liebenberg came to take me away from my office about noon.

The media had been locked out of the black townships by the stepped-up emergency regulations, and they had little to do. There was a protest meeting (against the restrictions and in

211

favour of my right to publish Tambo) going on in Burg Street outside the office where the police were to lead me out. Scores of journalists and many members of the public were present. I had been unaware of the build-up. The arrest became one of the day's stories from South Africa. Liebenberg, Mostert, and I literally walked into a horde of journalists. There were clicks and whirs. The police were unhappy about having their pictures taken but had to endure it. The security police did not like being photographed in South Africa. They were upset that they had been "ambushed" by scores of camera-wielding journalists. I pointed out to them as they drove me away in their car toward Caledon Square that even if I had wished to arrange a hot reception for them, I could not have achieved—nor expected—this.

As the guests were sitting down to lunch at the bank, I was over the way, a few blocks off, standing in the dock of the Cape Town Magistrate's Court. The place was deserted because it was lunch-time. The offence was quoting a banned or listed person, for which the legislature did not make any provision for a fine for an individual and which carried a maximum penalty of three years in prison. The prosecutor told the court that further charges might be added. That, we concluded, could be the Big One—up to ten years in jail for endangering the security of the state.

That formality over, and after promising the magistrate that I would report at Caledon Square police headquarters at 4 P.M. for fingerprinting, I was released on my own recognizances. There was no request to post bail.

I went to lunch, late. I have seldom had a better excuse.

The fingerprinting was absorbingly interesting. It was explained that all suspects in serious cases of crime had to be fingerprinted. Walter Judge, the managing director I had not consulted, but who was, as always, loyal and supportive to his editor, accompanied me. Lots of black ink was smeared on my fingers and thumbs, and they were rubbed on the official paper used for fingerprinting. I was assured that if I was acquitted of any crime, they would be destroyed and not kept by the police at their fingerprint headquarters in Pretoria.

212

When I went to the bathroom in Caledon Square to wash the black ink off, I surveyed with more than usual interest the area leading to the stairs. I had remembered the notorious stairs at Caledon Square where more than one political activist had allegedly fallen and been injured—or so the official version went.

As I idly thought about these things, Lieutenant Liebenberg headed fast toward me.

He was apologetic. "I'm sorry, Mr. Heard. We left out one thumb." Apparently thumbs have to be done twice in fingerprinting, and he had discovered one missing. There had been so much pressing and pushing and inking that I would not have noticed. So we traipsed back to the fingerprinting office, and the thumb was duly done, the process watched by my transfixed managing director . . . who was on his first visit to the bowels of Caledon Square.

I was asked by Reuters after the fingerprinting if I was prepared to risk jail for the sake of a free press, and I said: "There are very few things I am prepared to risk prison for, and one of them is freedom of expression. . . ."

I went off home to Hout Bay, and that weekend went snorkeling in the cold Atlantic.

The messages continued to flood in—from colleagues, black groups, the International Press Institute, publishers' bodies, newspapers, academics, ordinary people, from many parts of the world—most of whom thanked me for giving the public basic information. Ambassador Worrall in London said on television that the matter of my arrest could have been handled with "more finesse."[116]

On November 20 a birthday present was a visit by Mr. Palo Tshume. He had travelled six-hundred miles from Port Elizabeth, representing the "Pebco" community organization in that city, just to shake my hand, say thanks, and return.

I was not, however, elected man of the year by my company.

The managing director of the *Cape Times*, Walter Judge, had executed what he described as a "sideways leap" on reading the interview at home in his Monday morning newspaper, November 4, 1985. He was used to shocks on Monday, because of the South African habits of reckless driving and domestic mayhem at week-ends—always prominently reported on the front page. But he did not expect Tambo.

Judge was naturally miffed because he was not consulted, and he, quite correctly, handed the matter over to John King, managing director of South African Associated Newspapers (S.A.A.N), the parent company in Johannesburg. S.A.A.N. was rather grim.

Legal advice given in Johannesburg was discouraging. It began by asserting that there appeared to be no doubt that the editor had contravened Section (1) (p) of the Internal Security Act, and it was thought not impossible that a charge could be brought under Section 13 (1) (a) (v) which made it an offence to: ". . . encourage the achievement of any of the objects of the unlawful organization . . . or perform any other act of whatever nature which is calculated to further the achievement of any such object." It was felt that it could be argued in court that, in publishing a complete exposition of the approach of the ANC, the *Cape Times* performed an act calculated to further the achievement of the objects of the ANC. On the other hand, it was recognized as important that members of the public should know the objects of the ANC, and the informed hope was expressed that there would be no prosecution under this section, which carried a prison term of up to ten years.

In addition, the lawyers pointed out that Section 58 of the Internal Security Act provided for increased penalties where an offence was committed "by way of protest against any law." It was, however, judged a remote possibility that this would apply.

The lawyers said that directors of the S.A.A.N. company owning the *Cape Times* would be guilty unless it could be proved that the director did not take part in the commission of the offence and could not have prevented it. The lawyers did not fear that any director or manager of S.A.A.N. would be held liable for the actions of the editor. It seemed clear that my deliberate deci-

214

sion not to consult, at least, let the directors and managers off the hook.

The lawyers also noted that under the same Act there was provision for outright prohibition of publication of a newspaper. This had to follow ministerial consideration of a report by an advisory committee made up of a judge and two other persons. Although it was felt that a case could be made out for the prohibition, it was doubted that an advisory committee would agree with this as a result of a single action.

The lawyers, although doubting that in this single case I as editor had jeopardized the existence of the *Cape Times,* felt it could be a factor taken into account by the minister for future action against the paper.

There was some criticism of my actions, particularly non-consultation, but it was accepted that there could be a powerful case for mitigation of punishment.

Managing Director John King invited me to his office in Johannesburg (where I happened to be on business). Somewhat apologetically, he handed me a written rebuke dated November 6, 1985. It read:

> I am acutely distressed that you found it necessary to act in such a high-handed manner and publish the interview with Oliver Tambo (Cape Times November 4, 1985) without consultation with either the Managing Director of the Cape Times or myself.
>
> Your action is not only in breach of your conditions of appointment as editor but has placed the company in a most invidious position and prey to whatever action the Government may wish to exercise. Furthermore, while this one act may be unlikely to cause the prohibition of the Cape Times it will surely serve, together with any previous incidents, to limit the freedom of the paper to comment.
>
> I trust that in the future you will meticulously observe your responsibilities towards the company.

The rebuke could have been at least partly tactical, to have it on "on record" in case the matter got out of hand with the government. King was not at all unfriendly. There was a strong implication, though, that this hot-headed action in Cape Town could

215

complicate the cosmic things the company was doing behind the scenes with government in defence of free expression. I was made to feel a bit of an upstart; I was, sort of, ruining it all by running the Tambo interview.

The whole incident underpinned something that, to me, was grossly ironic. A mere interview was illegal in South Africa. Interviews were routine in a world where Palestinian leader Yassir Arafat was quoted in Israel, SWAPO guerilla leader Sam Nujoma in pre-independence Namibia, even Hitler in wartime Britain . . . but in South Africa knowing what others thought was *verboten,* and publication even earned a *company* rebuke.

Compensation for me was the continued flow of supportive messages. There were so many that they could not all be replied to personally, and thanks were noted in the columns of the newspaper. There was strong support from the fraternity of newspaper people worldwide. The International Press Institute, after a board meeting in Lisbon on November 8, 1985, described the court charges as "persecution, and selective punitive action." The *Guardian* of Britain, noting the three-year maximum sentence, wrote that "journalism is a deadly serious business at the Cape." The *Washington Post* was editorially supportive, as was the Johannesburg *Star,* whose editorial headline was: "Remove this tattered gag." The *Daily News* of Durban carried two editorials of support. A professor of journalism at Rhodes University, Gavin Stewart, wrote a letter which I think sums things up. See Appendix 2, p.256.

In Cape Town, lawyers were hired and we began the painstaking task of preparing a defence with the help of eminent counsel Sydney Kentridge, who had appeared for Steve Biko's family at his inquest and practised in Johannesburg and London. Matters that would be placed before the court were to include:

> The importance of publishing the interview, drawing on evidence from politicians, businessmen, and editors of other newspapers.
> The proper functions of the press, namely to publish both sides of the story as opposed to selective quotes, as had been the case.

216

The fact that the *Cape Times* had published articles covering a broad spectrum and had at times been critical of the ANC, particularly on the question of violence.

The fact that others had published statements by banned or listed persons and had not been prosecuted. To prove this, the defence would consider issuing subpoenas against attorneys-general, other editors, Chief Buthelezi, and Minister Le Grange.

I prepared myself for "vigorous cross examination" by the state on publication of the article, my motives, the fact it was against the law, why ministerial permission was not sought, my ideas on the rule of law and general philosophy. The lawyers warned that the security police would have a dossier on me, and that it would be available to the prosecution for cross-examination purposes.

Senior aides on the *Cape Times* scoured the library to collect items for my defence, including leaders on the ANC either written by myself or published while I was editor; articles showing the *Cape Times*'s attitude to the ANC; pieces showing that the *Cape Times* gave full coverage to everyone who warranted it. Gerald Shaw prepared a memorandum "Audi Alteram Partem," which detailed the paper's tradition of seeking the other viewpoint which went back to the paper's founding.

We were ready for a Supreme Court case early in 1986.

As we prepared, more compensation was to come. Not long after his letter of repudiation, King found himself commending me for the award of the Golden Pen of Freedom by the International Federation of Newspaper Publishers (FIEJ) based in Paris for "particularly deserving" deeds in the cause of the freedom of the press. The nomination had been made by the American Newspaper Publishers Association (ANPA) and the British Newspaper Society.

I heard that a dissident in Russia, Yury Shikhanovich, who had been in detention for many years because of his courageous *samizdat,* or underground, writings, had also been considered for the Golden Pen. I felt that his ordeal justified the award far more than mine. I felt this so strongly that, in my speech in Lisbon on receiving the award, I made an appeal to Soviet leader Gorbachev to release Shikhanovich—and I followed this up, rather ambitiously, with a letter to Gorbachev, delivered to the Soviet Embassy in London: "I should like to draw your attention to the enclosed address I gave in Lisbon recently—particularly the marked section concerning Dr. Yuri Shikhanovich.

"May I add a personal appeal to you to consider his case favourably."[117]

There was no reply. But *glasnost* finally caught up with Shikhanovich. He was pardoned and released in February 1987.

There was an invitation to address the Cape Town Press Club. The Japan Pen Club offered me guest membership, together with ten writers imprisoned in Vietnam, Turkey, and the Soviet Union—including a spirited dissident, Ukranian poet Irina Ratushinskaya. I travelled to the Hague to address the publishers' body of The Netherlands, and addressed the West German publishers in Bonn, and spoke at the International Press Institute annual assembly in Vienna. The year 1986 kept me busy, and the travelling led some journalists to complain that I was "Heard but not seen" in the office. The times were turbulent in South Africa, and I was acutely conscious of the need to be at my desk as much as possible.

The editorial staff of the *Cape Times*, a small band of journalists who had been through trying times covering the unrest, were immensely supportive. They sent a petition to Minister Le Grange asking him to drop charges. He said he found it "surprising that responsible journalists can regard an alleged breach of law passed by Parliament as a 'courageous decision'."[118]

My calculation all along had been that the authorities would duck a trial. Even if it went ahead, it would be a celebrated case, involving the fundamental right to know. The defence could, for instance, draw on Milton, Voltaire, the United States First Amendment, and other powerful free-expression sources and statements to make the point.

I was out on my own recognizances and was not held in custody. I appeared in court on remand several times. Then I was told that in the future my remands could be done in my absence. The prosecution seemed to be losing interest in a trial. There was a suggestion from the prosecution, through our lawyers, that if I pleaded guilty it might be possible to fine the company, which would mean no jail term (suspended or real) for me. This was declined. But the authorities were clearly unkeen on pursuing such a case in court. Suddenly, unilaterally, the state withdrew charges against me personally. They had found a way to get themselves off the hook. They issued summons against the S.A.A.N. company, which owned the *Cape Times,* and fined it a paltry three hundred rands, which was announced on August 13, 1986—nine months after the interview appeared. No one asked me about this; there was no deal that I was aware of. I could not insist on a trial, nor was I keen on one. The interview had been cheap at the price. I regretted nothing.

I met the attorney-general, Niel Rossouw, in St. George's Street, Cape Town, not long after. He was a decent, courteous man with strong Cape connections. We chatted. He said the outcome seemed the best way out for all; he smiled and said he had not wanted to see me go to jail. I always suspected that he had been under pressure from the political authorities to pursue the matter. Although attorneys-general enjoy wide powers in pursuing or dropping prosecutions, pressure from the cabinet was not unknown.

By fining the company, the state's face was saved. A conviction was secured. But I was scot-free.

The Tambo affair thus drew to a close.

The interview was referred to by an expert on the African National Congress, Dr. Tom Lodge, and the text handed into court as an exhibit in a trial in Johannesburg.[119]

Nelson Mandela, it seems, had become an avid reader of the *Cape Times*. He complained in March 1987 to his Cape Town lawyer, Hymie Bernadt, that he had not been receiving copies during the past month in his prison at Pollsmoor. I made sure the oversight was corrected; indeed, I personally handed Bernadt back copies for the past month. Mandela went out of his way to convey his thanks via Bernadt.

219

South African Associated Newspapers was in dire financial straits by 1986. It had a huge overdraft at the bank caused by newspaper trading losses in Johannesburg. In these crisis conditions, Stephen Mulholland left financial journalism and became managing director of S.A.A.N. on April 1, 1986. On the second, he swooped to Cape Town on a night plane and fired Walter Judge, local managing director of the *Cape Times*. Joel Mervis, in *The Fourth Estate*, reports Mulholland's belief that there was no place for Judge in a restructured *Cape Times*.

My colleague Judge—honest, decent, and capable—had kept the company's end up in Cape Town superbly. In line himself for the managing directorship of S.A.A.N. in the seventies, he had declined the job prospect. In highly competitive trading conditions, he had maintained the *Cape Times*'s profitability. Making dramatic breakthroughs into property and other advertising fields which had been the preserve of the rival *Argus* newspaper in Cape Town, he had tweaked the tail of the giant Johannesburg-based Argus Printing and Publishing Company. His efficiency and success could have justified professional envy in some S.A.A.N. quarters in Johannesburg. Judge was axed at a time when the mining houses, suddenly discovering their responsibilities as owners of the commercially warring English-language press, were moving—belatedly—to rationalize the industry to save money. He was portrayed as standing in the way of this necessary step. His "enforced retirement" was criticized in a letter to the S.A.A.N. chairman by a director, Leycester Walton (a former S.A.A.N. managing director and chairman of the local management board of the *Cape Times*). Walton, who had been abroad when Judge was fired, spoke of his "firstclass job" for the *Cape Times,* and discounted charges that it was Judge who had obstructed newspaper rationalization. Walton wrote (May 9, 1986): "A very senior and loyal Cape Times servant whose performance has been excellent finds that his immediate resignation is demanded without any explanation given."

The dramatic Judge firing, incidentally, gave Mulholland an early chance to show his managerial mettle. He was clearly out to be a "mover and shaker" as chief executive and saviour of S.A.A.N.

Joint operating agreements (J.O.A.s) were set up between S.A.A.N. papers and the more powerful Argus company. In Cape Town this meant heavy *Cape Times* staff redundancy, and a physical move by the editorial staff into the Argus building (happily renamed Newspaper House). Initially, there was much staff unhappiness and intrigue—including attempts, with which I was associated, to get local business interests to buy the *Cape Times* out of S.A.A.N. and return it to the independence it had enjoyed from its founding in 1876 up until 1973. The mine industry owners, partial as ever to monopolies, were not sellers—and I pointedly was told not to "interfere."

I was not politically popular with government nor with S.A.A.N. conservatives, and there were published rumours that I was next in line for firing, which Mulholland strenuously denied. Our paper's circulation had dipped after an earlier decision to raise its selling price above that of the *Argus* in order to maintain profitability in difficult times. But circulation recovery was around the corner, and the J.O.A. soon settled down well and guaranteed continuing profitability.

As August 1987 dawned, I had done sixteen years and some three thousand editorials as editor of the *Cape Times*. It was my turn for the chop.

CHAPTER SEVENTEEN

# OUT

## AUGUST 7, 1987

CAPE TOWN (AP) [August 7, 1987.]—Times Media Ltd., one of South Africa's major newspaper chains, has dismissed Anthony Heard as editor of the *Cape Times* without explanation.

Heard, 49, was with the *Cape Times,* the white-ruled country's oldest newspaper with a daily circulation of about 50,000, for 30 years and served as editor for 16 years. He crusaded vigorously at home and abroad against government press restrictions.

Times Media Ltd. made no mention of Heard's future and gave no reason for the dismissal, saying only that Heard had enjoyed a distinguished career and "after 16 years as editor it was felt that the time had come for a successor to be appointed" . . .

Under Heard's leadership, the *Cape Times* often tested press restrictions, imposed under President P. W. Botha's national emergency decree in June 1986. He encouraged his reporters to challenge government versions of continuing civil unrest and police actions to subdue it.

Heard was charged with violating the Internal Security Act by publishing on Nov. 4, 1985, a full-page interview with Oliver

Tambo, president of the outlawed African National Congress. It is illegal in South Africa to quote Tambo or other ANC officials without specific government permission.

The charges against Heard were withdrawn in July 1986. The newspaper group, then called South African Associated Newspapers, subsequently paid a small admission-of-guilt fine.

The black nationalist ANC is fighting to overthrow the white-led government of South Africa and dismantle the apartheid racial separation system.

## LAW AND CUSTOM

By law and custom, apartheid establishes a racially segregated society in which the 25.6 million blacks have no vote in national affairs. The five million whites control the economy and maintain separate districts, schools and health services.

The International Federation of Newspaper Publishers awarded Heard the Golden Pen of Freedom award in May 1986.

He gave speeches in several countries on press censorship in South Africa. He told the Dutch Newspaper Publishers' Association last November: "It is, unhappily, not possible to . . . say that the South African press is still free."

Heard said the press restrictions, now in force for most of the past 14 months, "make it difficult if not impossible to perform our simple but necessary task of informing the public of what is going on around them."

Tony Weaver, Western Cape vice-president of the South African Society of Journalists and assistant news editor at the *Cape Times,* was highly critical of the decision to replace Heard.

He said today: "Whatever weak excuses are given . . . (for dismissing Heard) there can be only one reason—buckling to government, police and right-wing pressure."


# AUGUST 12, 1987

You may assure Tony—indeed you may give him the categorical assurance—that our decision to appoint a new Editor had nothing whatsoever to do with his integrity or moral probity. If Tony so wishes we are prepared to issue a public statement to this effect. As we have said in public, the decision has been made for practical, commercial reasons, and our view that we need a new Editor to apply a fresh mind to the problem of increasing circulation, and tackle various managerial and related problems. —Statement by

224

Stephen Mulholland, managing director, Times Media Ltd (formerly S.A.A.N.), to Richard Rosenthal, attorney of Cape Town, August 12, 1987.

# EPILOGUE: SEASON OF REAPPEARANCES

Dismissal from the editorship of the *Cape Times,* in my view, was unimportant and my circumstances comfortable compared with happenings in South Africa.

Afrikaners were marching again. The "fighting commandos" and "private armies" mentioned by George Heard in his columns were regrouping. It was fifty years later. Afrikanerdom, once again, was bitterly divided.

Sons were taking up the armed struggle where fathers, grandfathers, and great-grandfathers had left off. War cries echoed those of the Boer Wars, Afrikaner rebellion in World War I, and pro-German violence on the home front in World War II. Now, in the 1990s, came a last-ditch, right-wing attempt to save the Afrikaner "volk" from the inevitable—integration with their fellow South Africans.

This time it was not the old Boer commandos, rebels, Ossewa-brandwag, or Stormjaers preparing for war. It was their political heirs, the Afrikaner Weerstandsbeweging (resistance movement) and a cacophony of other militant right-wing groups.

This time they were not marshalling their armed force against the British Empire or a pro-British South African government. They were aiming their anger and their violence at the government of a fellow-Afrikaner with impeccable Nationalist credentials, President Frederik W. de Klerk. He had dared to unban black nationalist organizations, release Nelson Mandela and others from prison, and loosen up political life. He had dared to make South Africa more normal—if not completely normal. The right wing charged that he had betrayed Afrikanerdom; that the country was moving to black rule . . . the end of the white man in Africa. They openly threatened a Third Boer War.

De Klerk found his life endangered as gravely as Afrikaner dissidents on the Left. An ironic thread that bound him to Nelson Mandela was the mutual possibility of assassination. He moved with speed and urgency in some areas of liberalization, but baulked at early and total repeal of some pillars of apartheid. He faced major crises in the area of human rights because of the alleged activities of death squads aimed against the Left. But he promised South Africans a negotiated future, with an end to discrimination and oppression. Time would tell whether he could deliver.

Meanwhile, black groupings which had been banned since 1960 and the Communist Party (banned ten years before that) emerged and blinked in the light of South African day. They prepared to fight legally the battle they had fought as exiles and underground guerillas. It was a season of reappearances. Once-young faces in radical politics were seen again, now aged. The masses marched and protested in the streets. There was an air of expectation after the release of Mandela, a rare man whose stature increased with freedom. But there was also division and enmity, particularly in the province of Natal.

The scene was set for the final reckoning between white and black. Two big questions were: how much violence would accompany the move to majority rule and what type of economy would a new South Africa construct. The alternative to a relatively quick and peaceful transfer of power under a workable economic system could be human chaos as in Lebanon or Kampuchea, economic collapse as in the Eastern bloc, and historic enmity as in Ulster. The hopeful scenario would make South Africa the generous giant of Africa, a non-racial example to the world, meshing together the best from available economic systems; the latter, a race war and economic disaster for the international community to worry about or forget.

After a massive, forty-year detour against the tide of post-war history, South Africa was exhausted by border wars, repression, riot, double-digit inflation, and racial bitterness. Communities were forced into racial mosaics. Many whites and blacks could not communicate properly, as equals, because of the years of apartheid. Finding one another was to be difficult. An unexpected by-product of apartheid was a plethora of counters, doors, and duplicated buildings and services—provided by zealots to accommodate the races separately. The country of little bells had become the country of banging doors.

Hopefully, most whites were being led into a realization that they would either settle with blacks or go under. The right-wing organizations were due to learn, or be taught, this lesson in the 1990s—some of them the hard way by running foul of ordinary law. Political and social justice before the year 2000 seemed a real prospect, given good leadership and good fortune.

There are different paths that lead out of Langa, but one I shall not forget. It was followed by many of the marchers who set out on that historic occasion on March 30, 1960, to walk in dignity to Cape Town. Langa was not much changed when I revisited it in 1990. The four-storey "single zones" stood as they did in 1960, with half-made pavements and litter strewn around—just as they had been when Lombard's body was found, except for a "Welcome Mandela" daubing on a wall. The red-roofed building of the old "Bantu commissioner's court," the seat of sausage-machine justice associated with the pass laws, still stood; but its function had ended with the abolition of those laws. It had become a police station. The court, a policeman said, had "gone to Athlone" nearby. The same gum trees bowed to the south-easter wind at the Langa entrance; the same modest single-storey houses, where the faces had been pressed to windows on the night of the Langa riot, stood there as before (though something new was hoardings offering residents new, permanent homes). The same untidy corrugated iron fencing was strung around houses outside Langa as one left. The same town of Pinelands lived its leafy white life hardly a stone's throw away. It was almost as if thirty years had not happened. But this time no permission was needed for whites to enter Langa, and there were more women and children in evidence.

The route of the upper part of the march had become a huge new freeway, the N2, which swung past a massively rebuilt

Groote Schuur Hospital—and then, as De Waal Drive, snaked down to the city past a shooting range where nervous whites practised with sidearms in a quarry. Shooting ranges had proliferated over the years; the most telling commentary on events was the fact that a well-known coffee house in a basement, called "Die Koffiehuis," which used to be frequented by the National Party establishment in the centre of the city, had itself become a shooting range. At a point near the hospital where De Waal Drive divided, a new freeway, Eastern Boulevard, dived to the right on a more direct route to the city. It passed through the barren, grassy fields, dotted with defiant mosques and churches, which were once District Six. What "group areas" did not achieve in destroying District Six, this freeway had finished off. The spot at the Jutland Flyover bridge where Philip Kgosana's crowd paused before marching into the city was unchanged, with those huge conifer trees, some bent by years of wind, giving shade. On the route from there down to the city, the old Roeland Street jail was closed, its renovated building housing the national archives. Caledon Square police station stood in the same forbidding red brick, its large wooden doors closed, and its innards smelling of law and order. Parliament, much extended and embellished in the portentous Botha era, stood a couple of blocks away. That was the place the marchers did not reach.

Dr. Verwoerd and his Bantustan ideology had finally departed. The National Party made the break under De Klerk after false starts under Botha. Indeed, the party had tried all brands of apartheid and showed none could work. By trying, they made the country the polecat of the world and all but ruined it.

Left to remind the nation of Verwoerd's era was a huge, forbidding-looking grey building jutting into the sky next to Parliament. It bore his name. Its windowpanes were given a gold tint to deflect the sun. Housing the cabinet and administrative offices of government in Cape Town, this building awaited the unfolding destiny of South Africa. In May 1990 I was in that building to hear the deep, insistent voice of Nelson Mandela addressing a press conference together with President De Klerk.

I thought: one day this building will be renamed.

# APPENDIX 1: INTERVIEW WITH OLIVER TAMBO

*There has been a flurry of talks with the African National Congress recently, including the leaders of big business and the Progressive Federal Party. These contacts have raised questions about where the ANC stands on critical issues. So far, everyone's view but that of the ANC has been given in South Africa. The Editor of the Cape Times, Anthony Heard, met the 68-year-old ANC leader Oliver Tambo in his North London home last week and conducted an interview with what came across as an essentially moderate black leader. The Cape Times publishes the full interview as a contribution to peaceful solutions in South Africa in a matter of over-whelming public importance.*

*The ANC is officially portrayed in South Africa as a communist, terrorist-type organization, almost presented to the public as demons. Now, since the public have no access to your views, how would you answer this, particularly the charge of being a communist-controlled organization?*

It is important to observe that this has been a persistent portrayal of the ANC by many people who are opposed to us. But the ANC is as ANC as it ever was. It is true that the ANC has members of the Communist Party who are members of the ANC. That has been the case almost since time immemorial. The ANC was established in 1912 and the SA Communist Party in 1921, and so there has been an overlapping of membership all along the line. But ANC members who are also members of the SACP make a very clear distinction between these two independent bodies. We co-operate a lot but the ANC is accepted by the SACP as leading the struggle. There is absolute loyalty to that position. It is often suggested that the ANC is controlled by the Communist Party . . . by communists. Well, I have been long enough in the ANC to know that that has never been true.

The Communist Party has its positions and the ANC has its positions. The ANC is guided in its policy and all its members are loyal to the Freedom Charter, and that is where you find all the positions of the ANC. They are reflected in the Freedom Charter. We don't depart from the Freedom Charter. So, there is no problem of the ANC being controlled. Now this is also extended to control by the Soviet Union; much of this is propaganda. We go to the Soviet Union as we go to Sweden and to Holland and to Italy to ask for assistance in one form or another. And in all these countries we do get assistance, and assistance is given quite unconditionally. The Western countries, who do support us and we very much appreciate the assistance they give us, do not give us weapons of course, because they generally do not approve and their laws do not allow it. But in the socialist countries we get the weapons, so we go there to get what we can't get elsewhere. And that's all there is in it.

*Are you getting more support from the West now?*

We are getting a great deal of support from the West, increasing support, in material terms, too; that support is growing.

*So the charge that you are a communist organization, you would reject strongly?*

We would reject that. We would say that there is a communist party. So we are fortunate because if one is looking for a communist party it is there, but the ANC is not the Communist Party.

Now, the other aspect of being terrorists: Again, there is a lot of exaggeration about this terrorism. Long before we had injured a soul, when we were very, very careful in our sabotage actions to avoid hurting anybody, and that is what we have been doing for the better part of 20 years now . . . even when we started, this was called terrorism. We knew what terrorism was and we thought that the people of South Africa are being misled about

232

what terrorism was. We could have been terrorists if we had wanted to, but we chose not to be. So even that has been an exaggeration. It is true that more recently, as for instance in May 1983 when a bomb exploded and others were attempted, this was stepping up things. It is proper to recognize that this was after 20 years at it. We started in 1961 and 20 years later you get a bomb exploding. We could have done this much, much earlier on numerous occasions. We did not want to be seen as terrorists; we are trying to put on pressure. And we have been notoriously restrained in our armed actions—notoriously.

*What future do you see for whites in the future South Africa?*

The ANC, and all of us in the ANC, have always considered and accepted that whites like ourselves belong to our country. They are compatriots, fellow-citizens. We took the earliest opportunity to dispel the notion that we were fighting to drive the whites out to somewhere and we made it clear that they belong to South Africa. They had their role to play as we would like to think we had a role to play although we are excluded. And so this has been basic. We have asked whites to join us in the struggle to get rid of the tensions that come with the apartheid system. We have hoped that we could together build the future non-racial South Africa, and by non-racial we really do mean non-racial. We mean a society in which each one feels he or she belongs together with everybody else, where the fact of race and colour is of no consequence, where people serve according to their abilities and their skills, where we together work to unite our people, and we have adopted policies which discourgaed the polarization of our people either into ethnic groups or into white versus black.

*And do you distinguish between any particular white group?*

No, no. Our charter says that South Africa belongs to all who live in it and we say that people who have chosen SA as their home are welcome there. There is plenty of room for them, and we should accept them as South Africans and they in turn should accept us as South Africans. This is the kind of society that we are hoping will emerge.

*Is there any reassurance or assurance that you could give whites about their physical sofety, their jobs and their home security under an ANC-led government? How would you address the question of their insecurity, which is manifest at the moment?*

What we would hope our white compatriots will learn to understand is that we don't really see them as whites in the first instance. We see them as fellow South Africans in the first instance. They are as good as black. In fact, let us say, they are Africans. We see them as Africans. We are all born there in that country, or most of us are. We live on this continent. It is our country. Let's move away from these distinctions of Europeans and non-Europeans, whites and non-whites.

*So, it is security for all, as it were?*

It is. It is security for all, and it would be in the interests of all of us that everybody feels secure. Everyone's property is secure; everyone's home is secure. The culture is secure. We believe our cultures will begin to merge. We have got a rich variety which, when it comes together, is really going to be something we can put out to the world. So all this would be respected. There would be room for it all. But the main thing is, and the sooner we begin to grapple with this problem the better, not to proceed on the basis that the Africans are going to do something to the non-Africans, but to begin on the basis that we all belong to that country. Let us not look at one another's colour. Let us not address that. Let us see one another merely as fellow-citizens.

*How do you view the business leaders, the PFP, the dominees who have been seeking talks with the ANC? How do you feel about this?*

We feel very good indeed because, you see, in the fifties when we were a legal organization we were getting across very effectively to the white community. The ANC was getting accepted and its objectives were getting generally accepted among the whites. We were uniting the country where apartheid separated it. Now this is because we had access.

I recall Chief Albert Lutuli (the late ANC leader) going to Cape Town. . . . And do you remember the effect he had, the impact he made. Well, when he came back to Johannesburg from that trip, there were thousands of white people at Park Station; thousands who came to meet him as a result of the impact he had made. So this is the kind of situation that had developed. Then we got banned and this contact was broken. And now the white community has been brought up to regard the ANC as something very, very dangerous. The one effect of this visit by the business people has been to open the lines of communication because I am sure they saw us as something very different from the way we had been projected all the time, and I think they said as much.

*Are you keeping in touch?*

We do keep in touch. And then we next looked forward to the visit of the young people. We thought what a good thing that they should get together and begin to look at their future together. This was a very good thing. And the contribution is not one-sided. It is not as if we are giving or receiving all the time. I think we are enriching one another with views about what should be done with our situation. We had hoped to see the ministers of religion who wanted to come. We thought that was another opportunity. Then of course the PFP came along and we had very good exchanges with them. All this is much-needed communication, especially at this time because at some point we have got to agree on what to do about our own future.

*Could you briefly set out your economic theory, particularly on questions like nationalization and wealth redistribution?*

I don't know if I would call it a theory. It appears in our charter and all we do is to interpret what the charter says. We have not attempted to depart from that in any way. We start with what the charter says and broadly the interpretation is that the state would control some of the industries, solely with a view to ensuring an equitable distribution of the wealth that we have and I think that this was at the back of the minds of the people who drew up the charter, and it was more than the ANC. We said our country is very wealthy, our country is poverty-stricken as far as the blacks are concerned, and by blacks I mean coloureds and everybody else. They are very poor. Even the whites are not really wealthy but the wealth is contained in the hands of a few. And we look at the country: 13 percent overcrowded by millions of landless people who are starving and dying.

What do you do about this? Where do you get the land from to give them? You have got to address that question. You have got to say how to end this poverty, how do we handle the wealth we produce in such a way that we can relieve some of these problems. The solution we saw was one of nationalization, and, of course, when we meet the business people they say that nationalization will destroy the South African economy.

*Do they accept some measure of redistribution?*

They seemed to. Yes they do. They accept some measure of redistribution. It is the method, the mechanism, how to achieve it—this is of course where we did not agree and could not agree. But they accepted, they understood, what we were trying to get at: That you cannot have a new South Africa which does not address this problem.

*What about private property; how far would nationalization extend, as you see it?*

It would be a mixed economy. And certainly nationalization would take into account the situation as we find it at the time—the realities of the situation in which we find ourselves. But there would be private ownership, there would be levels of private enterprise and it would all be geared to the situation that obtains at the time. Also, we don't envisage fighting in the streets over it. We think that we will have to approach this from the point of view of what the people want. If the people want one form of distribution above another, well, it must be like that.

*There would be a debate about the level of nationalization?*

Yes, there would be a debate.

*What sort of environment could that debate take place in? Would you see free media, free expression, freedom of newspapers?*

Absolutely.

*What about violence? In what circumstances would you as leader of the ANC be prepared to renounce violence and start talks? What are the circumstances that can bring that about because I think that's what, frankly, everyone wants, on all sides; in other words, the violence, on all sides, to stop. I am sure that no one wants it to go on forever.*

No, not even we. This question of violence worries many people. The unfortunate thing is that people tend to be worried about the violence that comes from the oppressed. And so the tendency is to want to know, as you want to know, on what terms would we end violence. Really, there would be no violence at all if we did not have the violence of the apartheid system. And even if there was, and there has been for two decades, it's been restrained. But if you look at what comes from the other side, during those two decades there has been massive violence. So we then have to say to ourselves: Of course we can stop our struggle, we can stop even our violent actions, but on that basis what would be the reason for that? And in return for what?

*Is there a possibility of a truce?*

There is always a possibility of a truce. We see the possibility of a truce. It would be very, very easy, if, for example, we started negotiations. We have said that negotiations can start, serious negotiations. . . .

*With the government?*

Yes, with the government, when they are ready because at the moment we think they are not ready. And we have said to them that if you wanted negotiations, we would not go into that without Nelson Mandela and the other political leaders and the political prisoners. Now, a serious indication of readiness for negotiations would be the release of all these leaders, because they have got to be part of the process of preparation for serious negotiations which will not just be talks for the sake of talking. It is quite conceivable that in that situation of preparing for negotiations and looking at necessary conditions and so on, this question could arise. But we have had a problem about just saying we are now suspending our struggle, which is what it would mean. . . .

*On one side, as it were?*

On one side, without any indication on the other side of their willingness to do anything about what every one of us knows is their violence. We have said: Lift the state of emergency, pull out the troops from the townships, and the police. And release the political prisoners. We have even said unban the ANC. Do all these things to create a climate.

*Which you would welcome?*

We would welcome a climate of that kind, and if the rest of the leaders were there I think it would be time to get together and put the question: Can we really do anything about this? Everybody would then be there. But we are getting this persistent refusal on the part of Botha either to release Nelson Mandela and the other political prisoners, and we say: What are you going to do with treason trials . . . it is simply a form of repression. Who are you going to negotiate with, if you want to negotiate. If he withdrew the treason trials and did all these things by way of lifting the pressures that rest on us, we would begin to see that the other side are ready to talk.

But we have argued that it is not necessary for hostilities to cease before negotiations start. . . . Before Nkomati accord, there were lengthy negotiations between the South Africans and others before there was any signing of an agreement. The agreement that was signed in Lusaka between the South Africans and the Angolans was preceded by a series of meetings and negotiations.

*Is anything going on at the moment . . . i.e., talks about talks between the ANC and the South African Government?*

No, nothing at all. Which is why we think that they are not ready to have any talks. They are not even ready for other people to talk to us. We are South Africans. If we meet we can only talk about our country. We are not going to fight about it. We talk about it, and they don't like this. But I think what they do not like is that in meeting we get to understand each other better, and we, the ANC, certainly benefit from these talks, and we would think that those we talk to also benefit. So this is moving in the direction of resolving our problems, but they are not prepared for that.

*Violence against people, civilians. What is the ANC's attitude on this, bearing in mind the fact that down the years the ANC has in my opinion held back to a great extent on what one might call indiscriminate violence or going for soft targets?*

I am glad you have put it that way, because it is often forgotten that we have been at the receiving end all the time, and we have held back. And it is not conceivable that we could go on like that indefinitely without anything changing. But one must see in this holding back the reluctance of the ANC on questions of violence. But when once, of course, we have decided we have got to fight then we must fight.

239

*What about soft targets?*

The question of soft targets has been exaggerated out of all proportion. As I have once had occasion to observe, when the police go into a township and shoot, when they did on the 21st March, repeating Sharpeville, they were hitting soft targets, and this whole year has been a year of shootings of, really, soft targets. So people are being killed. It has never been quite like this. But they are being shot and even children are being killed . . . so when the ANC talks about soft targets this creates an alarm and yet the ANC is going no further than saying that we have got to intensify our struggle if we are in a struggle. If we stop, we stop. But if we are in struggle and we feel the demand of the situation is that we struggle, then we must intensify that struggle. We have held back for too long. Now, if we do intensify we are not going to be choosing carefully to avoid hurting anybody, but we will move into military personnel, police and so on.

*But you won't go for civilians as such?*

No we will not go for civilians as such. We think that civilians will be hit as they are hit always. They were hit in Zimbabwe . . .

*In a crossfire situation?*

A crossfire situation, in any war situation.

*But not cinemas, and supermarkets and . . . ?*

We will not go into cinemas and bars and places like that. We won't do that. But we will certainly be looking for military personnel, police and so on.

*Why will you hold back, because often in a guerilla war the limits do get more and more extended? Is it a moral feeling about killing civilians, or what?*

240

Because we are not fighting against people, we are fighting against a system, and we can't kill people. Why? Why would we kill them? We cannot even kill whites because we are not fighting whites at all. We are fighting a system.

*On foreign policy, do you see SA as a pro-Western, non-aligned, or as a Soviet-socialist-leaning country? For instance, in the sale of minerals and raw materials—would these be denied to anyone? What about Commonwealth membership? Where do you see South Africa standing in the world?*

First of all, non-aligned in terms of East-West, developing trade with all the countries of the world, strengthening trade links, so maintaining the lines of trade for mutual benefit.

*So the Americans can be sure of getting their needs?*

The Americans will be sure to get it, if they are willing to pay for it. We would want to trade with all the countries of the world, in the interests of our own economy.

We would come back to the Commonwealth because the basis for the exclusion of South Africa would have gone. And we will establish very peaceful relations with countries. We will work very closely with the rest of the African continent, and certainly with the countries of Southern Africa. We would become members of SADDC or it might be called another name by then, and we could build together a small common market of our own. South Africa would therefore be admitted into this wider economic grouping than we have in Southern Africa. And we would be a very influential country in the world.

*Do you feel this would unleash resources that we have not been able to unleash?*

I am certain. I think the economy itself would be stimulated by the energies that would be unleashed, and the prospects of peace and stability. We think the country would be transformed, politically and socially and economically.

*I presume you favour sanctions. Do you to the point where people lose jobs and the economy suffers seriously?*

We think the economy must be put into difficulties because the economy strengthens the regime. It enables them to do all the things that they want to do. This question of losing jobs, for the victims of apartheid it is nothing. To be a victim of apartheid means to be many, many things above losing a job which you are losing all the time anyway. And the way we look at it is: The more effective the sanctions are, the less the scope and scale of conflict.

*If there was a new grouping in SA white politics, with liberal Afrikaners who were formerly Nationalists and Progressive Federal Party people like Slabbert forming a new bloc, would you be prepared to deal with them and on what basis?*

We have met Van Zyl Slabbert and we hope to meet various leaders of organizations. An organization that is opposed to the apartheid system we regard as on our side. I don't think that we would refuse contact with such an organization because we would see it moving in the direction that we are. We do of course encourage our white countrymen to mobilize and make their contribution to changing the apartheid system and on that basis we ought to be able to find a *modus operandi* with them.

*You strike me as a somewhat reluctant revolutionary. With what measure of enthusiasm did you turn to accept that there had to be violence? How did you yourself personally respond to this?*

I suppose I was angry and frustrated, like we all were, and I continued to be angry and frustrated, to feel that this system must be fought. But I was a full supporter of the policy of non-violence because we thought it would bring us the fulfilment of our objective. When that failed then we had to look for an alternative. We found the alternative in combining political and armed actions and it is one of those things that you have to do as there is no alternative. I don't think I am peculiar in this respect, I think that many people in the ANC would be glad if there was no need for violence, but the need is there and we have got to go ahead with it, bitter as it is.

It is painful to see anybody being killed, to see children being killed, no matter who kills them. The death of children is a painful thing and you do have to say what brought us to this situation where these things are happening. We naturally feel that it is the system that has made it impossible for us to avoid what we strove to avoid with such resolve when we were first confronted with this violence. But as individuals, and certainly as an individual, I don't like violence.

*You are enjoying great attention in London. To what do you ascribe this?*

I think generally, in many parts of the world there is a lot of interest in what is happening in SA, and people are discussing it. And when a member of the ANC in my position is around, many people want to try and understand where we go from here. What is more, the discussion now revolves around the question of what sort of South Africa. In the past there was just denunciation of apartheid and so on, but a new interest has emerged, an interest in what takes the place of what we are seeing now and how do we move from the present to something different. This represents real movement forward for us. We have reached the point where people are expecting change and are beginning to reflect what that change involves and this has been part of the interest. People want to know, when apartheid goes (because they are sure apartheid is going), what takes its place.

*To what extent is the current internal unrest in South Africa orchestrated by the ANC and to what extent is it spontaneous?*

Both words are not very applicable. There is a great deal of spontaneity in the sense that when you shoot at people they are

243

angered and want to do something in retaliation. You would not say that the ANC is orchestrating all these responses. They are almost natural. So there is an element of spontaneity. But I would not use the word orchestrated. I would say that the ANC has called on our people, and in some cases they are very disciplined about it, in others there are excesses; the ANC has said let us destroy these structures of separation and apartheid. That is where it starts. Now in this process other factors come in. The authorities come in and shoot and the people respond . . . and you have a situation of escalation which can tend to conceal the true nature of the conflict as being the people resisting the implementation of the apartheid system and preventing it from working. This is the essence.

# Appendix 2: For the Record

This is the letter of appointment which, essentially unchanged, was traditionally given to editors of the *Cape Times*.

---

## CAPE TIMES LIMITED

*Newspaper Proprietors*

77 BURG STREET · CAPE TOWN · P.O. BOX 11
*Telephone 41-3361 · Telegrams 'Times' · Telex No. 57522*

30th July, 1971

A.H. Heard, Esq.,
Cape Times Limited,
77 Burg Street,
CAPE TOWN.

Dear Mr. Heard,

You have been appointed Editor of the Cape Times on the following conditions:-

1. The appointment will take effect as from the 1st September, 1971.

2. Your salary will be at the rate of R900 per month.

3. You will be entitled to receive R165 per month as an entertainment and transport allowance.

4. Your services are to be available to the newspaper in a fulltime capacity and you will not engage yourself in any outside work or serve on any committee without permission in writing given by the Chairman of the Board.

5. Your engagement is subject to termination on six months' notice to that effect being given by you or by the Company. The Company has the right to pay six months' salary in lieu of such notice.

6. Provided they do not involve any departure from the established and recognised policy and practice of the Cape Times you will conform to all instructions and directions from time to time given by the Chairman of the Board of Directors on behalf of the Company.

/2.....

*Directors: C. S. Corder (Chairman), D. A. St. C. Hennessy, G. M. C. Crosswright (Managing), F. Fisher, S. L. Lloyd (Br.), I. G. MacPherson, C. C. Norris, R. B. Stuttaford*
*Alternates: E. A. Catamby, W. Judge, I. R. Bancroft Baker*

245

It is understood that:-

(a)  The aim of the paper should be to maintain its
     dignity and its reputation for accuracy and re-
     sponsibility.

(b)  In its tone the paper should avoid anything either
     by way of selection or presentation savouring of
     sensationalism.

(c)  Headlines should faithfully reflect the facts and
     importance of the news to which they are attached.

(d)  Criticism of public authorities and institutions
     on questions of fact, either by members of the staff,
     contributors or the public, should not be published
     unless and until those who are criticised have been
     given an opportunity to furnish their version of the
     facts or to present their side of the case.

7.   Both the Editor and the General Manager of the paper
are equally and independently responsible to the Board,
but it is important that a relationship of close co-
operation should be maintained in all matters affecting
the interests of the paper.  Matters in respect of which
there may be disagreement should be referred to the Chairman.

8.   The Editor shall not incur on behalf of the paper any
considerable additional expenditure without discussion with
the General Manager and approval by the Chairman.

     If you agree to the arrangement set out herein please
let me have a formal notification to that effect.

                         Yours faithfully,
                         CAPE TIMES LIMITED


                         CHAIRMAN

An example of the type of communication newspapers could receive before action was taken to stop publication at the height of the Information Scandal.

Telegramadres
Telegraphic address } "GOVAT"

Telefoon
Telephone } No. 45-3101

Privaatsak
Private bag } 9001

Kode
Code } 8001

J 459

Geliewe in u antwoord te verwys na
In reply please quote
No. 10.19/79/B1

DEPARTEMENT VAN JUSTISIE · DEPARTMENT OF JUSTICE
REPUBLIEK VAN SUID-AFRIKA · REPUBLIC OF SOUTH AFRICA

DIE ADJUNK-STAATSPROKUREUR
DEPUTY STATE ATTORNEY

2de VLOER, HOMES TRUSTGEBOU
2nd FLOOR, HOMES TRUST BUILDING

WAALSTRAAT
WALE STREET

KAAPSTAD
CAPE TOWN

8001

12 March 1979

The Editor
The Cape Times
CAPE TOWN
8001

Dear Sir

THE RHOODIE STORY

I write to you on the instructions of the Honourable Mr Justice R P B Erasmus, Adv G F Smalberger S C and Adv A J Lategan S C who presently comprise a commission of enquiry into alleged irregularities in the former Department of Information (hereinafter referred to as "the Commission").

In the editions of The Cape Times which appeared on 9, 10 and 12 March respectively, you published extensive reports on purported disclosures by dr Eschel Rhoodie concerning various matters which are presently being investigated by the Commission.

I refer you to the relevant Regulation promulgated in Government Gazette No 6211 of 7 November 1978 (Regulation Gazette No 2689) and for your information I quote Regulation 14:

    14.  No person shall insult, disparage or belittle the
         Commission or a member of the Commission or pre-
         judice, influence or anticipate the proceedings
         or findings of the Commission.

The Commission is of the opinion that the aforesaid reports are of a nature to prejudice, influence and anticipate the eventual findings of the Commission. Furthermore, it is clear that you intend to continue publishing further reports of a like nature.

The Commission therefore intends to bring an urgent application to the Supreme Court to interdict the further publication of such reports and we hereby give you notice that the papers are present-

2/ ........

247

ly being drawn and will be served on you as soon as they have
been completed.

The Commission intends to move as soon as possible for an interdict which will apply to tomorrow's edition of The Cape Times
as well as future editions, and this should be borne in mind by
you when tomorrow's edition is being prepared.


Yours faithfully


D G CONRADIE.
for DEPUTY STATE ATTORNEY
/HG

# Statement issued by the SA Media Council's Chairman, the Honourable Mr L de V van Winsen (former Appeal Court Judge), on Thursday, December 11, 1986.

Emergency regulations affecting the media and promulgated in today's Government Gazette extraordinary give rise to grave concern for the future of our country.

They constitute the most far-reaching constraints yet placed upon the free flow of news during the present crisis.

The existing situation poses a serious threat to people of all races, a situation which must be taken into account by the media in their coverage of current events.

As is stated in the preamble to the Media Council's Constitution, the press, radio and television services have as their prime function the duty to inform the public accurately and, where appropriate, to comment fairly on matters of public interest without fear or favour.

Their task is to keep the public reliably and timeously informed on all aspects of the situation to the best of their ability. Ignorance serves only to make the public more vulnerable to threats to their security.

The Media Council has felt obliged to warn against the consequences of previous restrictions imposed by the Government on the availability of informed news and comment. These latest regulations move even further in the same direction and will place the public at an even greater disadvantage.

There is a double jeopardy in that, in addition to depriving the public of vital information, the regulations seek also to deprive the public of the knowledge that they are being so deprived. This result is sought by preventing the media from drawing attention to the forced omission of certain news and views which omissions would lull the public into a false and potentially fatal sense of complacency.

Failure to draw attention to the risk entailed in the new regulations and to appeal for reconsideration would be a dereliction of the public responsibility delegated by the Media Council's charter.

CHAIRMAN

LDEVVW/RCS/sp

11 December 1986

# General Swart's famous "tee-shirt" order.

ORDER BY THE DIVISIONAL COMMISSIONER OF THE
SOUTH AFRICAN POLICE FOR THE WESTERN PROVINCE
DIVISION

Under the powers vested in me by Regulation 6 of the
Regulations promulgated under the Public Safety Act,
1953 (Act no 3 of 1953) by Proclamation R201 of
26 October 1985, I, CHRISTOFFEL ANTHONIE SWART
Divisional Commissioner of the South African
Police for the Western Province Division,
hereby issue with effect from 30th JANUARY 1986
up to and including 15 FEBRUARY 1986 with reference
to the Magisterial Districts of BELLVILLE, GOODWOOD,
KUILSRIVER, SIMONSTOWN, THE CAPE and WYNBERG the order
contained in the Schedule

## S C H E D U L E

No person shall in any place affix, display or distribute ·
any placard, banner, sticker, pamphlet, clothing or similar
object on or in which any viewpoint of a political nature
or in relation to any system of Government or Constitutional
policy is expressed, advocated or propagated.


Signed at CAPE TOWN this 29th day of JANUARY 1986

                                                    Brigadier
DIVISIONAL COMMISSIONER : SOUTH AFRICAN POLICE
WESTERN PROVINCE DIVISION
C  A  SWART

The code of conduct in terms of which signatory members of the Newpaper Press Union operated as part of their voluntary self-disciplinary arrangements.

# CODE OF CONDUCT

## 1. Preamble

The freedom of the media is indivisible from, and subject to the same legal and moral restraints as that of the individual and rests on the public's fundamental right to be informed.

## 2. Reporting of news

2.1 The media shall be obliged to report news truthfully, accurately and objectively.

2.2 News shall be presented in the correct context and in a balanced manner, without intentional or negligent departure from the facts whether by:

    2.2.1 distortion, exaggeration or misrepresentation;

    2.2.2 material omissions; or

    2.2.3 summarisation.

2.3 Only what may reasonably be true having regard to the source of the news, may be presented as facts, and such facts shall be published fairly with due regard to context and importance. Where a report is not based on facts or is founded on opinion, allegation, rumour or supposition, it shall be presented in such manner as to indicate this clearly.

2.4 Where there is reason to doubt the correctness of a report and it is practicable to verify the correctness thereof, it shall be verified. Where it has not been practicable to verify the correctness of a report, this shall be mentioned in such report.

2.5 Where it subsequently appears that a published or broadcast report was incorrect in a material respect, it shall be rectified spontaneously and without reservation or delay. The correction shall be presented with a degree of prominence which is adequate and fair so as readily to attract attention.

2.6 Reports, photographs or sketches relative to matters involving indecency or obscenity shall be presented with due sensitivity towards the prevailing moral climate. In particular, the press and television services shall avoid the publication of obscene and lascivious matter.

2.7 The identity of rape victims and other victims of sexual violence shall not be published or broadcast without the consent of the victim.

## 3. Comment

3.1 The media shall be entitled to comment upon or criticise any actions or events of public importance provided such comments or criticisms are fairly and honestly made.

3.2 Comment shall be presented in such manner that it appears clearly that it is comment, and shall be made on facts truly stated or fairly indicated and referred to.

3.3 Comment shall be an honest expression of opinion, without malice or dishonest motives, and shall take fair account of all available facts which are material to the matter commented upon.

## 4. Special provisions relating to the Press

4.1 Headlines and captions to pictures shall give a reasonable reflection of the contents of the report or picture in question.

4.2 Posters shall not exaggerate and shall give a reasonable reflection of the contents of the reports in question.

## 5. Privacy

5.1 In so far as both news and comment are concerned, the media shall exercise exceptional care and consideration in matters involving the private lives and concerns of individuals, bearing in mind that the right to privacy may be overriden by a legitimate public interest.

## 6. Payment for articles

6.1 No payment shall be made for feature articles or programmes to persons engaged in crime or other notorious misbehaviour.

## 7. General

7.1 Due care and responsibility shall be exercised by the media with regard to:

    7.1.1 subjects that may cause enmity or give offence in racial, ethnic, religious or cultural matters, or incite persons to contravene the law;

    7.1.2 matters that may detrimentally affect the peace and good order, the safety and defence of the Republic and its people;

    7.1.3 the presentation of brutality, violence and atrocities.

10

251

The document P. W. Botha wanted the "establishment newspapers" to agree to in 1986—and which they turned down.

## REQUEST TO THE NEWSPAPER PRESS UNION OF SOUTH AFRICA

In order to terminate the state of emergency as soon as possible the Government requires the co-operation of members of the Newspaper Press Union of South Africa to discipline themselves, preferably on a voluntary basis, along the following guide-lines: -

1. Not to give reporters and other news staff in their service assignments which would require their presence at scenes of arrest, unlawful or restricted gatherings and actions by the security forces.

2. Not to publish statements and reports which may have the effect of inciting or encouraging members of the public to commit or to participate in acts of a subversive nature, for example -

(a)    to resist or oppose the Government in any steps it may take to terminate the state of emergency or to restore peace in the country;
(b)    to participate in or to support school and consumer boycotts;
(c)    to participate in or to support actions of civil disobedience by refusing for example to comply with the provisions of any law or to pay rent or service fees to local authorities;
(d)    to stay away from work for polititical considerations or to participate in unlawful strikes;
(e)    to attend unlawful or other gatherings on which restrictions were placed by law;
(f)    to support or to subject themselves to the authority of unlawful structures usurping the functions of local authorities and courts of law.

3. Not to publish any news or comment on the following matters unless particulars of such matters were released by a Government spokesman: -

(a)    any actions by the security forces to terminate any unrest;
(b)    the movements and employment of the security forces;
(c)    the time, date, place and purpose of unlawful gatherings, including gatherings on which restrictions were placed by law;

(d)   the extent to which school and consumer boycotts, stayaway actions, unlawful strikes and actions of civil disobedience are supported by the public;

(e)   the manner in which members of the public are intimidated to participate in such boycotts, actions and strikes;

(f)   the extent to which alternative structures usurping the functions of local authorities and courts of law are effective;

(g)   the statements of persons against whom steps under the security laws or the emergency regulations are in force, insofar as such statements may threaten the safety of the public or the maintenance of public order or may delay the termination of the state of emergency;

(h)   the circumstances of arrest or the circumstances of, or treatment in detention of persons who are or were detained under the emrgency regulations;

(i)   the release of such persons;

(j)   allegations of assaults on detainees, unless found by a court of law to be true.

4.  Not to publish a publication containing blank spaces or any obliteration or deletion of part of the text of a report or of a photograph it that blank space, obliteration or deletion is intended to be understood as a reference to this request by the Government.

5.  Not to publish any photographs or other visual material -

(a)   of any unrest or actions by the security forces or of any incidents occurring in the course thereof, including the damaging or destruction of property or the injuring or killing of persons;

(b)   of any damaged or destroyed property or injured or dead persons or other visible signs of violence on the scene where unrest or security action is taking or has taken place;

(c)   of any injuries sustained by any person during unrest or security action.

If the Newspaper Press Union of South Africa voluntarily co-operates in the above regard, the Government undertakes to exempt the members of the Newspaper Press Union from the present provisions of the emergency and also to exclude them from the operation of any further emergency regulations which may be published later.

The difficulties social clubs had with South African racial law. One example from the Cape Town Press Club.

Cape Town
Press Club
P.O. Box 3816
Cape Town    8000

Kaapstadse
Perskiub
Posbus 3816
Kaapstad

March 17, 1978

The Press Club has run into problems concerning the laws governing licenced premises.

Recently a police officer from the liquor squad visited the club premises in the Cafe Royal Restaurant and warned the manager that he should not admit people who were not white.

The club chairman took up the matter at Ministerial level the same day but failed to elicit any assurance of help. It was subsequently decided, at the Minister's suggestion, to write to the chairman of the Liquor Licencing Board, explaining the background of the club, its aims and its operation, and requesting permission to admit all members.

In the meantime the club chairman has undertaken to speak to the Divisional Commisioner of Police in an attempt to effect a stand-by solution, pending the Board's reply.

Would members please bear in mind that neither the club as a whole nor the committee in particular want or accept premises which are restricted by race.

The problem is being dealt with as a matter of urgency, and in the meantime the decision as to whether to visit the club premises or not must be left to individual consciences.

The committee does not believe, however, that boycotting the premises would serve any useful purpose. No such gesture is necessary, since no-one needs convincing, and we all know what we want.

An obvious question is: why were we not aware that such a situation could arise? The reply is simply that the hotel owner took up the question with the Department of Justice in Pretoria before the Press Club takeover, and was informed that there would be no problem (as long as there was no dancing!) and that the question of admission should be left to his discretion. No member was turned away for reasons of race.

The hotel manager has been forced to comply with the police warning.

Your understanding would be appreciated.

Note: Copies of this letter are being prepared and will be posted to all members.

Signed

. (ALAN DUGGAN)
Chairman (House Committee)

254

Cape Town Press Club
P O Box 3816
Cape Town    8000

Kaapstadse Persklub
Posbus 3816
Kaapstad

IMPORTANT NOTICE TO MEMBERS

Re: Premises at the Cafe Royal
Restaurant

We are happy to inform you that we
are now able to comply with the
requirements of the Liquor Board
as applied to all clubs in South
Africa without "international"
status.

What this means in effect is that
all members and signed-in guests
are free and welcome to make use of
the club premises during the
stipulated hours.


ALAN DUGGAN
House Committee Chairman

BELANGRIKE KENNISGEWING AAN LEDE

i/s: Perseel by die Cafe Royal
Restaurant

Ons is bly om u mee te deel dat ons
nou in staat is om die vereistes
van die Drankraad na te kom wat op
alle klubs in Suid-Afrika sonder
"internasionale" status van toepassing
is.

Wat dit beteken, is dat dit alle lede
en ingetekende gaste vry staan om
van die klub se perseel gedurende die
vasgestelde tydperke gebruik te maak,
en u is welkom om dit te doen.


ALAN DUGGAN
Voorsitter, Huiskomitee

A word of appreciation after the Tambo interview from a professor of journalism.

## Department of Journalism & Media Studies
### RHODES UNIVERSITY·GRAHAMSTOWN

PO Box 94,Grahamstown,6140 South Africa•Telephone(0461)2023x47•Telex 24-4223 SA•Telegrams Rhodescol

November 15, 1985

The Editor
Cape Times
PO Box 11
Cape Town
8000

Dear Sir

I congratulate the Cape Times on its courageous decision to publish the interview with Mr Oliver Tambo.

For a generation -- 25 years -- public debate in South Africa has been maimed by the exclusion of the most vigorous opponents of racism. For three-quarters of a century, perhaps more, people other than whites have been allowed into the main political arena only on suffrance.

A whole generation of South Africans has never legally heard the voices of the African National Congress and the Pan Africanist Congress; another generation has apparently forgotten that the pleas of Ex-Chief Albert Luthuli and Mr Robert Sobukwe, and of many of their successors, are pleas for tolerance and humanity.

Newspapers -- and other media -- have more than a right to make public all the voices contributing to the political debate in their country; they have a duty to do so. The right was made a criminal offence by the signature of a cabinet minister: no more is required to outlaw any organization, to silence any person, or to make a potential criminal of any editor.

GM Stewart
Professor of Journalism
Rhodes University

# NOTES

1. *Lectures on the English Comic Writers* (Oxford University Press, 1907), 1.

2. *Cape Times,* March 22, 1960.

3. Hansard Record of Debates, March 21, 1960, column 3732.

4. *Cape Times,* May 12,1960.

5. Ibid.

6. J. G. N. Strauss testimonial, dated September 5, 1983.

7. Joel Mervis, *The Fourth Estate* (Johannesburg: Jonathan Ball publishers, 1989), 235.

8. Ibid.

9. Ibid, 236.

10. Article by ex-SABC staffer Percy Baneshik in the *Star,* Johannesburg, December 7, 1974.

11. *Sunday Times,* April 21, 1940; also cited in Mervis, *The Fourth Estate.*

12. Mervis, *The Fourth Estate,* 241.

13. Ibid, April 21, 1940.

14. Ibid.

15. J. F. J. van Rensburg, *Some Facts about the Ossewa-brandwag,* (Pro Ecclesia Publishers, 1944), 54.

16. Columns by Donald Woods in *Cape Times,* March 8 and April 16, 1976.

17. Vida Heard's recollection.

18. Mohandas K. Gandhi, *Autobiography* (New York: Dover Publishers Inc., 1983), 97.

19. Report of speech in Parliament by Cabinet Minister Eric Louw, *Cape Times,* March 30, 1949, in which he quoted the *Sun.*

20. Speech, January 16, 1949, at Randfontein, Transvaal.

21. Ibid.

22. *Cape Times,* March 30, 1949.

23. Mark Twain, *Following the Equator* (New York and London: Harper and Brothers), vol. II, 343.

24. Ibid, 406.

25. A. N. Pelzer, ed., *Verwoerd Speaks* (A.P.B. Publishers, 1966), xxviii.

26. Beach notice observed by author, 1989.

27. Ibid, 203–30.

28. Dr. Piet Cillié in an article in *Die Suid Afrikaan,* late spring issue, 1985. Cillié wrote: "What this experiment in the human ordering of affairs also achieved for the better, was that the option of total race and territorial segregation was, hopefully, closed for good" (translated from Afrikaans).

29. The Johannesburg *Star,* July 14, 1984.

30. Unpublished SAPA report, March 16, 1950.

31. As published in the monthly *Contact* newspaper, April 1960.

32. Terblanche article in *Huisgenoot* magazine, April 14, 1960, 9.

33. As published in *Contact,* April 16, 1960.

34. Ibid.

35. Ibid.

36. *Huisgenoot* article, April 14, 1960.

37. Ibid.

38. *Move Your Shadow,* (Penguin Books, 1985), 319.

39. See account by Tom Lodge in *Black Politics in South Africa since 1945* (Longmans, 1983).

40. See, for instance, ibid., 221.

41. Ibid, 325.

42. Ibid., 315.

43. Ibid., 316.

44. *Cape Times,* April 20, 1961.

45. C. J. Driver, *Patrick Duncan, South African and Pan-African* (Heinemann).

46. *Verwoerd Speaks* (A.P.B. publishers, 1966), xv.

47. Ibid., 83.

48. *Verwoerd Speaks,* ibid, 397.

49. *Cape Times,* June 1, 1960.

50. *Cape Times,* February 22, 1962.

51. *Cape Times,* March 9, 1983.

52. Roger Williams, written memoire, September 25, 1989.

53. Ibid.

54. *Cape Times,* March 27, 1963.

55. *Cape Times,* August 11, 1977.

56. *Burger* report, May 15, 1978.

57. Speech delivered to S.A. Institute of Race Relations Conference, January 1977. Quoted in Michael Savage's *The Cost of Apartheid,* inaugural lecture as professor of sociology, University of Cape Town, August 27, 1986.

58. Ibid.

59. Helen Suzman's written account, in a letter to me, December 7, 1989.

60. Ibid.

61. Private talk, May 30, 1974.

62. Norton's memorandum to Press Commission.

63. Personal discussion.

64. Personal discussion, May 30, 1974.

65. Winston Churchill, *History of the English-speaking Peoples,* arranged into one volume by H. S. Commager (Toronto, Montreal: McLelland and Stewart, 1956), 460.

66. February 24, 1975.

67. Discussion, November 27, 1973.

68. Private talk with editors, November 13, 1973.

69. Discussion, February 14, 1975.

70. *Inside Boss* (Penguin Books,1981), 578.

71. Evidence to Erasmus commission into Information Scandal, quoted in *Weekly Mail,* December 6-14, 1989, 13.

72. 1986 edition published by Butterworths, Durban.

73. Communication by NPU to its members, September 3, 1980.

74. Letter dated February 28, 1982.

75. Editorial, November 16, 1978.

76. Discussion between minister of defence and editors, December 9, 1975.

77. Dispatch sent 1658 hours, April 3, 1978.

78. Memo, September 2, 1975.

79. Note sent on August 10, 1977.

80. Note dated May 17, 1978.

81. Human Rights Commission, quoted in *Weekly Mail,* December 6-14 issue, 1989, 6.

82. Letter from Senator C. F. Clarkson, minister of the interior, to editors dated September 14, 1945, which came into my possession. Translated from Afrikaans.

83. Statement by M. V. Jooste, president of the N.P.U., January 21, 1962.

84. Private memorandum from Norton.

85. *Daily Dispatch,* July 26, 1985.

86. Editorial in *Cape Times,* June 9, 1972.

87. Report in The *Argus,* September 17, 1988.

88. *Cape Times* editorial, March 1, 1974.

89. Personal memoire of meeting, July 7, 1977.

90. July 13, 1979.

91. Joint statement by universities of Cape Town and Stellenbosch, May 13, 1976.

92. Referred to in *Cape Times* editorial August 15, 1962.

93. Sent October 26, 1976, just before midnight.

94. Report on page 8 headlined: "PAC, ANC attack West on SA," October 27, 1976.

95. Note on February 2, 1978.

96. *Cape Times,* October 21, 1977.

97. *Financial Mail* editorial, December 7, 1984.

98. Broadcast delivered October 15, 1985.

99. Speech, October 29, 1985.

100. *Argus* report, February 13, 1984.

101. Ibid.

102. E.g., in Parliament, July 12, 1984.

103. Sent January 30, 1987.

104. Sent March 22, 1987.

105. Sent July 17, 1985.

106. Column in *Beeld,* January 9, 1981.

107. N.P.U. minutes of meeting with Le Grange, May 14, 1985.

108. Report in the *Times,* October 17, 1985.

109. Ibid.

110. October 27, 1985.

111. Interview defending TV coverage restrictions by ambassador Worrall, who was later to join the opposition Democratic

Party; S.A. Broadcasting Corporation "Netwerk" programme, November 18, 1985.

112.  Letter dated July 30, 1971—see Appendix 2, p. 000.

113.  James Thurber's "The Sheep in Wolf's Clothing," *Fables for Our Time.*

114.  *Cape Times,* November 4, 1985.

115.  The *Burger* report, November 5, 1985.

116.  South African Broadcasting Company "Netwerk" programme. Ibid.

117.  Letter of June 6, 1986.

118.  Letter of November 15, 1985.

119.  *The state versus J.B. Leepile and J.M. Ngidi,* November 1985.

# INDEX

175; "racial editions" experiment, 175; under–age street newspaper sellers, 176; big walk, 176; courtesy titles for blacks, 176; use of "guerilla" and "terrorist," 177; help on reform moves, 179–83; published Tambo and Sibeko at UN (1976), 186; published Woods, 188–89; joint operating agreement, and profitability, 221

*Cape Times* Fresh Air Camp racial problem, 171–74

*Cape Times* driver (Richard Lombard) killed, 3

Cape Town: Mother City and environs described, 53–59; colonial history, 56; racial attitudes, 58–59, 72–73; muggings, 65

Cape Town City Council, 58

Cape Town Press Club, 173

Cape and Transvaal Printers, 133

Carlyle, Stewart: press gallery colleague, 126

Casspirs: police vehicle, 12

Cato Manor: police deaths (1960), 6; squatter area, 43

Centlivres, Chief Justice Albert van de Sandt, 77, 120

Churchill, Winston, 56

Chelsea Court, Durban, 39

Chinese and race classification, 79

Christian National Education, 42

Cillié, Dr. Piet: editor of *Burger*, 81

*Citizen* newspaper and information scandal, 139

Clark, U.S. Senator Dick, 139

Clarkson, Senator C. H.: letter to editors after wartime censorship ends, 160

Coetzee, Gen. Johann: police commissioner, acts against *Cape Times*, 166–67

Colenso battlefield, 34

Coloured Affairs Department (C.A.D.), 109

"Coloured" people, xiii, 5; and apartheid, 57, 60, 111; and black liberation, 62; frustration over race classification, 63; "try for white" in the north, 63–64; municipal councillors unseated, 72; lost common–roll vote, 77

Commonwealth: break with South Africa (1961), 50 ; Tambo on Commonwealth, 200

Communism, 20, 21, 200

Comrades Marathon, 41

Cope, John: editor of the *Forum*, 23

Copeland, Tom: *Cape Times* political correspondent, 186

*Contact*: liberal newspaper, 92, 103

Corder, Clive Sinclair, chairman of *Cape Times*, 175

Cornwall, England, 28, 201

Cronwright, Guy: managing director of *Cape Times*, 20

Crossroads squatter camp, 55

*Cry, the Beloved Country* (Paton), 37, 120

*Daily Dispatch*, 134, 140; boycott by United Democratic Front and settlement, 163–64

Dalling, David, M. P: discloses terrorism reporting guidelines, 161–62

Dar–es–Salaam, 73, 196

Darroll, Roland, 74; and railway sign, 73

Darwin, Charles: visited Cape, 56

Dawood, Hadji Ismael: and Upington trip (1957), 75

Day, Chris: and information scandal book, 139

Day, Sir Robin: of B.B.C., 209

De'Ath, George: journalist killed in township, 166

Defence agreement with press, 146

Defence department notes to newspaper editors, 154, 155

Defence Special Account, 139

Gallow, doorman: saved *Cape Times* building, 157

Gandar, Laurence: crusading liberal editor of *Rand Daily Mail,* 120, 177; prisons trial, 147

Gandhi (Mohandas K), Mahatma: train incident, 35

Gibson, Rex: editor of *Sunday Express* (later of the *Mail*), 140

Glenwood High School, Durban, 44

*Good Hope:* frigate on which George Heard served, 22

Gorbachev, Soviet leader: letter sent, 218

Graaff, Sir de Villiers: leader of United Party, 104

Grahamstown, 39

Greeff, Secretary for Justice C. J.: sees Kgosana, 100–01

Groote Schuur Hospital: marchers pass (1960), 90

Group Areas Act, 60, 61, 108, 113

Greenacres store, Durban, 49

*Guardian,* London, 201

Guguletu Seven police killings and *Cape Times,* 166–67

Hadeda birds, 42

Havenga, N. C.: finance minister, budget scooped, 15, 28

Hazlitt, William: essayist, 2, 14

Heard, Anthony Hazlitt: birth, upbringing, 13; beach life, 44–47; bicycle incident, 49; Zulu–Indian incident, 39; West Street incident, 49; London (1954–55), 50–51; taught Afrikaans by George Manuel, 67; statement to commission on Kgosana assurance, 98; parliamentary press gallery, 103; London office, 124; editor, *Cape Times,* 132; information scandal, 141–45; Tambo interview and repercussions, 195–221; dismissal, 223–25

Heard, Arthur Henry: George's father, 13

Heard, George Arthur: birth, upbringing, education, 13–14; early career: *Farmers Weekly, Friend,* 14; *Rand Daily Mail, Sunday Times,* 15–21; scoops 1937 budget, 15; summoned, sentenced, order discharged, 16; role in war vote of 1939 recognized, 17; on O.B. death list, 20; public speaking, 20; political views, 20, 30; sacked from *Mail,* 21; joins navy, 21; turns down UK job offer, 21; returns to S. Africa, plans to edit *Photonews,* 23; A–Bomb dropped, 23; disappears, 24; theories, 25, 28; O.B. assassin in Cape Town, 26; Name on Plymouth war memorial, 28; John Vorster on Heard disappearance, 28

Heard, Janet: daughter of Anthony, 119, 210

Heard, Raymond Elliott: brother of Anthony, 31, 46

Heard, Val: former wife, 210

Heard, Vicki: daughter, 119, 208

Heard, Vida: no pension after husband's disappearance, 28; old age in Cornwall, England, 28; concern for beach boy sons, 46; and Tambo interview, 201

Hennessy, D. A St. C.: chairman of *Cape Times,* writes to Botha, 152

Herbst, Terry McComb, 9, 12

Herbstein acting justice: on George Heard's disappearance, 24

Hertzog, Prime Minister J. B. M.: lost war vote, 16–17; on Cape "Native" franchise, 59

Heunis, Cabinet Minister Chris, 119, 148

"High Court of Parliament" and enlarged Senate manoeuvre, 77

Hitler, 16, 68, 79

1963 freedom, 89–90; task force, 90; Poqo violent offshoot, 101; break with ANC, 103

Park, Sir Maitland: editor of *Cape Times* recommended by Kipling, 134n.

Parliament: effect of Sharpeville/Langa, 5; missed by mass march on Cape Town, 95–96

Pass laws, 4, 109

Paton, Alan: author, 36, 104, 120

Payne, Bill, 41

Payne Brothers store: Durban, 49

Pelser, Justice Minister Peet, 186

Pelzer, Professor A. N.: on Verwoerd, 105

*Photonews*, 23

Pforzheim, Germany: where Swales won V. C., 41

Piet Retief: eastern Transvaal, 63

Pietermaritzburg (or Maritzburg), Natal, 35, 41

Pinelands "garden city, " adjacent to Langa, 7–8

Pitman's College, High Holborn, London, 50

Plural relations: department for blacks, 109

Plymouth, England, 28

"Polecat of the world," 79

Population Registration Act: race classification, 79, 82, 179

Poqo, violent offshoot from PAC, 101, 128

Portscatho, Cornwall, 201

Portuguese grip in Africa ends, 113, 131

*Post* newspaper effectively banned, 137

Powell, Enoch: anti–immigration speech, 51

Pratt, David: shot and injured Verwoerd at Rand Show, 111, 177

Press Commission, 132

Press Council (originally Board of Reference, later Media Council), 137, 160

*Private Eye* on Verwoerd assassination, 126

Progressive Party, 92, 104, 105, 113

Promotion of Bantu Self–Government Act, 79

Protection of Information (official secrets) Act, 146

Publications and Entertainments Act censorship: NPU members exempt, 161

"Quislings" in wartime South Africa, 18

Quito, Ecuador: where Rhoodie traced, 141

Racial code on I.D. documents, 116

Racial planning for white security, 8

Racial definitions, xiii

Ramphele and Wilson study on poverty, 36, 67, 69

Rand Club, 175

*Rand Daily Mail*, 15, 86, 120; and information scandal 139–44

Ratel vehicle, 12

Ratushinskaya, Irina: Ukranian poet, 218

Reay, Col. J. A. C., 91, 100

Reform pressures, 178–79

Relly, Gavin: head of Anglo–American Corporation, 193

Rhodes, Cecil John: diamond magnate, empire–builder, 56, 133

Rhodesia's unilateral declaration of independence, 113, 123, 124

Rhoodie, Dr. Eschel, 129–30; information scandal, 139–44; on newpaper informers, 142–43

Right–wing opposition, 178

Rorke's Drift battle, 34

Rosenthal, Richard: attorney, 225

Rossouw, Niel: attorney–general of Cape, 219

Russell, David: banned priest, 78

Russell, J. Hamilton, M.P.: and enlarged Senate remark, 77–78

Russell, Most Rev. Philip: archbishop of Cape Town, 211

Sachs, Albie, 127
St. George's Cathedral incident (1972),166
St. Leger, F. Y., founder of *Cape Times*, 132
Sanctions, 179
Sandy Bay nudist beach, Cape Town, 54
San people: earliest inhabitants, 56
Sauer, Cabinet Minister Paul: Humansdorp speech (1960), 177
Savage, Prof. Michael: on cost of apartheid, 121
Savimbi, Jonas: Angola guerilla leader, 130
Scarecrows in *A Tale of Two Cities*, 118
Schoeman, leader of House of Assembly Ben, 126
Schwarz, Harry, M. P.: and Rand Club, 175
Scorpio right-wing urban terrorism, 156
Scott, John: columnist of *Cape Times*, 135
Segal, Ronald: editor of *Africa South*, 197
Selassie, Emperor Haile, of Ethiopia, 79
Senate: and enlargement, 77
Separate Amenities Act, 61
Sewgolum, golfer Papwa: and apartheid, 79–80, 130
Shaka of Zulus ("Black Napoleon"), 37
Sharpeville, 4–5, 87, 109
Shaw, Gerald: of *Cape Times*, 85–87, 126, 153, 180, 204, 217
Shikhanovich, Yury: Soviet detainee, 217, 218
Sibeko, David: of PAC, 185–86
Simons, Dr. Harry Jack, 74
Simon's Town group areas, 114
Sisulu, Zwelakhe, 169

Slabbert, Frederik van Zyl: opposition leader, fire at home, 156
Smit, Dr. D. L., M. P.: on "breach of faith," 101
Smit, Dr. Robert: aspirant M.P. murdered with wife Jean–Cora, 142
Smith, Adam, 48
Smith, Cyrus: defence public relations officer, 154
Smith, Ian: white Rhodesian leader, 123, 124
Smuts, General J. C.: and war vote, 17; refusal to arm blacks in war, 19n.; on 1949 Durban riots, 38
"Snake Pit," London, 50
Sobukwe, Robert: PAC leader, 89, 93, 94, 103, 134
Sophiatown, 109
South African Air Force, 42
South African Associated Newspapers (later Times Media Ltd.), 133, 152; and Tambo interview, 214–15, 219, 223–25; financial difficulties and joint operating agreements, 220–21
South African Broadcasting Corporation and pro–Nazis, 17–18
South African Council of Churches, 120
South African Morning Newspapers, 123; and information scandal, 139–44
South African rand, xiii
South Beach, Durban, 43, 47
South West Africa (Namibia) war, 113
Sparks, Allister: editor of *Rand Daily Mail*, 141; and role in information scandal disclosures, 140–41
Spionkop battlefield, 35
Sports boycott success, 80
Springbok cricket team and Durban High, 41
Springbok Legion, 21
Sri Lanka (Ceylon), 51
*Star*, Johannesburg, 77, 149

Vanderbijlpark, 5

Van der Ross, Dr. Dick , 177n.

Van der Westhuizen, Col. J. H.: security chief, 99

Van Rensburg, Dr. J. F. J. (Hans): leader of Ossewa–brandwag, 19; attacks *Sunday Times* and editor Levy,19; Group Areas Board job, 20, 113; crisis of conscience, 113–14

Van Riebeeck, Jan: started Cape refreshment station (1652), 62

*Vaderland,* Johannesburg, 185

Verwoerd, Prime Minister Dr. H. F.: and African representation in Parliament, 59; personal value of packed Senate, 77; Russell incident, 78; Bantustan "vision," 79; Swellendam speech, 80; government's style in unrest, 99; thesis, 106; schemes for South Africa, 106–12; birth in Netherlands; education, 105; on pass laws, 108; assassination attempt by Pratt, 111–12; recovery, white dove falters, 112; assassination in Parliament, 112, 125–26; miscalculated African numbers, 178

Victoria Cross, 34, 41

Victoria Embankment, Durban, 39

Visser, George Cloete: investigated George Heard's disappearance, 25

Viviers, Koos: editor of *Eastern Province Herald* (and later *Cape Times*), 158

*Volksblad,* Bloemfontein: on George Heard budget scoop, 15

Vorster, Balthazar John: O. B. "general," 20; prime minister, 20; on George Heard disappearance, 28; and African Resistance Movement, 74–75; apartheid relaxed in hotels, sport, 76; calls off English cricket tour, 80; as deputy minister, watches Cape Town march, 92–93; "smashed" communism, Poqo 127;

detente effort in Africa, 129; ditches Ian Smith, 130; on fall of Portuguese empire in Africa, 131; personal relations with journalists, 133–34; beliefs, 135–36; compared with Botha, 137; on Rhodesia, 137; information scandal, 139–44; reveals Angola invasion in private talk, 153; "informal emergency" attempt, 162; also 127, 178

Vosloo, Ton: editor of *Beeld,* on negotiating with the ANC, 192–93

Waldheim Dr. Kurt: UN secretary–general, 138

Walton, Leycester: director of S.A.A.N., on Walter Judge, 220

War vote in Parliament (1939), 16; and George Heard's role, 16, 17

Waterford non–racial school, Swaziland, 33

Weaver, Tony: journalist, 167, 224

*Weekly Mail,* 149

Weenen slaughter of Boer families, 34

Welsh, David, 165

Welwitschia plant, 159

West Coast described, 55–56

Western Cape African removal scheme, 110–11

Western Cape Traders' Association, 211

Western Cape winter rainfall: significance for early settlers, 55–56

West Street, Durban, 49

Wiley, John, M.P. and cabinet minister, 173, 174

Williams, Roger: of *Cape Times,* 114

Wilson, Harold: attempts to settle Rhodesian crisis, 123

Windhoek unrest, 6

Wind of change speech by Macmillan, 106

Windrum, Serjeant–Major Charlie, 66

Wilson and Ramphele study on poverty, 36n., 67n., 69

Woods, Donald: banned editor of *Daily Dispatch*, 134, 203; riles P. W. Botha, 152–53, 159n.; quoted by *Cape Times*, 188–89
Woods, Wendy, 188
Woodstock train smash: racial death toll, 119
*World* newspaper banned by Vorster, 137

Worrall, Dr. Denis: ambassador to London, 188–89, 213, 258–59n.

Xhosa, 35

Zulus, 32, 34, 35; riots (1949), 37–40; and beaches, 46

Anthony Hazlitt Heard was born in Johannesburg, South Africa, in 1937. Heard was awarded the Golden Pen of Freedom by the International Federation of Newspaper Publishers and the Pringle Medal for the Defense of Freedom of the Press by the Southern African Society of Journalists. Heard is now an internationally syndicated freelance columnist. He lives in Cape Town with his wife, Mary Ann Barker.